BEYOND THE
GREAT WAR

Pierre Lierneux & Natasja Peeters (eds.)

BEYOND THE
GREAT WAR

Belgium 1918-1928

LANNOO

WWW.LANNOO.COM

Register on our website to receive a regular newsletter
with information about new books and
interesting exclusive offers.

Editing
Pierre Lierneux
Natasja Peeters

Editor's board
Wannes Devos
Manuel Duran
Emilie Gaillard
Kevin Gony
Pierre Lierneux
Natasja Peeters
Sandrine Smets
Jan Van der Fraenen
Olivier Van der Wilt
Piet Veldeman

Text editing
Emmanuel Brutsaert
Yves Perger
Filip Van Brabander

Visual editing
Jan Van der Fraenen

Photo editing
Guy Deploige
Luc Vandeweghe

Translations
Telelingua International

TELELINGUA
Crossing Language Borders

Ruth Lemmens
Diane Vanthemsche

Cover design
Mieke Verloigne, Studio Lannoo
with the cooperation of Patricia van Reeth

Cover photos
Josephine Baker, 1926-1927 (Lucien Waléry)
Run for veterans, England 1926 (photographer unknown)

Layout
Keppie & Keppie

© Lannoo Publishers nv, Tielt, 2018 and the authors
D/2018/45/599 – ISBN 978 94 014 5529 9– NUR 688

CONTENTS

8850

PREFACE

Michel Jaupart

On 11 November 1918 at 11 a.m. the armistice trumpet announces the end of the most terrible war ever to have ravaged Europe. That same trumpet also proclaims the end of the Russian, German, Austrian and Ottoman empires. It rings out for 9,500,000 deadly casualties, 20,000,000 wounded and 10,000,000 disappearances. Moreover, it heralds both the end of an era and the emergence of a new society, thriving on hope but also undermined by hitherto unseen tensions and imbued with a brutality and violence of a new kind, industrial in size and inhuman on every level...

For millions of fighters and for their families, the 1918 armistice promises a new future. However, it is not synonymous with worldwide peace, in spite of the *"No more war"* bellowed by veterans as soon as fighting stops and in spite of the League of Nations wishing, in 1924, to outlaw war and to establish peace through arbitration.

The Allied powers take pride in a great victory, although it has come at an unfathomable human cost burdening European societies for years on end. Soldiers can finally return home, but all is not well. Mere days after the armistice, fights erupt in Germany, in Austria and in Hungary, putting communist factions wishing to install a proletarian dictatorship at odds with conservative movements.

Conflicts arise in the east too. When Russia is devastated by civil war, Western powers send out units to support the white counter-revolution. The former Ottoman Empire is wrecked by civil and international wars from May 1919 onwards. Elsewhere, in Poland, in Czechoslovakia, in the Baltic States, in Finland guns continue to be heard as well...!

The 1920s truly deserve the epithet "Roaring Twenties", as both new generations and those who survived the war dream of a new world and go all out to forget the atrocities of war. However, the same decade witnesses the rise of frustrations, not only in defeated Germany and Austria, but also in Italy who feels short-changed and believes the Allies did not compensate for the sacrifices brought in their favour.

Closely observed by the public, a car with an American Red Cross camera team drives through the streets of Brussels in mid-November 1918. The Germans have just left the city. Lieutenant H.E. Du Bois and Captain Ernest Meadows probably are the first Allies to enter the capital after the armistice. The Joyous Entry by the royal family and the army only takes place on November 22, 1918. (Library of Congress, Washington, 2017683173)

July 1919, liberation festivities in Heist-op-den-Berg. Once the Versailles Treaty is signed, many towns and villages all over the country celebrate the official end of the First World War. Lots of liberation parties also take place in November 1919. (Gemeentearchief Heist-op-den-Berg, Henri De Wolf collection)

In the USSR, communism puts its foot down, although the country is subjected both to civil war and to repression by the newly constituted Cheka, forerunner of the GPU and the KGB. As Lenin is laid to rest in his Red Square mausoleum, Stalin starts his unstoppable ascension.

While the world is enthused by jazz, that new and exciting sound coming from the United States; while Art Deco replaces Art Nouveau; while André Gide, Paul Morand, Raymond Radiguet, Joseph Kessel and Colette revolutionise literature; while André Breton writes his manifesto of surrealism; while communist parties emerge all over Europe in the hope of taking control, Benito Mussolini in Italy and Adolf Hitler in Germany talk of grandeur, of power and of creating empires that would be the heirs of Antique Rome or an imaginary Germania. Europe dances when Mussolini marches on Rome in 1922 and seizes power; it still dances in 1933 when Hitler becomes Chancellor.

In Belgium, as in other places, war accelerates social reform. Universal suffrage is introduced and enables all men to participate in political life, and the first social laws assist war victims. Meanwhile, military cemeteries and monuments honouring the dead testify to the bloody price paid by everyone.

It is the story of this troubled era that the exhibition "Beyond the Great War: 1918–1928" wishes to tell and that the publication you are holding illustrates. I hope this book is a stimulating one and that it will make readers see how the First World War – often referred to as the Great War – influenced our history and how we still live with its consequences to this day.

Such is my goal, and it has also been the drive of my collaborators and all those who participated in the creation of this exhibition and of this book. I seize the opportunity to thank them all for their remarkable work.

INTRODUCTION

BEYOND THE GREAT WAR?
BELGIUM FROM 1918 TO 1928

Luc De Vos

By 1918, 1914 and the *Belle Époque* seemed a distant memory. In those short years Europe and, in fact, the world had changed fundamentally. War, and certainly a war on that scale, deeply affects man and society, involving, as it does, the most extreme emotions: love and hate, trust and betrayal... What is good, what is bad? Ethical norms are severely tested. On the other hand, it is in battle that war-related discoveries are made. But does that outweigh the huge material losses? In the First World War more was afoot. Contemporary historians are right in saying that the twentieth century began not in 1900 but during the First World War.

The nineteenth century had already been characterised by a great acceleration of history. That was when the ideals of the Enlightenment were really disseminated. The Industrial Revolution, born in England in the eighteenth century, had spread throughout Europe. A world leader since the sixteenth century, Western Europe now ruled supreme, colonising the majority of the globe. The United Kingdom and France shared Africa; Belgium, through its monarch, gained the Congo, the heart of Africa. It was supposed to act as a sort of buffer, mirroring the role our country fulfilled in Europe. France appropriated the highly profitable Indochina, and the United Kingdom crowned its monarch Empress of India. Even China, immense though it was, suffered – economically at least – at the hands of what were actually relatively small European states: the United Kingdom, France and the German Empire.

In the nineteenth century Italy was unified and the German peoples united. Those unifications were, however, relative: Austria and Switzerland remained separate states, and the actual German Empire – with Berlin as the capital – consisted of four kingdoms and twenty counties and duchies. The autonomy of those parts was huge. The intellec-

A Belgian boy, wearing a pre-war Belgian side cap and holding a small Belgian flag, poses next to a German artillery piece in Arlon, November 1918. The war is also over for the German soldiers in the background.
(War Heritage Institute, Brussels, B.1.84.21)

tuals dreamed of "Germany", but the people preferred their familiar *Heimat*. It is certainly true that the German Empire, a confederation, defined foreign policy. The industrial might of the most populated country in Western and Central Europe gave it a privileged position. As a latecomer, Germany had ended up with only the crumbs from the ultimate wave of colonisation. But in continental Europe it was the dominant power.

In the nineteenth century there were relatively few wars. The century began with the collapse of the Napoleonic Empire and there were, of course, the small wars of unification of Italy and "Germany" and the wars of Balkan liberation. Amongst these, the war of 1870 between France and the German peoples stands out, since it led to not only the foundation of the Second German Empire under Wilhelm I, but manifestly demonstrated the waning power of France. For centuries the threat to our regions had come from the south. Now there was a new threat in the east.

It was during the nineteenth century that all the ideologies that were so important to the twentieth century were formed. Socialism and its more extreme form, communism, were born, and liberalism came of age. At the same time, the seeds of fascism were sown. In Russia the First World War would bring about the collapse of the established order, as communism triumphed.

Industrialisation and, with it, the exponential increase in the population of Western Europe, made the mobilisation of mass armies possible, and conscription was a fact virtually everywhere. Generalised basic education allowed national feelings to pervade a nation's own population. Suffrage was still very limited and, for women, nonexistent.

In the 1890s and early 1900s, alliances were born, as France, the United Kingdom and Russia tried to rein in the German Empire. Meanwhile, the small states of the Netherlands, Belgium, Switzerland and the Scandinavian countries looked on anxiously, hoping that their neutrality meant they would steer clear of acts of war.

Many economists believed that war in Europe was no longer possible, given the commercial entanglement and high costs. However, they underestimated the inventiveness of the Europeans: autarchy, money printing and sky-high taxes proved to be the solution. For France, the United Kingdom, Italy and Belgium the colonial empires provided breathing space.

The First World War, which has long been known as the Great War – or the European War to the Americans – was an all-out war in which everyone and everything was deployed. The people of the empires came to fight in Western Europe and the Middle East and replaced the workers in the factories and on the farms. Refugees from Belgium, among other places, helped the factories stay operational in the United Kingdom and France, and the Germans used people from the occupied countries to work behind the front in their fields and factories. Poles, Czechs, Slovaks, Arabs, Senegalese, Indochinese, Indians, and a host of others increasingly wondered why they had to fight and work for their masters: the Germans, Russians, French and British. New Zealanders,

November 1918. Soon after liberation Antwerp citizens flood the *De Keyserlei*.
(National Archives and Records Administration, Washington, 165-WW-79A-4)

Australians and Canadians fought enthusiastically for the British motherland, yet were aware of their individuality and dreamed of being self-governing. Everywhere, women were being employed in production, to emancipatory effect.

The United States, in contravention of the Monroe Doctrine, came to join the fight in Europe, bringing fresh blood and powerful American industry that ultimately tipped the balance in the Allies' favour. But their intervention on the old continent gave the new continent a headache, and after the war the United States would return to isolationism.

In the First World War the essence of battle also changed. By the end of 1914, the huge increase in firepower in terms of loading, precision and discharge rate had brought a stabilisation of the fronts, but not without dramatic losses. On 22 August 1914 around 27,000 French soldiers were killed in the Belgian and French Ardennes, and in September of the same year the German armies suffered the deaths of 71,000 troops. Trenches, barbed wire and most of all firepower formed the basis of the fundamental problem of the First World War: how could you break through a front? All kinds of technical inventions and tactical procedures were used in the search for a solution until, ultimately, came the tank. That tank, used properly, would bring the solution in the Second World War.

The First World War, meanwhile, started rashly: contemporaries believed that if differences of opinion could not be set aside diplomatically, a war would provide the

Ypres, 1919. Returning to the areas that were devastated by war is not easy. Rubble has to be cleared before rebuilding can start. Many people are overwhelmed by what appears to be an insurmountable task.
(Imperial War Museum, London, Ivan L. Bawtree, Q100483)

solution. The Germans in particular thought that they deserved a better place in the world. The French and British, on the other hand, did not wish to relinquish their position of power. In 1914 people had no idea that the war would last as long as it did or have such drastic consequences. It was the beginning of the decline of Western Europe; in Germany they even spoke of the downfall of the Western world.

The First World War ended with a series of treaties, the most important of which was the Treaty of Versailles. The peace treaty was ruthless and caused a great deal of ill-will in Germany; people were looking for someone to blame for the "stab in the back", singling out Jews and communists. Many see the Treaty of Versailles as a cause of the outbreak of the Second World War. There are some colleagues who dub the period 1914–1945 the Thirty Years' War: one generation, hit by two terrible wars. Following in France's wake, Belgium shed its mandatory armed and guaranteed neutrality, which caused great dismay in Flanders. King Albert, too, was not happy with that evolution.

Vast numbers died in the First World War: around ten million soldiers and the same number of civilians, though half the number of deaths were attributable to Spanish flu, a disease that held a weakened population in its grip. For a long time, or at least until the Second World War, we thought that it was the most terrible of wars. Is that not ethnocentric European thinking?

Every war has an aftermath, so too, the Great War. Materially and mentally, countries had to be rebuilt. On the battlefield the ground literally had to be levelled. Countries that were once rich – France, the United Kingdom, Belgium and Germany – were now groaning under the weight of debt and sought to avoid their obligations through inflation and taxes that, for that era, were sky-high.

In towns and villages, men with one arm or one leg were a common sight. The *gueules cassées* hid their disfigured faces behind masks. Even the smallest villages unveiled monuments to their fallen sons. Hundreds of military cemeteries dotted the landscape. Widows, mothers and fathers made pilgrimages to Flanders Fields, to the Somme and Verdun... Veterans' associations were born. Some tried to reclaim their lost youth with drink and dancing, a period that later became known as the Roaring Twenties.

The political landscape was completely redrawn. The Socialists broke through everywhere, partly due to the introduction of universal single suffrage. But more authoritarian parties also came into being. In the countries that had lost the war, a climate of revolution reigned. Even art was shaken up by a revolution: Cubism, Fauvism and Dadaism were among the forms breaking with the norm.

A multitude of historians have studied 1918 and the aftermath of the First World War up to 1928, each focusing on their own domain of expertise. Alongside their own research they have been able to use the many new publications that appeared particularly in 2014. However cruel war may be, the study of this international conflict and its aftermath are fascinating episodes in the history of mankind. For the Germans it was the *Urkatastrophe*. The slogan "No more war" was everywhere, culminating in 1928 in the Briand-Kellogg Pact. This "General Treaty for Renunciation of War as an Instrument of National Policy" garnered great optimism. But to no avail: the Second World War was to bring even more upheaval.

1

THE WAR YEAR 1918

Tom Simoens

At the beginning of 1918 the Allies' strategic situation is not looking particularly rosy. The previous year had failed to live up to their sky-high expectations: the French-British offensives had stalled on the heights of the Chemin des Dames and in the Passchendaele mud, and more than half the French divisions are facing mutiny. The German Empire holds better cards. After Romania, Russia also signs an armistice in December 1917, and on the 3rd of March 1918 Lenin and the Bolsheviks, after a new German advance, even swallow the humiliating Treaty of Brest-Litovsk. For the Germans, the Russian capitulation comes as a relief. For the first time, the German military leaders, Paul von Hindenburg and Erich Ludendorff, join forces for a decisive campaign on the Western Front. The Germans, nonetheless, leave more than a million troops in the east, to secure the captured territories, so German supremacy on the Western Front is limited to 191 divisions to the Allied powers' 175. In absolute figures, both parties are evenly matched, with around four million troops. The Germans do not have much choice: they need to pursue a quick victory. Millions of American soldiers are on their way to Europe, and within a few months the Allies will have more soldiers than the Germans. At the same time, the British naval blockade is strangling the German economy, leading to strikes and production problems. The German population is starving.

September 1918, in the vicinity of Ypres. According to the original caption of the photo, a Belgian soldier holding a trench knife helps a German soldier clamber out of a shattered German bunker. Belgian artillery fire in preparation of the attack on 28 September 1918 had indeed been both intense and destructive.
(War Heritage Institute, Brussels, EST-1-813/44)

The German Spring Offensives

The Germans have a few military trump cards that make it seem as if a quick victory is within their grasp.[1] Since 1915 they have been experimenting with new assault tactics. They replace the tightly packed waves of soldiers with smaller groups of specially trained stormtroopers with unprecedented firepower: from hand grenades and flamethrowers to light machine guns and mortars. Their job is to advance as quickly as possible and encircle the enemy defence nests. Clearing the trenches and shelters becomes a job for the second wave of infantrymen. In this manner, the stormtroopers generate speed and continuity and sometimes hit upon enemy artillery positions or commando posts. Moreover, the Germans prevent days of artillery bombardment designed to level the path for the infantry by blasting away at everything, but which, in practice, has tended not to be very profitable. The new German approach opts for short but heavy barrage on the most important enemy positions several hours before the assault by the stormtroopers. Just before the start of the assault, poison gas causes confusion. Then a rolling barrage forces the Allied soldiers to entrench themselves, which means they cannot use their machine guns. These tactical innovations have already led to spectacular victories in 1917 on the Eastern Front (Riga) and on the Italian Front (Caporetto). Nevertheless, the German war machine also has a few weak points: there is a significant shortage of horses, carts and trucks. Those logistical problems are the biggest cause of the failure of the German offensives of 1918.

The offensives begin on the 21ˢᵗ of March 1918. Ludendorff aims his attack arrows at the British with Operation Michael, a reference to the patron saint of the German Empire. He hopes to break through the British Front between Arras and Saint-Quentin, thereby cutting off the British and Belgians from the French forces. From day one, it becomes clear that the German advance is formidable. However, the French come to Britain's aid, and the German tactical victory yields no strategic breakthrough. Two weeks later Operation Michael is history. This pattern typifies the German Spring Offensives: following a promising breakthrough, the advance falters after several days or weeks because the Allied reserves arrive faster than the German reinforcements. However, the German territorial gain, in some places as much as sixty kilometres deep, is unprecedented. The French, British, and Belgians too, are becoming particularly nervous and, as a matter of urgency, start to extend and occupy their lines of defence a long way to the rear. For the Allies it is all hands on deck. Political and military differences of opinion are set aside, and the French general Ferdinand Foch is appointed "coordinator of the Allied forces" five days after the start of Operation Michael. In the months that follow his powers are expanded. From now on, Foch can quickly send aeroplanes, tanks, cavalry and infantry to sectors under threat.

These measures are much needed. From the 9th of April onwards, the Germans start to batter the British again near the Lys. Passchendaele, the ridge at Messines and even the Kemmelberg are lost. Again, the French save the day. After three weeks, Operation Georgette ceases. The Belgians, too, share the hits this time at Merkem, but they stand fast. The failed German attack, carried out without much artillery support, gives the Belgian army confidence.

The military tipping point of the war

Yet Ludendorff still believes that the Allies are gradually reaching breaking point. He aims his sights at the French with new combat operations in May and June. Just like in 1914, the Germans reach the Marne and panic breaks out in Paris. On the 15th of July 1918 the final German attack begins near Reims. The French successfully fend off the Germans; their defence is now a match for the German assault tactics. After only three days

In the spring of 1918 the Germans pull out all the stops in the hope of breaking through the western front. On 14 April 1918 the British Middlesex Regiment guards improvised barricades in the streets of the French city of Bailleul. The city nevertheless falls into German hands. However, the German offensive is contained soon afterwards. (National Archives and Records Administration, Washington, 165-BO-1515)

the French counterattack. The Germans are forced to retreat. Ludendorff takes a gamble... and loses. Between the 15th and the 18th of July, the 1918 campaign – and in some sense even the whole war – tips. The weight of the Americans is decisive: in May they carry out an initial attack, and in July already eight American divisions take part in the fighting near Reims. Ludendorff feels a storm coming. He cancels the next offensive and gets the German army to defend again. The initiative now lies with the Allies.

The balance sheet of the German Spring Offensives is catastrophic. Although the German territorial gains are considerable and unprecedented for the Western Front, they bring new problems more than anything. Before the Spring Offensives the German troops occupy the well-structured positions of the *Hindenburgstellung*; after the offensives they occupy a new frontline without much cohesion, which, because of its many bulges, ends up being more than 120 kilometres longer. Not a single strategic target is reached. At the final count, German losses are 800,000 – often their best soldiers – leaving a shattered fighting force to defend poorly prepared and difficult-to-maintain positions. Still, Paul von Hindenburg and Erich von Ludendorff do not give up the fight, believing that it is unlikely that the war will be settled in 1918 since the Allies have been hit too hard by the Spring Offensives. Moreover, they are not expecting the American divisions at the front very quickly or in large numbers. Their optimism proves unfounded: the summer of 1918 becomes the military turning point of the war. In the months of July and August 1918 the initiative definitely goes to the Allies, who capitalise on their numerical superiority in terms of soldiers, ammunition, aeroplanes and tanks.

This is possible thanks to improvements at strategic, operational and tactical levels. At a strategic level everything is finally arranged. Ferdinand Foch fully embraces his role as coordinator. Admittedly, he still has to negotiate with his most important colleagues: his fellow countryman Philippe Pétain, the Briton Douglas Haig and the American general John Pershing. The four of them determine the military strategy. Most observers think that the liberation offensive will not be possible until 1919. Pending that ultimate offensive, Foch wants to take the Germans by the throat and conquer major railways. This will cause the logistical support for the offensive planned in 1919 to run smoother. So, in the summer of 1918, Foch organises a series of smaller, less ambitious attacks along the whole of the front. That those ultimately unfold into the liberation offensive is not something he predicts at the time.

At operational level the Allied generals – reluctantly – comply with the military restrictions of that time. They know that their troops can break through the first German lines, but at the same time realise that an offensive to unsettle the whole German Front is not a viable option. The infantry needs the protective umbrella of the artillery in order to conquer and occupy territory. Hence, where necessary, they work in stages ("bite and hold") from now on. After each attack ("bite"), they take a break ("hold"), to allow logistics and artillery to push forward.

At a tactical level, the Allies apply the new assault tactics that the Germans used to cause them so much pain in the spring of 2018. On 4 July, the British test this new procedure for a successful attack at Hamel. Thanks to acoustic tracking methods, they are able to perfectly locate and neutralise the German cannons, while a shifting curtain of artillery grenades silences the German machine guns (rolling barrage). On the battlefield itself, two events make it clear that the tide has turned. In addition to the Franco-American counterattack on the 18th of July, which we have already mentioned, on the 8th of August Foch and Haig bring together around 600 tanks and at least as many aeroplanes for an attack at Amiens. In the space of four days they push back the Germans. Almost half the German losses are surrendering soldiers. The German military apparatus appears to collapse. Ludendorff later describes that 8th of August as "the dark day of the German Army".

The successes gradually open the Allies' eyes: does this mean that victory in 1918 is still within their grasp? The strength in German numbers decreased since March 1918 by a million troops, while on the other side of no-man's-land one and a half million American soldiers throw themselves into the fight with unprecedented and naive enthusiasm.

The Hundred Days campaign

Foch does not want to pass up his chance and begins to order a series of bigger offensives. From 26 September, the French, Americans and British head off on the attack. Two days later, the Belgians also launch their first major offensive since 1914. Ludendorff has yet another nervous breakdown. On the side of the Allies, everything gains momentum.

Even King Albert changes tack, having spent four years refusing to take part in the French and British offensives. He accepts Foch's invitation to take part in the major offensives. The offensive approach is immediately felt in the Belgian trenches. With bigger raids, the Belgian army tries to push the jumping-off line for the liberation offensive as far forward as possible. On the 11th of September the King accepts command of the newly founded *Legergroep Vlaanderen* (Flanders Army Group), consisting of Belgian, British and French divisions. Later, two American divisions join them. The practical leadership of the army group is in the hands of the French general Jean-Marie Degoutte. At the beginning of September the Belgian front units are given instructions to start the mass logistical preparations for the imminent offensive and the subsequent advance. The Belgian army is able to bring 170,000 troops and more than 1,000 artillery pieces into the field. The French and the British, too, bring in artillery to support the Belgian advance. However, the preparations do not go smoothly: there is not much time to turn this multi-national army group into a well-oiled machine. Three weeks

before the start of the offensive, the attack plans still had to be written. The manoeuvres that are eventually worked out are sometimes too complicated for the limited means of communication of the time. Furthermore, several orders arrive late, or attacks that had been cancelled take place after all. However, the supremacy of the Allies is great so that even the difficult preparation does not throw a spanner in the works: there are ten undermanned German divisions against 29 divisions of the Flanders Army Group.

French soldiers have their picture taken next to the German negotiators' car in Homblières on 8 November 1918. A few hours earlier a German delegation led by General Detlof von Winterfeldt and the chairman of the German armistice commission Matthias Erzberger has reported to the first French lines. The delegation then takes the train to Rethondes near Compiègne, where Allied supreme commander Ferdinand Foch dictates the 34 armistice conditions. The armistice is proclaimed on 11 November 1918 at 11 a.m.

(Imperial War Museum, London, Q47865, G. Gessat)

The 28ᵗʰ of September: the time has come

The first target of the Flanders Army Group is the *Flandern II Stellung* on the crest of the hill that stretches from Klerken (near Dixmude) via Passchendaele to the south of Ypres.[2] At 2:30 in the morning, the artillery launches the impressive display. The shelling is brief but overwhelming and gives the infantrymen courage; three hours later, they go over the top. They follow the rolling barrage. The advance goes very smoothly, but due to a delay on the Belgian side, the strong *Flandern II Stellung* has not fallen by evening. Yet the Flanders Army Group advances at least eight kilometres. On the 29th of September the British, French and Belgians finally break through the German position. Then, the offensive falls silent at the following German position, the *Flandern I Stellung*. There, the resistance proves to be much tougher than expected. Moreover, the infantrymen are exhausted and supplies are running low. The artillery needs to move on, and that takes time. A logistics break is urgently needed. After the advance of twelve to fifteen kilometres ("bite"), it is time for the break ("hold").

On the 14th of October the Flanders Army Group is ready for the second bite. The artillery preparations remain very limited this time, to increase the element of surprise. The setup succeeds and the Flanders Army Group breaks through the *Flandern I Stellung*. That day, a further eight kilometres of territory are gained. The Germans now move from one improvised position to the next: from *Flandern I Stellung* they head back behind the Lys and the Diverting Canal of the Lys *(Lysstellung)* and at the beginning of November behind the Ghent-Terneuzen canal and the Scheldt *(Gent-Hermann-Stellung)*. They defend the area between these positions with machine guns and artillery fire.

However, the British, French and Americans are unstoppable. On the 20th of October they cross the Lys and on the 3rd of November the Scheldt. On the 30th of October the third phase of the offensive breaks out after a second logistics pause. Meanwhile, the Belgian divisions have also left the Yser Front between Nieuwpoort and Dixmude behind them and liberated the Belgian coast. The Germans do not give up the fight and continue to work feverishly on the *Antwerpen-Maasstellung*. However, the Armistice of the 11th of November 1918 makes a fourth phase redundant. In the space of 45 days the Flanders Army Group has advanced around 60 kilometres and liberated the largest part of West and East Flanders and Hainaut. The armistice line runs via Ghent, through Zottegem and Geraardsbergen to Bergen. German resistance was fiercer than predicted. As a result, Belgian losses are high: 3,336 killed and 27,000 wounded. On the German side, given the chaos of those days, there are no known figures of the losses.

German soldiers on the *Hohenzollernbrücke* in Cologne, November 1918. The armistice conditions proclaimed on 11 November 1918 dictate that the German army must leave all occupied territories within a fortnight and evacuate the left bank of the Rhine. Soldiers are welcomed as heroes at the German border. The Belgian and Luxemburg territories are, however, only fully vacated on 30 November.
(National Archives and Records Administration, Washington, 165-WW-158C-5)

The Armistice of 11 November 1918

On paper, the German military position in November does not seem too bad. They still occupy more than half of Belgian territory and the north-eastern corner of France. Only at the Swiss border do the Allies succeed in penetrating into German territory, albeit into Alsace-Lorraine, the part of France that the Germans took over after the war of 1870–1871. However, the military, economic, social, diplomatic and political situation is far less rosy. The threat of a communist coup is real. Desertion and mutiny are soaring. In the space of little over a month the Bulgarians, Ottomans (Turks) and even the Austrians throw in the towel. After two changes in the post of Chancellor, Ludendorff's resignation and flight to Sweden, and finally Kaiser Wilhelm II's departure in exile to the Netherlands, a delegation from the German Empire signs the armistice in Compiègne. On the 11th of November 1918 at eleven o'clock in the morning, the guns fall silent.

For the soldiers, the final days of the war were alienating. They knew full well that the ceasefire was close and yet they still had to carry on fighting. On the 10th of November the rumour mill was working overtime: everywhere, soldiers were talking about the imminent armistice. The rumours were confirmed in the early morning of the 11th of November, as most of their officers learned that the guns would fall silent at eleven o'clock. Yet the fighting continued until the clock struck eleven. Here and there, Allied units continued to advance, while in some places the Germans responded aggressively. Just before the armistice took effect on the 11th of November, the Belgians, too, secured a final success when they moved into Ghent, which had been evacuated by the Germans.

On 10 November, the artillery unit of Belgian René Deckers found itself at a position near De Pinte. René was among those to hear that day that an armistice would be signed, although – as is often the way with rumours that are grossly exaggerated by soldiers – he was a step ahead of events. The next day, René heard at five o'clock in the morning that the armistice would take effect six hours later. "We were delirious with joy. (…) Peace! Peace! Peace! … that's wonderful!" but he also added that on 11 November the Germans were still shooting at five to eleven. That same day, in his units barracks in Ruiselede, infantryman Florimond Pynaert also heard the cannons roaring so loudly that he had doubts: "At two minutes to eleven the cannons were still firing away. Eleven o'clock came and the cannons fell silent: their sad song was over." Elsewhere conditions were no longer as bad. Valère De Boodt was confronted by Germans on the 11th of November. His unit was situated on the left bank of the Scheldt at Zevergem, while the Germans were entrenched on the other side of the Scheldt in Schelderode. In the night of the 10th to the 11th November, from his outpost, Valère saw several German scouts on the opposite bank of the Scheldt, but he and his colleagues left them undisturbed. When they were informed at eight o'clock the following day that the guns would fall silent three hours later, it seemed surreal because the German artillery continued to blast. Until eleven o'clock, then it suddenly went quiet on the Scheldt, too.

Unfortunately, not all the soldiers lived to experience the joyful event. The Belgian Marcel Terfve died of his injuries at quarter to eleven. He was possibly the last Belgian soldier to die before the armistice, although doubtless many other wounded shared his sad fate in the minutes, hours or days that followed. The last Briton killed was George Ellison. He had been at war since August 1914, but an hour and a half before the armistice he was felled by a bullet while patrolling near Bergen (Mons). Not far from there, the last Canadian was killed: soldier George Price, who two minutes before the armistice took a German sniper's bullet to the heart when his unit was combing a village. Shortly before that, a German bullet felled the last French *poilu*, Augustin Trébuchon, in the vicinity of Sedan. Soldier Henry Gunther – of German origin of all things – was, in turn, the last American to be killed in battle. Shortly before eleven o'clock he stormed a German machine gun nest, a heroic deed that cost him his life. Nevertheless, news of the armistice spread like wildfire among the Americans, as well. Allegedly, even the German machine gunners gave the sign that peace had almost arrived, yet Gunther still continued his fateful action, and the Germans opened fire at close range.

The armistice brought four years of misery to an end. In Belgium, it was also the beginning of several turbulent weeks, with mutinous German soldiers causing a stir and looting the country for a final time, while the Belgian population settled its accounts with anyone who had too close links with the German occupation. To weaken the impending chaos, on the 11th of November the King invited the most important political leaders from occupied Belgium to his headquarters in Loppem near Bruges. At that meeting, important decisions were made. Decisions that would change the political landscape in Belgium forever.

2

BETWEEN WAR AND PEACE

NOVEMBER 1918. THE RETURN OF THE KING

———

Emmanuel Gerard

By the beginning of October 1918, the end of the war was in sight. The Allied offensive on the Western Front was successful and forced the German army to retreat. The *Reich* ended up isolated as, one by one, its Bulgarian, Ottoman and Austrian allies quit. When, on 3 October, the new German Chancellor Max von Baden asked the US President Woodrow Wilson to begin peace negotiations and showed that he was prepared for an armistice, it was clear to everyone that the countdown had begun for Germany. How would the war end for Belgium?

On 11 November 1918 Spanish diplomat Pedro Saura, Liberal politician Paul-Emile Janson and Socialist politician Eduard Anseele inform King Albert, who resides at Loppem Castle, of tensions in Brussels. Janson and Anseele also submit a post-war political programme. (War Heritage Institute, Brussels, B.1.72.19)

Countdown to armistice

On the western flank of the Allied offensive, the Flanders Army Group was on the move under the command of King Albert, and by the end of October the Province of West Flanders had been recaptured. On the 24th of October the royal family left its residence in De Panne to settle in the castle of Baron Albert van Caloen in Loppem near Bruges. The following day, King Albert made his formal entrance into the capital of West Flanders.[1]

Belgian soldiers parade through the streets of Ghent during the Joyous Entry by the royal family and the army on 13 November. The royal family and the army already visited Bruges; Antwerp, Brussels and Liège are next in line. (War Heritage Institute, Brussels, PK 14)

In Brussels the Belgian authorities were preparing for the return of the government. By this point it was clear that in the event of an armistice the Germans would have to fully evacuate the occupied territory. Former minister Michel Levie, the government's official representative, installed a ten-man government committee composed of the three parties. Its task, in consultation with the judicial authorities, consisted of preventing a power vacuum, and in maintaining public order in the transition period, while the actual authority in the occupied country and in Brussels lay with the powerful *Comité*

National de Secours et d'Alimentation (CNSA) and with its leader, the banker Emile Francqui. It was he who gave the orders during those days.

The political parties were also preparing for the end of the war. Catholics, Liberals and Socialists alike wanted a government of national union to rebuild the country, but their conditions for participation differed. Liberals and Socialists, the former opposition, were claiming a fifty-fifty composition of the cabinet, even though the Catholic party had an absolute majority in Parliament. The *Parti Ouvrier Belge* (POB), the Belgian Workers' Party, confirmed the demands that it had already made: immediate introduction of universal single suffrage from the age of 21, abolition of Article 310 of the Criminal Code punishing strike action, and acknowledgement of the right of association for officials. The Liberal party followed suit. It also demanded the immediate introduction of universal single suffrage at 21, i.e., without following constitutional law procedure, but expressly objected to giving women the vote. The Catholic party was divided. It had been in power for more than thirty years and some politicians did not want to simply cede power through a voting reform that would end up benefiting the opposition of the left. However, a group of Catholics had gathered around Henri Jaspar, a prominent Brussels lawyer; they were pursuing a loyal cooperation with Liberals and Socialists, and sidelined the conservative group surrounding Charles Woeste.

The political consultation was abruptly interrupted by dramatic events in Germany. War fatigue, the bitterness surrounding the defeat, and the example of the Bolshevik revolution in Russia were at work. The mutiny of the German fleet in Kiel at the beginning of November was the sign for a general revolution, with workers' and soldiers' councils taking over power in a number of cities. On the 9th of November the Socialists in Berlin declared the republic. *Kaiser* Wilhelm II abdicated at his headquarters in Spa and fled to the Netherlands. The events in Germany put wind in the sails of the Belgian Socialists, even though the POB leadership distanced itself from the revolution. And in bourgeois circles they strengthened the position of those who supported democratic reforms to prevent worse.

The repercussions of the revolution in Berlin were felt immediately among the German occupying troops in Brussels, where on the 10th of November, rebellion broke out. Thousands of soldiers trooped together to Place Poelaert, before heading to Rue de la Loi and occupying the headquarters, based in Parliament. The red flag was hoisted at the Palace of the Nation and a soldiers' and workers' council was formed, which took over power from the German occupying administration. Political prisoners, deserters, prisoners of war, and even common law criminals were released, giving rise to a dangerous situation in the capital. In some places there were shootouts among German soldiers, and looting took place. Among the fatalities were civilians.[2]

Gentlemen, I convey the army's salute! On 22 November 1918 King Albert honours the army, the occupied populations and the war victims in his parliamentary address. In his lengthy speech from the throne he then presents the post-war political agenda and promises numerous reforms.
(War Heritage Institute, Brussels, B.1.104.24)

Loppem

When, on Monday the 11th of November at 11 a.m., the Armistice took effect, events followed in quick succession. The previous evening Emile Francqui had, at the request of the Spanish Ambassador Marquis de Villalobar, decided to send a delegation to the King, asking him to return to Brussels with his troops as soon as possible and to restore order there. In the early hours of the 11th of November the Liberal politician Paul-Emile Janson, accompanied by the Spanish Consul Pedro Saura, left for Loppem. In Ghent, they were joined by the Socialist Edward Anseele, acting mayor of the city. The company was received by King Albert shortly after midday. Saura and Janson reported events in Brussels, with Janson and Anseele explaining the political situation. Later, some would – wrongly – allege that they had threatened revolution and that was how they forced the King to make concessions.[3] The King, who had been tempted to make reforms for quite some time, immediately decided to hold a series of meetings, and handed Janson a list of persons who were invited to Loppem. When it came to the troops, they were unable to get to Brussels any sooner: according to the armistice agreement the German army had until the 17ᵗʰ of November to withdraw and until that date the Allied troops could not breach the demarcation line established on the 11ᵗʰ of November.

The Belgian government, which had left Le Havre at the beginning of November and based itself in Bruges, had understood for some time that after the end of the conflict they would have to pass the baton to politicians from the occupied nation. In the afternoon of 13 November, the ministers decided to make their portfolio available, once back in the capital. The prospect of a triumphant return to the King's side, however, was shattered when, that evening in Loppem, cabinet leader Gerard Cooreman tendered his resignation during a meeting with the King. It was a surprising twist, which was greeted by the Catholic ministers with incomprehension and fierce criticism. What had prompted this about-turn? On the morning of that same 13ᵗʰ of November, the King had made his formal entrance in Ghent and had a meeting with Francqui. The leader of the CNSA had come to greet the King together with the Grand Marshal and the Spanish Ambassador and they had once again urged a quick dispatch of troops to maintain order in Brussels. But in the discussion with the King, Francqui had raised other matters. According to the CNSA leader, when the King returned, he would have to be accompanied by a new team and announce a generous programme of reforms. In his conversation with the King that evening, Cooreman came to terms with that position.[4]

In the early hours of the 14ᵗʰ of November, a caravan of cars carrying around fifteen politicians left Halle Gate in Brussels bound for Loppem. That same day, Léon Delacroix, a Catholic lawyer and, along with Jaspar, a close colleague of Francqui's in the CNSA, was charged by the King with forming a new government. In the countless meetings that Delacroix had, he had no choice but to acquiesce to the demands of the united opposition: parity between Left and Right and immediate introduction of universal single suffrage for men over 21, but no women's suffrage.

Brussels

It was the formation of the government that explained why the King's return to Brussels did not happen until the 22ⁿᵈ of November, even though the city had already been evacuated by the Germans on the 17ᵗʰ of November. First, on 19 November, Albert visited liberated Antwerp, and then on 21 November the royal family left their residence in Loppem. That evening, at the Palace of Laeken, the new ministers took the oath before the King: six Catholics, three Liberals and three Socialists, just as the united opposition demanded. Léon Delacroix became the new Prime Minister.

On Friday the 22nd of November, King Albert made his formal entrance in Brussels at the head of his troops. On his grey, with Queen Elisabeth at his side, and flanked by Belgian generals and Allied commanders, he rode into the city through the Flemish Gate, surrounded by jubilant crowds. The King made his way to the Palace of the Nation, where he spoke to the united Chambers shortly after midday: "I bring you greetings from the Army. We have come from the Yser, our soldiers and I, after passing through liberated towns and country." After this poetic opening, he rendered account for his conduct during the war and gave an explanation of the military operations. Then he moved on to the political element. In his famous speech from the throne, he set out the landmarks for the coming period, repeatedly interrupted by enthusiastic applause and hurrahs: "It is conceivable that the noble union of which Belgium has given so admirable an example during the War should give place on the morrow of the liberation of our territory to a resumption of barren quarrels. This union should remain a reality in present circumstances (...)." He unveiled the programme of the new government: immediate introduction of universal single suffrage for men over 21, abolition of Article 310, and the principles of a higher education in Dutch in Ghent. The Members of Parliament sat up in surprise and applauded, although many realised that nothing would be as before. Belgium had entered the era of democracy. Due to the unusual circumstances of the formation of the government and the prominent position of Liberals and Socialists, in conservative milieus the picture emerged of the "Loppem Coup".[5]

BELGIUM IN THE LAST MONTH OF WAR

Jan Van der Fraenen

S ince the 11th of October 1916, Belgium had been in a state of siege. The Belgian military government was able to take exceptional measures that also applied to the civilian population, but it was also burdened with additional responsibilities to its citizens. With this in mind, the *Service de Liaison avec la Population* was set up within the army. Better known as the *Office de Liaison avec la Population* (OLP), the department was effectively able to be deployed as of October 1918, with British, French, American and Belgian troops liberating the first Belgian towns and villages. The OLP's most important task was to take care of the liberated Belgian people by, among other things, providing sufficient food.[6] This was essential, having become a scarce commodity during the final months of the war. In many places the retreating Germans had looted food stocks, production was at a standstill and, on top of that, the thousands of refugees were disrupting the carefully constructed food distribution network. Throughout the country, there was a dire shortage of bread, milk and fresh meat. On the 7th of November the first Belgian train carrying flour and emergency rations arrived in the British zone, in the south of the country, with a second train en route and a third preparing to depart.[7] Overall, the British would hand out more than a million rations, with 110,000 of these being on the 12th of November alone. It was not until the second half of November that food supplies from the Belgian government would be fully back up and running again.

October 1918, Bruges. Locals ransack the house of a supposed activist. After the country's liberation, many Belgians turn against collaborators, activists and war profiteers. Belongings are destroyed and the heads of many "wandering" Belgians are shaved. Thousands are taken into custody. Belgian authorities do not condone this popular fury, but cannot prevent street repression.
(War Heritage Institute, Brussels, B.1.73.4)

British servicemen distribute food in a liberated village in the north of France, as people both there and in Belgium are obviously hungry. When the Allied troops enter liberated towns and villages they hand out millions of rations.
(War Heritage Institute, Brussels, B.7.23.1)

A population under pressure

Given the shortage of food and the lack of doctors and medicines, contagious diseases like typhoid fever, tuberculosis and dysentery were rife. In addition, the Spanish flu was responsible for many deaths. Few places were spared the aggressive virus: in many regions the military authorities reported epidemics. In Nederbrakel, in the period from the 10th of October to the 13th of November, Spanish flu claimed the lives of 90 out of a population of 5,300. At the end of November the French were reporting that many cases of flu were occurring in their occupied zone in Belgium and that mortality was quite high. In Laplaigne in the south-west of the province of Hainaut, there were a hundred cases of Spanish flu on the 11th of November and no doctor to care for the sick. In Celles near Tournai a doctor reported that the mortality rate was five times higher than normal. Although partly down to the Spanish flu, it was also down to the exhaustion of the population: by then, the inhabitants of the village had been without fresh meat for four months. Elsewhere in Hainaut, in La Glanerie, a severe influenza epidemic was raging and refugees were being evacuated as a precaution. A British army doctor tried to help the sick, but by the 9th of November three hundred villagers – roughly two thirds of the village – were already ill. According to a report from a Belgian doctor, a third of the population in the wider vicinity of the village were "dead men walking". He wrote that the Spanish flu "is decimating the population".[8]

Belgium saw a huge rise in mortality during the war, especially in 1918. Whereas in 1913 108,296 deaths had been registered, in 1918 this figure was 157,340. Added to that were the more than 40,000 Belgian soldiers who died during the war, deceased deportees and other civilian casualties. Sociologist Ernest Mahaim calculated in 1926 that between 1914 and 1918 623,503 Belgians died as a result of the war. It is a number that does not compare with the high losses of other warring nations. Yet the war still shook up Belgium at a demographic level. Far fewer marriages took place, a fall of 48% on average. In West Flanders the number of marriages fell by 63%, and this also had consequences for the number of births. In 1913 birth numbers in Belgium were 170,102, falling to only 85,056 in 1918, before rising again in 1919 to 128,236.[9]

Seeking revenge

Even before the end of the war, the Belgian government in Le Havre had decided to prosecute traitors. To this end, the OLP worked closely together with the *Sûreté Militaire de l'Armée de Campagne*. Upon liberation, triage centres were set up, where suspects were locked up and interrogated. Although both authorities did their best to arrest suspects as soon as possible after liberation, the public took matters into their own hands. In Aalter, the arrival of the Belgian troops was the starting signal for heavy looting. One Belgian officer had the words *"verboden voor de Belgen"* ("no Belgians allowed") painted on the facades of bars with German sympathies, and for that very reason the houses were looted and ransacked. In Bruges the police had to intervene to quell the public anger that led to incidents in the city during which fifty troublemakers were arrested, hundreds of official police reports written out and five hundred searches of premises conducted. On the 11th of November 1918 around 25 homes in Ghent were looted and smeared with the word *landverrader* (traitor). Women had their hair cut off and a man was shot dead while trying to protect his home. General Louis Bernheim had to act and call on the people to calm down. "Deplorable lootings," he called them, "under the pretext of punishing residents who have shown themselves to be too sympathetic to the Germans."[10] Bernheim called on the courts to do their work, and with regard to the activists, a great many of whom fled to Germany or the Netherlands or were arrested. In Namur there were further incidents at the beginning of December: more than a thousand civilians and British soldiers, acting on rumours, laid siege to, looted and ransacked homes of inhabitants who were under suspicion. The *Rijkswacht* (gendarmerie or state police) were forced to intervene and arrested 62 people. And 12 newly released Italian prisoners of war were also picked up. In Molenbeek and Schaarbeek police watched soldiers armed with scissors cut off the hair of several women. In Evere at the end of November, 15 women who were rumoured to be consorting with Germans were arrested before having their hair cut and their clothes removed, under intense public interest. Clothed in just a shirt and with a German spiked helmet on their heads, the women were driven through the streets of Evere on a cart.[11]

Banditry

At the end of December 1918 in Heusden near Destelbergen, a group of young men were harassing two women, intending to cut off their hair. One of the women pulled a knife and stabbed one of the assailants. "The public expresses the hope that appropriate measures will be taken to prevent the spread of immoral behaviour, such as cutting off hair, to avoid regretting any terrible consequences," wrote the local newspaper *De Gentenaar – De Landwacht* about the incidents, continuing: "The young people have no work; people are poverty-stricken; everyone is turning feral, stringent measures are needed to prevent Belgium becoming a den of thieves and murderers."[12] The population was impoverished and there was no strong government apparatus; it was the ideal breeding ground for the banditry that had increased dramatically during the war and which persisted long after the armistice.[13] The same newspaper also reported the brutal robbery of a farming family, in which the two daughters were killed and the father seriously injured.[14] In other parts of the country bandits and gangs also made the area unsafe. *Rijkswacht* brigades asked for reinforcements to counter the growing criminality and to rein in banditry.

Destroyed towns, villages and landscapes

At the front, many towns and villages were wiped from the map. During the final days of the war, huge amounts of damage were caused to buildings and roads that for a long time had been spared by the war. The *Dienst Verwoeste Gewesten* (Office of Devastated Regions), set up in April 1919, adopted 241 municipalities that needed help with reconstruction. Around 100,000 private buildings needed to be restored or reconstructed, with more than 70,000 of those having been completely destroyed. In the adopted municipalities of the Devastated Regions, the government itself took responsibility for the restoration of public buildings: 163 town halls, 237 churches, 392

View of the large assembly hall at the *Ateliers de Constructions Electriques de Charleroi* prior to 1914.
During occupation the workshops fall into the hands of the German occupier, who pillages the building.
(Archives Royal Palace, Albums AE. 443A)

schools and 402 other buildings. Outside the Devastated Regions, the government financed a further 1,300 public buildings. Countless roads and bridges also needed to be repaired. Furthermore, around two thousand kilometres of railway track needed to be re-laid, 1,100 kilometres of which had been completely destroyed. And 1,649 kilometres of the 2,709 kilometres of branch lines had been affected. The war had also had a huge impact on the landscape itself: for four years, salty seawater had been poisoning the farmlands between Nieuport and Dixmude. The front was littered with tonnes of unexploded ammunition and the soil was heavily contaminated with warped steel. In Belgium, between 80,000 and 125,000 hectares of agricultural land was unusable, accounting for 3% to 5% of the nation's total agricultural area.

View of the large assembly hall at the *Ateliers de Constructions Electriques de Charleroi* after German occupation. The occupier used the building and stole all construction equipment. Once clearance is completed, rebuilding can begin. (Archives Royal Palace, Albums AE 443A)

An economy in ruins

The economic balance sheet from the war was dramatic: farming had to cope with a sharp reduction in the number of livestock, and industry suffered severely. Of the 2,554 coking plants that existed in 1914, only 993 were able to be quickly restarted. A total of 1,192 furnaces had been badly damaged and 369 completely destroyed. Of the 57 blast furnaces for the steel industry, only 11 had been spared; the others had been badly damaged or reduced to ash. Many steelworks had been dismantled. Quarries lay dormant and most industries lacked the raw materials to restart production. Moreover, every branch of industry and all the factories and workshops had suffered particularly from the constant requisitioning of machinery, tools, leather, metal, etc. However, the greatest disaster was not the systematic dismantling of Belgian industry, but the complete crippling of all production. Factories were closed, workers were unemployed, the port of Antwerp was shut, there were no imports and the shops were empty.

To work!

After the armistice, 600,000 Belgians were still abroad. With the Germans pulling out and the end of hostilities, the refugees gradually returned. Prisoners of war, the interned, political prisoners and deportees also came back. The reintegration of both soldiers and civilians into a fundamentally changed society was no easy task. King Albert realised only too well the task facing the country. On the 22th of November, he succinctly summarised it in his address to the Chamber and Senate: *"Aan het werk dus, Mijne Heeren"* ("So to work, Gentlemen!").[15]

FROM OCCUPATION TO OCCUPATION. THE FOREIGN PRESENCE IN BELGIUM, 1918–1919

Jan Van der Fraenen

During the final offensive of the First World War, the Belgian and Allied troops of the Flanders Army Group abandoned the desolate and depopulated war-torn landscape, as the war moved to the still-populated parts of the country. Day after day, hamlets, villages and towns returned to Allied hands. The liberation itself had been thoroughly prepared at the administrative level. All Allied divisions had a Belgian liaison officer who was responsible for the fortunes of the Belgian people, who were no longer occupied by the Germans but by other foreign troops. Local government – where there was one – was given a lot of additional responsibilities. The army was responsible for clearing the battlefields, but it fell to the municipality to collect all the abandoned military equipment. Nothing was allowed to fall into the hands of the civilian population. Law enforcement also came under the jurisdiction of local government. Lastly, local government had to do everything it could to secure its archives and to protect its monuments from destruction and fire. Here, it got help from the liberators, regardless of their nationality. Historical and cultural heritage – such as monuments, churches, town halls, museums and libraries – were protected by the army. Billeting was strictly forbidden, unless there was no other option. Only when the occupation was of a prolonged duration did local government have to take responsibility for the safeguarding of heritage. The liberators, however, did more than protect monuments. They helped supply the distressed population with enough food. The Belgian government relied on Allied aid to keep two million Belgians going for 20 days.

Australian soldiers use their spare time to explore their surroundings. Group visits to cities and monuments are also scheduled. On 16 February 1918 they have their picture taken with a few children in front of a Brussels tourist hotspot. (Australian War Memorial, Canberra, E04308)

January 1919. Belgian soldiers with the occupation army check a cart on the *Oberkasseler Brücke* crossing the Rhine at Düsseldorf. The tram is used as a passport control office. In early January 1919 revolts led by Spartacists break out in several German cities. Many Germans flee the city in search of safety.
(National Archives of Belgium, Brussels, F1546, 2771)

On the day of the armistice, only part of Belgian territory was in Allied hands. However, the terms of the armistice stipulated that the territories of Belgium and Luxembourg were to be evacuated by the Germans at the end of November. Belgium was then liberated from the German yoke, and the Allied troops gained full control of the country. Hostilities may have ended, but peace was some way off. This would not be signed until the end of June 1919 in Paris. The Flanders Army Group was disbanded on the 18th of November 1918, but neither the Belgian nor the Allied troops returned home immediately: the possibility that war might resume was not inconceivable. On the 14th of December the armistice agreement was temporarily extended until the middle of January 1919. Both parties subsequently extended the agreement once more, by a month, and after that for an indefinite period.

Belgium as transit nation

The armistice agreement stipulated that the German army was to withdraw behind a 10-kilometre wide neutral zone on the right bank of the Rhine. Starting on the 26th of November, the first Allied troops crossed the German border and organised four occupied zones on the left bank of the Rhine. Seven million Germans thus ended up under Allied control. The Belgian army was assigned a zone from Düsseldorf to the Dutch border. The Americans sent around 240,000 soldiers from the newly founded Third Army to Germany; as of January 1919 this became the American Forces in Germany. For the British, the 2nd Army was given the honour of moving into Germany; this later became the British Army of the Rhine. The French were put in charge of the largest zone, occupying it with at least 21 divisions.[16]

As a result, Belgium unwittingly became a transit zone following the armistice. With its extensive transport network, the country was squeezed between the former front and, behind it, the developed logistics bases in France and Great Britain on the one hand, and between Germany with the Allied occupation zones on the other. With its many supply routes, the country therefore became the ideal operational base for the occupation in Germany. Hundreds of thousands of troops from all over the world passed through Belgium, making ample use of the road network. The available part of the railway network became overburdened, just as the French network. In the spring of 1919 the American army briefly considered demobilising the troops via the port of Antwerp, before deciding on the French ports. This derailed the plans of the Belgian government, which had hoped to put the port of Antwerp on the map. Later that year the Americans would use the port of Antwerp for the transport of equipment and weapons.

Troops en route to and from Germany were billeted in the country. After the German occupation, many places again had soldiers staying. This time, however, there were no Germans, but Americans, British, Australians, New Zealanders, French or Canadians. The reception was mostly kind. Canadians in Nivelles at the end of November 1918, for example, enjoyed warm accommodation, soft beds and "eight thousand bottles of wine."[17] In Verviers, soldiers from New Zealand were welcomed enthusiastically midway through December, with men, cars and horses being decorated with banners and flowers.[18]

Waiting for repatriation

The overseas troops from Britain were waiting for a "quick" repatriation. After a brief presence in Germany, the Australian and New Zealand soldiers were pulled out. Demobilisation did not begin until February 1919. At least 180,000 soldiers had to return

In the last months of war the Allied armies take thousands of German prisoners of war, who are then locked up in temporary camps. After the armistice these prisoners are put to work, clearing battlefields and dismantling ammunition. They can only return home by late 1919. (War Heritage Institute, Brussels, B.2.31.54.25332)

by ship to the other side of the world. Meanwhile, "fighting morale" had to be replaced by "reconstruction morale": preparing the men for a life after the army. School education had been provided during the war, but the armistice fundamentally disrupted these programmes. When the Australians were billeted in and around Charleroi, it was very difficult to restart lessons. There were too many interruptions due to leave and official orders and there was the repatriation scheme. Furthermore, huge delays prevented enough text books and teaching materials from being obtained. Just over the

Belgian border, a huge technical school was set up. It was equipped with machinery requisitioned and then abandoned by the Germans. In total, two thousand soldiers would take lessons there. Australian troops could also take lessons at the *Université du Travail* in Charleroi. In addition, the Australians set up a primary, secondary and business school. At least 47,000 soldiers would take lessons at a school both during and after the war. For American soldiers, space was freed up at Belgian universities, but the American army had already sent students to England and France.

51

Getting an education is far from being the only thing that the soldiers from the Allied armies did. They took part in sports events, physical training, classic military drills *and* the nightlife. The theatre company of the 3rd Canadian Division, the Dumbells, was renowned during the war, playing *H.M.S. Pinafore* to packed houses in Charleroi for 32 days. The "warm, friendly attitude of the Belgians (…)" further eased the long wait for their repatriation, "as did the conducted tours to Brussels, Waterloo, and elsewhere."[19] The Canadians also enjoyed regular tours to various towns and cities. They, too, were in our country getting ready for their repatriation, having taken part in the Allied occupation in Germany for a short time. However, Canadian doctors reported that the visits to cities like Brussels, Namur and Liège were not without their consequences. Between February and May 1919 they had to wage a constant battle against venereal disease, a genuine plague that first appeared during the Rhine occupation. The first Canadians left Belgium at the beginning of February, the last at the beginning of May. The New Zealanders left in March, and the last Australians left the country in May. The French had already left Belgium at the end of 1918.

In addition to the tens of thousands of billeted Allied troops, thousands of Russian prisoners of war also ended up in Belgium. They had been released by the Germans, but had no funds and could not yet be repatriated. The government suggested accommodating these Russians temporarily in a camp in Houthem near Veurne. Around five thousand Russian soldiers were waiting there for their repatriation, but the Allied powers would have preferred to deploy these men in the fight against Bolshevism. Due to a lack of regulation, training and resources, little became of this plan. It was not until July 1920 that they eventually went back to Russia.[20]

Relationships

The presence of all these troops brought with it vast amounts of supplies. In addition to the hundreds of thousands of rations that the Allied troops shared with the population, a great number of Belgians also made extensive use of the Allied armies' medical provisions. The Belgians were able to count on a great deal of sympathy from the foreign armies. One American officer even wanted to adopt an orphaned Belgian boy who was serving as his errand boy. More than one foreign soldier married a Belgian woman. In the French port town of Brest, the Americans installed special barracks for the soldiers who were married to Italian, French, British or Belgian women. Quite a few Belgians served in the American military. Honoré Devoldere from Izegem left for America in 1912 and joined the army. After mediation from the Palace, he was given two weeks' leave in February 1919 to visit his wife in Belgium.

The presence of so many foreign troops also had a flip side. In the Council of Ministers at the beginning of January 1919, King Albert reported that there were at least 40 foreign divisions in the country, accounting for around 700,000 men. Those Allied troops naturally put public resources under severe pressure. This caused a lot of tension. The Americans were annoyed at the Belgian attitude to ammunition storage depots: they seized six thousand tons of German ammunition but were not allowed to destroy, stockpile or transport it, given the danger that gas grenades represented. The Belgian government agreed to take on the responsibility for the ammunitions but only in exchange for a large quantity of seized construction materials.

Clearing the battlefields

During the war the Belgian army captured 19,000 prisoners of war. From March 1918 onwards, these men were deployed on French soil as a labour force for the Belgian army. After the armistice they were immediately released but grouped in various camps throughout the country. Many of them were deployed to clear the battlefields in West Flanders and others had to help gather weaponries and ammunition. Accidents were not uncommon. It was not until the autumn of 1919 that the Belgian government repatriated the German prisoners of war, as provided for in the Treaty of Versailles. Twenty Germans stayed behind in Diest to exert pressure: it was a way of making sure that all Belgian prisoners would return from Germany. The last Germans were not released until the end of January 1920.[21]

It was not only Germans who were deployed to clear the former battlefields. The Allied forces were only too happy to deploy their overseas colonial troops on this thankless and dangerous task. The *travailleurs annamites* – workers from Indochina – carried out dangerous work on the front after the armistice. Workers from the Chinese Labour Corps helped to clear the front and bury the dead. Though these Chinese *coolies* built up a sound reputation during the war as reliable workers, these *Tsjings* ("Chinks" would have been the English equivalent at the time) gained a bad name due to alleged thefts and violence after the armistice. In September the Corps was replaced by the Indian Labour Corps, which consisted of civilians in British military service. With the help of these hundreds of foreign workers, Belgium was able to begin the long process of rebuilding.

THE RETURN
TO BELGIUM IN 1918–1919

———

Michaël Amara

The closing weeks of 1918 and the whole of 1919 were marked by the return home of hundreds of thousands of Belgians who had been forced abroad or into unoccupied Belgium by the war. The great majority of these were refugees. When the armistice was signed, some 600,000 Belgian civilians were still living abroad. There were more than 300,000 in France, just under 180,000 in Great Britain, and approximately 100,000 in the Netherlands. In addition to these civilians, there were tens of thousands of soldiers, those who had been at the front or in the rearguard bases of the Belgian army in France, plus more than 30,000 soldiers who had been interned in the Netherlands in 1914, and 40,000 prisoners of war returning from Germany.

The refugees

In England, the repatriation of the exiles started at the end of November 1918. A few days after the signing of the armistice, the London government contacted the Belgian authorities to announce their intention to repatriate the refugees quickly. Nobody could be unaware that the closure of the wartime factories would soon be putting tens of thousands of Belgian workers out of work. In this context, the repatriation operations was seen as a priority. At the end of 1918, the lack of boats, and the dockers' strikes slowed the operations down somewhat, but this did not weaken the resolve of the authorities of either country to expedite matters. In January 1919, the Ministry of Shipping made four cruise ships available, and from that point on, thousands crossed the Channel every day. In order to speed up repatriation, the British Government agreed to bear the travelling expenses of those who were unable to pay for the crossing. Others set

The first ship carrying refugees from Great Britain arrives in Ostend after the armistice.
The trip also heralds the re-launch of passenger traffic between Dover and Ostend in 1918.
(National Archives and Records Administration, Washington, 165-WW-179B-009)

October 1918. The Allied liberation offensive not only chases Germans out of occupied territory but also engenders a massive outflow of refugees, as was the case in 1914. French and Belgian civilians flee the violence of war and seek shelter in The Netherlands. Carrying all they possess, they reach Weert station, just across the Belgian border, by open freight train carriages.
(Nationaal Archief, Spaarnestad collection, Het Leven, SFA022802985)

out under their own steam. In the early spring of 1919, only a handful of refugees were left on the other side of the Channel.

The repatriation of Belgians from the Netherlands was just as quick. From December 1918, the first internees and their families came back into the country by rail. After obtaining passes issued by the Belgian authorities, some tens of thousands of refugees followed suit. In mid-January 1919, between 60% and 70% of the 100,000 refugees who had still been living in the Netherlands at the time of the armistice had already returned. The refugee camps closed down one by one in the February of 1919, and the refugee aid arrangements were terminated a few weeks later. In the summer of 1919, almost all the Belgians were back home. One of the ironies of history; in 1921, the installations of two of the old refugee camps were dismantled and sent to France to house the homeless of the Lens and Liévin regions.[22]

The highest number of refugees had been in France, which is where repatriation turned out to be the most complicated. The work of the officials from the *Office de Rapatriement Belge* sent throughout the country was not easy. More than 300,000 Belgians had to be repatriated, but due to the destruction of the railway lines and the shortage of rolling stock, the repatriation operation did not really get underway until the spring of 1919. In April, more than 1,200 Belgians entrained in Nantes after listening to a speech by the mayor boasting of the indestructible links which would unite Belgians and French from then on. Scenes like this were reproduced throughout the country. Refugee allowances were stopped from the 15th of July 1919, except in the case of Belgians originating from around 40 communities in Western Flanders which had been destroyed.

For them, their troubles did not end with the war. By the beginning of 1919, more than 65,000 homes had been destroyed or damaged in Western Flanders. Due to inadequate funding, temporary housing was only being built sporadically, and it turned out to be very uncomfortable. Many people were forced to live there for months, or even years. Some, faced with the destruction and the loss of all their property, refused to go back. In fact, France was the only host country where a sizeable proportion of the Belgian diaspora stayed for good. It is difficult to calculate how many Belgians decided not to come back. However, there can be no doubt that they contributed considerably to the increase in the number of Belgians registered in Normandy, the Somme, and the agricultural areas to the south of Paris. Many farmers who had signed agricultural leases stayed on the land. Others decided not to come back because they had married locals.[23]

The prisoners

The return of the Belgians who had been in Germany started at the end of 1918. The civilian prisoners were the first to be repatriated. At the end of the war, there were still some 600 of these who were repatriated from November onward. Back from captivity, the mayors of Brussels and Ghent made triumphal entries into their cities. The 11th of November Armistice Agreement had provided for immediate repatriation of soldiers who had been prisoners of war in Germany. Between December 1918 and January 1919, more than 40,000 men returned to the country. About 30,000 of these travelled by train, and more than 4,000 by boat. The others returned under their own steam, after being released by their ex-jailers; these had in the meantime become members of revolutionary committees. By the end of January 1919, all that were left were those too ill to be moved, the members of certain rescue committees with the task of winding up their organisations, a few prisoners who had come back late from their sub-camps, and a handful of Belgians who wanted to settle down in Germany. Once back in the country, like the interned soldiers, all the ex-prisoners of war benefited from compensation of 50 francs, one month's paid leave, and some clothing. The civilian prisoners were granted assistance of 150 francs.[24]

In the Council of Ministers on 10 December 1918, the King insisted that "the return of the prisoners of war, internees, and Belgian refugees abroad must be organised in the best conditions, they must be welcomed with a certain ceremony, and on their return to Belgium they must be provided with every possible comfort and the moral assistance to which they are entitled."[25] However, this wish to celebrate the reunion of Belgians at home and from abroad received a feeble response. The returning refugees were met by general indifference. Over the years, each side had built its own idea of the other. Away from occupied Belgium, part of the diaspora had acquired a very negative image of the Belgians who had stayed behind. Some felt that prolonged contact with the Germans had spoiled whole swathes of Belgian society. In liberated Belgium, the stereotype of the gilded exile from a privileged class was to last well beyond the armistice. These misconceptions often forced the returned exiles, accused of having run away from the privations and brutality inflicted by the enemy, into a defensive stance against Belgians who they, in turn, suspected of being too accommodating to the Germans. The interned soldiers who had spent the whole war in the Netherlands did not escape from this vilification. They were seen as shirkers, and even traitors, and were conspicuous by their absence from the post-war patriotic celebrations. As for the ex-military prisoners of war, they had to start a long struggle to obtain full recognition for their trials and tribulations.

Oblivion

These latent misunderstandings resulted in the relegation of the experience of the returning Belgians to a kind of general oblivion. After 1918, the Belgian experience of war was seen only in the context of occupied Belgium and the Front. As a result, people who had survived the war outside the occupied territory or the Yser often decided not to attempt to join the pantheon of World War I heroes. Refugees kept quiet, receding further into oblivion. There is hardly any trace of ex-refugee associations and no press coverage at all. The rare monuments to the exile of the Belgians are abroad, not in Belgium. Many tried to melt into the crowd, concealing their own experience of the war.

In view of this silence, it has become difficult to assess the real conditions of the return of the exiles. There can be no doubt that there were many difficulties. In their absence, their homes had often been occupied or visited. The billeting of the German troops, the influx of French evacuees, and then the housing of the Allied troops had caused housing shortages, and to make up for this the houses or apartments of those who had left were sometimes used. These problems were exacerbated by those faced by children returning to their schools, and families who had been separated for many years

Thousands of Belgians flee to the United Kingdom during the war. Birtley in the north of England thus sees the creation of Elisabethville, a village exclusively housing Belgian refugees and Belgian soldiers no longer fit for service. Most of them work in the local weapon industry, the National Projectile Factory at Birtley. Once armistice is called these Belgian labourers are no longer needed and all Belgian are repatriated. The first train leaves the factory grounds on 7 December 1918. (Newcastle City Library, Local Studies Collection)

had to learn to live together again. Although the armistice was the signal for the immense majority of Belgians who had spent the war abroad to return, their troubles were far from over.

3

A NEW WORLD

THE POST-WAR PEACE TREATIES

Catherine Lanneau

On 11 November 1918, Germany had neither been defeated within its own borders nor fundamentally weakened. The Allies saw Bolshevik Russia, although diminished by the Brest-Litovsk Treaty, as a pressing danger. In addition, the experience of the war had been different, on the one hand, for the French (and the Belgians), whose territory had been totally or partly occupied and who wanted their security guaranteed as a priority and, on the other, for the British and Americans, who considered that German economic recovery should not be made impossible. In the light of these opposing attitudes, it is easy to understand why the Versailles Treaty and the subsequent treaties, known as the "Paris Suburban Treaties", very quickly came to be seen by some as ill-considered and creating exasperating obstacles, while others saw them as unable to guarantee the security of the continent.[1]

Even before the Versailles Treaty settles the dismantlement of German armed forces, the armistice conditions stipulate that German equipment is to be handed over to the Allies. On 2 December 1918 the U155 (the former *Handels U-Boot 'Deutschland'*), flying the German flag, arrives at the London Tower Bridge by way of the Thames. The vessel that sank 42 Allied and neutral ships is first exhibited and later scrapped. The ship even claims additional victims while it is being wrecked: five labourers die in an explosion in 1921.

(National Archives and Records Administration, Washington, 165-WW-330C-021)

The Treaty of Versailles

The Peace Conference opened in Paris on the 18ᵗʰ of January 1919. Initially, many journalists were present, but as they were only invited to the plenary sessions, they lost interest, and those who stayed on had to make do with more or less controlled leaks. In
line with Wilson's 14 Points, the Conference should have promoted open diplomacy
and respected the rights of peoples to self-determination. However, this was not to be.
A directorate of the five "main allied powers and partners" (France, Great Britain, the
United States, Italy, and Japan) took control, but soon it was mainly the "Big Four",
represented by Clemenceau, Lloyd George, Wilson, and Orlando, who were involved,
until Italy, frustrated in its ambitions over Fiume and Dalmatia, temporarily walked
out. The other "allied and partner" nations took part in plenary sessions and in the
work of the 52 preparatory commissions but had little to do with the major decisions.
Finally, Germany, the object of the first peace treaty being prepared, was not admitted
to the negotiating table and was barely able to make a few minor comments when the
draft text was forwarded to it at the beginning of May 1919.

Signed on 28 June 1919 in the Hall of Mirrors of the palace, the very place where the
German Empire had been proclaimed in 1871, the Treaty of Versailles consisted of 15 parts,
the first of which was the League of Nations (LN) Convention, a collective security instrument which was doomed to failure in the absence of a system for applying automatic
military sanctions if it were breached. Part XIII established the International Labour Office (ILO) calling for the establishment of "universal peace" based on "social justice". Its
general principles included the adoption of the eight-hour working day with a weekly
break, as well as the abolition of child labour and equal pay for men and women.

Article 231 of the Treaty of Versailles made Germany and its allies solely responsible
"for causing all the loss and damage to which the Allied and Associated Governments
and their nationals have been subjected as a consequence of the war imposed upon
them by the aggression of Germany and her allies." This moral condemnation, which
was aimed at justifying the principle of reparations, was to have considerable psychological consequences. It was accompanied by an obligation to hand over war criminals
to the Allies. The Treaty also required the arraignment of William II to be judged by a
special tribunal of the Five "for a supreme offence against international morality and
the sanctity of treaties."

In territorial terms, Germany lost 13% of its territory and 10% of its population. Article 80 of the Treaty banned in advance any *Anschluss* of Austria, declaring its independence to be inalienable. Alsace-Moselle returned to France, which, in compensation for the destruction of its mines in the North, was granted ownership of those of the
Saar, a territory placed under the control of the LN pending a plebiscite to be held
within 15 years. Belgium received full sovereignty of Moresnet-neutre, and obtained

the "Circles" of Eupen and Malmedy, following a public consultation, the questionable organisation of which was to be described locally as a bad Belgian joke. The border between Germany and Denmark was also to be redrawn following plebiscites which, held at the beginning of 1920, ended with the annexing by Denmark of Northern Schleswig, which was then renamed Southern Jutland. To the East, Poland received Posnania and part of Eastern Prussia. It had access to the Baltic via the "Danzig Corridor", Danzig having been declared a free city under the responsibility of the LN. Eastern Prussia was thus separated from the rest of Germany, and also lost Memel, which was placed under allied administration until its forced annexation by Lithuania in 1923. In Silesia, the small Hlučín Region was allocated to Czechoslovakia, while another zone, in High Silesia, was the object of a plebiscite between Germany and Poland on 20 March 1921, against a background of popular insurrections orchestrated by the Poles. Although the outcome tended to be in favour of Germany, the arrangement settled on by the LN gave Poland the main part of the Silesian "industrial triangle".

The German possessions outside Europe were allocated in the form of LN mandates. So in Western Africa, the Cameroons were entrusted to France, apart from 10% of the territory, which came under British administration, while two thirds of Togo were assigned to France and one third to the UK. In Eastern Africa, the UK also obtained Tanganyika, while South West Africa – now Namibia – was passed to the South African Union, New Guinea and Nauru to Australia, and Samoa to New Zealand, three British dominions. Belgium, for its part, received Ruanda-Urundi. Finally, Japan gained administration of the Mariana, Marshall and Caroline Islands in the Pacific, plus the German territories and concessions in China (Shandong) until the latter took them back in 1922.

On the military side, the Treaty of Versailles provided for the dissolution of the German High Command and a ban on Germany having heavy artillery, an airforce, tanks, submarines or battleships. Military service of any kind was also proscribed. The German land forces were restricted to 100,000 professionals and the naval forces to 15,000. The Allies also imposed occupation of the left bank of the Rhine, for release in three instalments in 5, 10 and 15 years on condition that Germany complied with these requirements. They were also to keep the three bridgeheads around Mainz, Coblenz and Cologne. In addition, a demilitarised zone 50 km deep was set up on a permanent basis on the right bank.

With regard to reparations, the Allies, obsessed with one-upmanship, failed to set the sum to be claimed from Germany. They declared that a figure must be set by May 1921, but initially required a provisional 20 billion gold marks, to be handed over "whether in gold, commodities, ships, securities or otherwise". Belgium specifically obtained reimbursement by Germany of its war debts (Art. 232) plus compensation for the burning of the Louvain University Library and the return of looted works of art

(Art. 247). In order to contribute to the recovery of the countries affected, Germany had to agree to hand over a large part of its merchant navy, plus livestock, machinery, rolling stock, coal, minerals, and chemicals. In addition, the economic and financial clauses of the Treaty made it responsible for the maintenance of all the occupying armies in Germany territory and imposed various customs and commercial restrictions on it for the first five years of implementation of the Treaty. Finally, the main German waterways were internationalised.

The Treaty of Versailles, felt by a humiliated nation to be a *Diktat*, came into force on 10 January 1920 and soon became fuel for the resurgence of an aggressive German nationalism. Its harshness was also criticised in the English-speaking countries.[2] On the other hand, nationalist circles, in particular in France and Belgium, saw it as a source of insecurity, as it did not disarm Germany and did not even guarantee definitive occupation of the Rhineland. The text was submitted to the American Senate on two occasions and finally rejected on 19 March 1920, which de facto invalidated the Treaty of Guarantee which the United States had promised France. In the aftermath, Great Britain also withdrew. So it seemed vital for Paris to obtain a military agreement with Belgium and negotiate "rear alliances" in Central Europe.

The Treaty of Saint-Germain

The Treaty of Versailles was taken as the model or matrix for the other peace treaties imposed on Austria (Saint-Germain), Bulgaria (Neuilly), Hungary (Trianon), and Turkey (Sèvres) in 1919–1920. These all took the LN Convention as their starting point, reproduced the provisions creating the ILO, and implied acknowledgement of moral responsibility for starting the war. Colonial interests and interests "outside Europe" were covered by specific clauses in the Saint-Germain and Trianon Treaties. The requirements regarding reparations are set out formally in all the treaties, except for that of Sèvres, which includes a specific clause on the protection of minorities, a question which, in the Saint-Germain, Neuilly, and Trianon Treaties, is included in the European political clauses. It should be noted that, with regard to respect for minorities, treaties of guarantee were also imposed on Greece, Yugoslavia, Romania, Armenia, Czechoslovakia, and Poland. In addition, the various treaties abolished military service, greatly reducing the size of the armies in question and their weaponry, and banning the possession of a naval or air force. Finally, they contained financial and economic clauses and provisions regarding prisoners of war, lines of communication and air navigation, which were comparable to those of Versailles.

Chronologically speaking, the second peace treaty was that of Saint-Germain, which, signed by Austria on 10 September 1919, formalised the breakup of the

Several allied commissions assembling in Paris draft the peace conditions to be imposed on Germany.
The issue of responsibility is also broached: Germany is blamed for the First World War.
The debate on the *Kriegsschuldfrage* lingers on throughout the 20ᵗʰ century.
(National Archives and Records Administration, Washington, 165-WW-400A-14)

Austro-Hungarian Empire, which had already collapsed shortly before the end of the
war due to declarations of independence by its members and by the proclamation of the
Republik Deutschösterreich.[3] While this name clearly indicates the wish for *Anschluss*,
this was formally rejected by the Allies in the Treaties of Versailles and Saint-Germain.
The dismembered Austria was now reduced to 83,000 km², only 15% of which was
arable land; it had a population of 6.5 million, one third of which was concentrated in
Vienna. It had lost Istria and Trentino-Alto Adige/South Tyrol to Italy; the Sudeten
region, Bohemia and Moravia to Czechoslovakia; Galicia to Poland; Bukovina to Romania; Dalmatia, Carniola, South Styria and a small part of Carinthia to the Kingdom
of Serbs, Croats and Slovenes, which was renamed Yugoslavia in 1929. Bosnia-Herzegovina, which had been ruled by the Austro-Hungarian Empire since 1908, also became
Yugoslavian. In Article 95 of the Treaty, Austria also waived "all rights, titles, and privileges whatever" in or over any territory outside Europe (Morocco, Egypt, Siam, China).
Its army was reduced to 30,000 professionals. The Treaty of Saint-Germain came into
force on 16 July 1920.

A NEW WORLD

The Treaty of Neuilly

The Treaty of Neuilly, imposed on Bulgaria on 27 November 1919, had several territorial implications, including some confirming or correcting the effects of the Second Balkan War (1913).[4] The country definitively lost Southern Dobrudja to Romania, the part of Macedonia obtained in 1913 to the future Yugoslavia, and Western Thrace to Greece, but under Allied administration. This meant that Bulgaria lost its access to the Aegean Sea. There was to be an exchange of populations with Greece, with some 50,000 Bulgarians leaving Greece and 40,000 Greeks leaving Bulgaria. Tens of thousands of Bulgarians from Thrace, Macedonia and Dobrudja also returned. Bulgaria's army was also reduced to 20,000 professionals. The resentment caused by the Neuilly Treaty, which came into force on 9 August 1920, was to be one of the causes of the rapprochement between Bulgaria and Germany, against a background of denunciation of unfair clauses.

The Treaty of Trianon

For Hungary, the Treaty of Trianon of 4 June 1920 still bears the hallmark of an unresolved national drama – a country reduced to one third of its 1914 area, with 3 million Hungarians living beyond its borders and 800,000 inhabitants belonging to minorities.[5] Under the authoritarian regime of Admiral Horthy, which ended the short Communist experiment of Bela Kun, the status of victim pointed the way to a revisionist policy, which finally led to an alliance with Nazi Germany. Specifically, Hungary lost Slovakia and Subcarpathian Ruthenia to Czechoslovakia; Transylvania and the eastern part of the Banat of Temeswar to Romania; and Croatia-Slavonia, Prekmurje, Batschka and the western part of Banat to the future Yugoslavia – which also gained Bosnia-Herzegovina, previously annexed to the Austro-Hungarian Empire. In addition, Hungary ceded Burgenland to Austria, except for the Sopron / Ödenburg region, which, by plebiscite of December 1921, confirmed its wish to remain Hungarian. The city of Fiume / Rijeka was disputed between Italy and Yugoslavia. It was the object of the famous coup by the Italian poet Gabriele d'Annunzio (1919–1920), expelled under the Rapallo Treaty (November 1920), under which the city became a Free State until its annexation by Fascist Italy in 1924. Under Article 79 of the Treaty, Hungary waived "all rights, titles, and privileges" covering all territories outside Europe (Morocco, Egypt, Siam, China). Its army was reduced to 35,000 professionals. The Treaty of Trianon came into force on 26 July 1921.

The Treaty of Sèvres

The last peace treaty was signed at Sèvres on 10 August 1920 with Turkey, represented at that time by the last Ottoman Sultan, Mehmed VI.[6] Since the Mudros Armistice of 30 October 1918, the French, British and Italians had gained control of various Ottoman territories. A few months later, the Greeks moved into Smyrna. The Turkish territorial possessions were reduced by the Treaty to the region of Istanbul / Constantinople and Anatolia. Italy's possession of Rhodes and the Dodecanese was confirmed. An autonomous Kurdistan and an independent Armenia are provided for in the text, but within undefined borders. Greece received Eastern Thrace and the Imbros and Tenedos Islands, plus Smyrna and Western Anatolia, subject to a plebiscite being held in five years' time. As a result of discussions held in San Remo in April/May 1920, France was called to run Syria and the Lebanon under LN mandates. The same applied to the United Kingdom with regard to Palestine and Mesopotamia (the modern-day Iraq). Arabia, under the name Hedjaz, became autonomous, under British influence, as was already the case for Egypt. The Straits were demilitarised and opened up to all foreign warships under the surveillance of the Straits Commission. Police and special troop numbers were restricted to 50,000 men plus the Sultan's personal guard. As for the capitulations, the extra-territorial advantages granted to the foreigners, these were re-established and amplified.

Refusing to recognise a treaty they felt to be one-sided, the Turkish nationalists intensified their military actions. They were working under Mustapha Kemal who, since April 1920, had been running their own government and their Great National Assembly from Ankara, in opposition to the Sultan's power base in Istanbul. The Turkish nationalists turned against the Republic of Armenia, which quickly had to give up its hopes for independence; the territory was to continue to be shared between Turkey and Bolshevik Russia. The Allies, although they had promised support for these people who were recently the target of genocidal massacres, proved to be powerless. The armed struggle also continued with the Greeks, against whom the Turks achieved several victories in 1921. In March of that year, under the Treaty of Moscow, Turkey recovered two Armenian districts, Kars and Ardahan; in June, Italy evacuated Adalia; in October, France gave up almost all of Cilicia and, de facto, recognised the Ankara Government. The year 1922 was crucial: the French and the Italians evacuated the Dardanelles, to the great annoyance of the British, who were still supporting the Greeks. The latter were violently expelled from Smyrna by the Turks, who perpetrated massacres and burned the city. At the beginning of November 1922, the Sultanate was abolished, and Kemal was, de facto, alone at the helm. On 29 October 1923, the Republic was proclaimed, and Mustapha Kemal was elected President.

The German delegation has little or no input in the imposed peace conditions. The victorious countries meet among themselves in various locations in Paris. The Germans are only invited to participate in the Versailles conference. (War Heritage Institute, Brussels, B.1.72.6.22)

In December 1922, an international conference was opened in Lausanne, recognising the failure of the Sèvres Treaty, which had never been ratified by all the signatories. The Treaty of Lausanne, concluded on 24 July 1923, consisted of five parts: political, financial and economic clauses; lines of communication and health matters; and miscellaneous clauses. So there was no longer any question of sanctions, military clauses, or any moral responsibility of Turkey. The text confirmed the mandates of the LN set forth at Sèvres, but erased independent Armenia and the autonomy of Kurdistan. Turkey recovered the whole of Asia Minor and Eastern Thrace, which gave rise, via an appended convention, to a two-way exodus of more than one and a half million people, Turks from Greece and Greeks from Turkey. The capitulations were abolished and the Straits, although demilitarised and open to all, were replaced under Turkish sovereignty. The Treaty came into force on 30 August 1924.

With the exception of the Lausanne Treaty, the peace treaties which put an end to the First World War did not survive the upheavals of the 1930s and the start of the second conflict. In fact, the outcome was worse – they became mere bogeymen, threatening shadows in the dark. The most recent historiography, however, tends to be less condemnatory of their authors, who were prisoners of their own views of the world.

THE CREATION OF
THE LEAGUE OF NATIONS

Jean-Michel Sterkendries

T he world has never been able to eliminate the scourge of war. After the Thirty Years' War, the Treaties of Westphalia attempted to establish a very relative international order. The French Revolution and Empire were followed by the so-called "Concert of Europe", which was highly ineffective and ceased to exist when two blocks of opposing alliances were drawn up. The early years of the 20th century once again saw a march to war. There were many forces working for peace, such as the socialist and trade union movements, the spirit the Churches tried to instil, and even the ambition to see international law upheld, which led to the founding of the International Court of Justice in The Hague. But all the grounds for hope they had given rise to were swept away by excessively aggressive nationalism. In 1914, Europe, followed by a large part of the rest of the world, plunged into an abyss. Four years later, there had been some ten million deaths, with devastation and material losses without number; empires had fallen, societies had been destroyed, and misery was widespread.

What could be done to ensure that the abomination that had taken place would be "the war to end all wars", the *"Der des Ders"*? The idea resurfaced of building up a new international order, backed by a society or "League of Nations". This was not a new idea but rather an expression which Emmanuel Kant had already used in his day. The great French statesman Léon Bourgeois, who campaigned tirelessly for peace, had already written a book about it in 1910. In September 1915, while war was raging, the Cabinet in London was doing its utmost to gain support from America, which was still neutral. The Foreign Office was already well aware of the idealism of Thomas Woodrow Wilson, who had won the presidential election in the United States in November 1912. In order to persuade him to join the conflict on the side of the democratic nations, His Majesty's Secretary of State, Edward Grey, sent him a proposal – to what extent would

The first plenary meeting of the League of Nations General Assembly takes place in Geneva (Switzerland) on 15 November 1920. It is chaired by the Belgian Paul Hymans and 41 countries participate. The meeting lasts until 18 December 1920. (Archives United Nations, Geneva)

November 1920. Group portrait of the Belgian League of Nations delegation. The third person from the left is Paul Hymans, the General Assembly's first chairman. At the far right is newly appointed Minister of Finances and future Prime Minister Georges Theunis. (Archives United Nations, Geneva)

the President be interested in the creation of an international organisation responsible for the peaceful settlement of conflicts and disarmament?[7]

The favourite child of President Wilson

The idea did not originate with Wilson, but when he started to take an interest in it in 1916, he became its most enthusiastic supporter. It was he who was to take up the project and literally impose it on his counterparts at the so-called Peace Conference.

It is known that the United States had carefully held aloof from the war until April 1917. When they did decide to join, it was not as allies of the *Entente* powers, but as a partner nation. The course of the war demonstrated the great rise in power of the star-spangled Republic. It is all too often forgotten that, from the start of their intervention, the US Navy immediately began to give major support to the naval forces of the *Entente*. On the Continent, their land forces were only to enter the fight a year further on into the War, but that was exactly when the balance of power started to tilt. And, in the meantime, the Europeans had become in debt to the United States to an extent which nobody could have imagined in the pre-War period. A lot has been written about the near-mystical character of President Wilson and his messianic vision of the part the United States were called to play in the world. The son of a Presbyterian minister, Wilson was a high-flying academic who had taught at the prestigious Princeton University; he had been the incumbent of the White House since March 1913. In 1916, he was re-elected after campaigning with the slogan "He kept us out of war". This, however, had not prevented him from making many attempts – in vain – to promote the return to peace. The Belgians were also well aware that the Americans were very active in providing humanitarian aid. After all, it was the Commission for relief in Belgium which, between 1914 and 1917, saved occupied Belgium from famine. According to Wilson, "*Realpolitik* had failed; and peace must now be founded on an international organisation and on bringing democracy to the world."[8] It was the latter that was the guarantee of peace. The fall of the Tsarist aristocracy and a sudden injection of democracy in Russia had arrived in February/March 1917 in the nick of time for America to be able to claim that it was joining the fray on the side of the democratic nations. But Wilson also wanted to stand outside the scrum and act as referee. A commission of experts, headed by Wilson's right-hand man, Colonel Edward Mandell House, was put in charge of studying the hard facts of a peace settlement.[9]

This was when, in Russia, the so-called October Revolution broke out. On the 8th of November 1917, Lenin proposed a peace with no annexations or compensation. The American president jumped at this opportunity to make his country the champion of the democratic reorganisation of the world. On the 8th of January 1918, President Wilson presented his famous fourteen-point peace programme to Congress. The main principles are well known – no more secret diplomacy, freedom of the seas, restoration of the integrity and independence of Belgium, restoration of a Polish state, the right of peoples to self-determination, and, last but not least, a fourteenth point which stipulated that "A general association of nations must be formed under specific covenants for the purpose of affording mutual guarantees of political independence and territorial integrity to great and small states alike".

However well-meaning these intentions, they were not easy to accept for those who were preparing to make a very hard peace settlement with Germany. The obvious wish of the American president to dominate the discussions also caused annoyance. The words attributed to Clemenceau were frequently repeated: "... God himself was content with ten commandments; Wilson is giving us fourteen." But what was clear was that it was Wilson who was in a position of strength at that point. In the closing days of October 1918, the Allied victory was no longer in doubt. In fact, it was only at this moment that the fourteen points were really discussed – and disputed more than once – by the French and British partners. At the great meeting held at the Quai d'Orsay on the 29th of October, Clemenceau objected specifically to the fourteenth point regarding a "League of Nations", which he found lacking in clarity. Other points were severely criticised by both Lloyd George and Clemenceau. They were unenthusiastic, to say the

November 1920. View of the *Salle de Réformation* during a League of Nations meeting. Between 1920 and 1930 the General Assembly meets in this former Geneva concert hall. (Archives United Nations, Geneva)

least. But the American pressure was enormous. The ubiquitous Colonel House made it perfectly clear that if his president's advice was not followed, he could not exclude the possibility of a separate peace with Germany.[10]

Meanwhile, in the preceding days, calls for peace to be prepared under the aegis of the United States had been coming from Germany itself. The Government of the Reich made it known several times in the course of October that it accepted Wilson's

fourteen points as a basis for future peace talks. So there would be a League of Nations, which would require a constitutional agreement. This was drawn up during the peace conference held from the 3rd of February to the 11th of April 1919 at the Hôtel Crillon in Paris. The Commission was chaired by Wilson himself, with the inevitable Colonel House alongside; Belgium was represented by its Liberal Minister of Foreign Affairs, Paul Hymans.

The final text contains 26 articles defining the fundamental aims (respect for international law, abolition of secret diplomacy, resolution of conflicts by arbitration) as well as the functions of the main organs of the future organisation. Wilson got the essential parts of what he wanted but had to make concessions. One of the aims of the future League of Nations was to achieve a general reduction in armaments, but the French delegation succeeded in having this provision made immediately applicable only to the losers. It also succeeded in obtaining the proviso that Germany would only be able to join the League of Nations after a certain period had elapsed. The French, however, were still not fully satisfied. Léon Bourgeois pleaded eloquently but in vain for the League of Nations to be given an international force in charge of applying any military sanctions; this was not upheld. Wilson declared in effect that he felt that if the League of Nations were to be armed, this would mean prolonging a post-War coalition against Germany. The English-speaking side also very probably felt that an "army of the League of Nations" would be too heavily dominated by the French.

In other words, it was fated never to happen, and this created a weakness in the League of Nations which would be taken advantage of at a later date. In practice, what this meant was that the only sanctions the League of Nations could take boiled down to the commercial and financial relationships covered by Article 16 of the Pact, the efficacy of which was to turn out to be unreliable. The Belgians also had more than one good reason for being disappointed. A headquarters had to be chosen for the future organisation. Paul Hymans pleaded on behalf of Brussels but was unable to convince the other members. And yet there were plenty of arguments for this. The Belgian Minister had declared: "... the choice of the country where the headquarters of the League of Nations will be established will mean a great honour for that country, and Belgium believes that it is entitled to claim this and aspire to this moral compensation (...). Throughout the War, Belgium was the symbol of the cause of Right and rendered services to this cause which earned it the gratitude of the world."[11] Although this declaration was met with sympathy, the majority of the members of the Commission still voted against Brussels. What they wanted was a League of Nations which would be forward-looking rather than anchored in what could be seen as the resentments of the past. The final choice was Geneva, because it wasn't a capital, it belonged to a neutral country, Jean-Jacques Rousseau and the international Red Cross were associated with it ... this was what the optimists would soon be calling "The Geneva Spirit".

From Wilson's dream to reality

Finally, the League of Nations would only represent a very small part of the international community. The losers would not be admitted, at least not immediately. As Jean

Monnet was to say, "the absence of Germany vitiated the very foundation of the principle of a true League of Nations."[12] Russia, in the throes of civil war, was not invited to the Peace Conference. Its future was uncertain, and nobody knew which Russians should be invited. In addition, Clemenceau would not hear of admitting to membership a country which he considered to have betrayed the Allied cause by its defection. It should also be noted that, even though this may be anecdotal, Pope Benedict XV did not look kindly on the birth of the League of Nations. In fact, the Holy See had been excluded from the Peace Conference at the specific request of Italy. Further, Benedict XV saw the League of Nations as the creation of Protestants, Socialists and Freemasons. So the League of Nations did not seem to have a smooth start. The membership would not include either Germany or the USSR. And worst of all, the United States had no intention of joining, either.

A few days before the end of the War, on the 5th of November 1918, the American legislative elections were won by the Republicans, who would henceforth have the majority in both the Chamber and the Senate. The new President of the Senate Foreign Relations Committee was Henry Cabot Lodge, the man who had led the opposition against Wilson. The latter had also bungled. Wanting to make his mark in Versailles as the arbitrator of the Peace, he had left the United States for several months, with the result that he had lost contact with his Congress and public opinion. In addition, the American delegation accompanying the President consisted of no fewer than 1,300 people, with not a Republican in sight. In the course of 1919, the President of the United States spent more time in France than in his own country, something that had never happened before.

This did not go down well on the other side of the Atlantic, and the Republicans had no problems in producing their campaign slogan "Back to normalcy", while isolationist feeling grew. At the same time, the Commission headed by Cabot Lodge severely criticised the draft United Nations Convention and put forward a slew of amendments. In particular, it could not approve provisions which could lead to the LN deciding to bring the United States into war at some point in the future, this being the sacrosanct prerogative of Congress. But Wilson was single-minded and was not prepared to compromise. In September 1919, he undertook an exhausting tour of the United States to persuade his people. And drama ensued. On the 2nd of October he had a stroke, and he returned to the White House an invalid, no longer capable of dealing with affairs of State. The Treaty of Versailles was never ratified by the United States, and they did not join the League of Nations. The presidential elections of November 1920 were won with a clear majority by Republican Warren G. Harding. America returned to isolationism. In other words, the League of Nations had got off to a bad start.

The organs of the League of Nations

Nevertheless, its institutions were set up. On the 10th of January 1920, when the Treaty of Versailles came into force, the League of Nations was officially established. It had three main bodies: a General Assembly, a Council and a Secretariat.

Each member nation had one vote within the Assembly. The Assembly held at least one session a year, theoretically in September. It elected non-permanent members of the Council and judges at the Permanent Court of International Justice. In most cases, decisions could only be passed by unanimity. The members naturally had to adhere to the values defined in the Convention. Every candidate nation had to give effective guarantees of adhering to these values. It then had to be approved in the Assembly with a majority of at least two thirds of the vote.

The first meeting of the Assembly was held in Geneva on the 15th of November 1920, chaired by Paul Hymans, an honour for Belgium. This great Belgian statesman would, in fact, be the only person to hold this seat twice, in 1920–1921 and 1932–1933. It was possible to join the League of Nations, it was possible to leave (by giving two years' notice), and it was possible to be excluded – and all these scenarios took place. A large number of South American nations, which had adhered to the Convention at the beginning, fairly soon withdrew from the organisation which did not include the United States and looked a little too much like a club for European conquerors. Germany, which was not admitted until 1926, walked out in 1933. Japan, a founding member and, furthermore, represented on the Council, also left the League of Nations in 1933. Much the same happened with Italy; a founding member represented on the Council, it left in 1937. The USSR only joined the League of Nations in 1934 – and was then excluded in 1939. One strange case is that of Yugoslavia,[13] a founding member which left the League of Nations but subsequently returned and stayed until the end.

The Council was considered to be the real executive body of the League of Nations. Initially, it was made up of four permanent members: the United Kingdom, France, Italy and Japan; they were joined by four non-permanent members elected for a three-year term. The first non-permanent members were Belgium, Brazil, Greece and Spain. In principle, the Council met five times a year. The first meeting was on the 16th of January 1920, and was chaired by Léon Bourgeois. Membership of the Council had to be changed several times. When Germany joined the League of Nations in 1926, it became the fifth permanent member, but subsequently, as already mentioned, Germany, Japan, and Italy left, which removed practically all its substance and made it inoperative. The number of non-permanent members also changed several times, rising to six (1922), then nine (1926), and finally eleven (1933).

The Secretariat was the permanent body that assured the daily functioning of the League of Nations. It prepared the agendas for the Council and the Assembly, and published the minutes of the meetings and the reports. The three official languages of the LN were English, French and Spanish. There was even some discussion of adopting Esperanto, but this came to nothing. The Secretariat had to have up to 670 staff and experts, headed by a Secretary General. President Wilson had insisted on this position being held by British national Sir Eric Drummond. This time, his advice was taken, and nobody ever came to regret it. Drummond carried out his task brilliantly, from 1919 to 1933. And one of his assistants was none other than Jean Monnet.

Alongside these three main bodies were an International Permanent Court of Justice, the International Labour Office, and several specialist commissions. The International Permanent Court of Justice, located in The Hague, was in charge of dealing with disputes between States and ruling on armed conflicts. The International Labour Organisation (ILO) is worthy of special mention, because some good did come of the Versailles Treaty. This was where a chapter was first prepared on the organisation of social relations by creating an International Labour Organisation, which was associated with the League of Nations from the start. Its mission consisted of improving the conditions of workers and promoting greater social justice in the world. The ILO was very active, and its role was to be positive. Many international norms and conventions were drafted, covering working hours, protection for women and children, the principle of trade union freedom, etc.

Finally, the League of Nations was backed by specialist commissions and committees: the Health Committee, the Commission for Refugees, the Slavery Commission, and the International Commission on Intellectual Cooperation. A Mandates Commission was also set up for the administration of the ex-German and Ottoman colonies allocated to the conquerors, with the aim of preparing them for independence. It has to be said, however, that this system of mandates was largely a whitewash. In practice there was little difference between the handling of the colonies and the mandate territories.

Last but not least, a Disarmament Commission was to head a universal arms reduction, which should have been one of the surest guarantees of maintaining peace. This was a complete failure.

The balance sheet

At first sight, it seems easy to produce a balance sheet of the results of the League of Nations. Just 20 years after its creation, it was unable to prevent the unleashing of the deadliest conflict in history. The word "bankrupt" springs to mind. However, not everything was on the debit side, and in the euphoria of the twenties, "The Geneva

The German delegation poses in front of Hotel Métropole in Geneva. Chancellor Hans Luther (sitting on the left) and Minister of Foreign Affairs Gustav Stresemann (sitting on the right) are the delegation's protagonists. The German delegation is not admitted to the League of Nations before March 1926 and Germany only becomes a member in September 1926. It then is the Council's fifth permanent member.
(Bundesarchiv, Koblenz, Bild 102-02388/photo: Georg Pahl)

Spirit" was talked of with optimism. Several successes can be entered on the assets side of the new organisation. Examples of this are the Upper Silesia Crisis of 1921 involving Poland and Germany; the settling of the Corfu crisis between Italy and Greece in 1923; the arbitration of the conflict between Sweden and Finland over the Aland Islands; the Saar Government for a 15-year period and the holding of the referendum which was to result in its union with Germany. In Liberia, it put an end to labour trafficking and forced labour. Although often derided, the Permanent Court of International Justice had paved the way for the future. And the work of the International Labour Organisation also bore fruit in several areas.

Unfortunately, the list of failures is longer and more serious. The attempted universal disarmament was a total failure. The League of Nations was powerless against many shows of strength: the occupation of the Ruhr by France and Belgium from 1923 to 1925, the invasion of Manchuria by Japan in 1931, the manic rearmament of Germany under Hitler, the Italian aggression in Ethiopia in 1935, the remilitarisation of the left bank of the Rhine in 1936, the annexation of Austria by Nazi Germany in 1938, the annexation of Sudetenland during the same year, the invasion of Bohemia and Moravia and their placing under protectorate by Germany in 1939 and, at the same time, Italy's invasion of Albania. This was a time of impotence. On the 1st of September 1939, Nazi Germany invaded Poland, and the worst was yet to come. The hope for a fair, sustainable peace had evaporated once again.

BELGIAN COLONIAL ASPIRATIONS IN VERSAILLES

Enika Ngongo

Belgians thought that being represented at Versailles would mean they could sit down at the negotiating table and discuss the fate of the ex-German colonies.[14] As the winner of the African campaigns of Tabora and Mahenge (in actual Tanzania) and conqueror of the rich Ruanda-Urundi,[15] Belgium thinks it holds a valuable pawn which it could use to gain access to the Atlantic Ocean after bargaining with Portugal, as well as a review of certain clauses agreed at the Berlin Conference of 1885 and the Brussels Conference of 1890, which it saw as obstacles to the development of the Belgian Congo. With the control of all the trading on the Congo River, Belgium would become an acknowledged imperial power in Africa, with the same status as France and Great Britain.

The Belgians and the colonial question

However, once in Versailles, it soon became obvious to the members of the Belgian delegation that Belgium was not going to be permitted to sit with the other nations interested in a new share-out of Africa.[16] In mid-February, the settlement of colonial affairs was still going against its interests. On the one hand, Portugal would never agree to negotiate its colonies and had no interest in new territories that were totally alien to it. On the other, the theory of mandates overturned the scenarios that the Belgian delegation had envisaged up to that point.[17] If Belgians were to declare any intention of abandoning Ruanda-Urundi, the League of Nations would probably appoint a new

Belgian topographers with the *Comité Spécial du Katanga* at work. After the First World War the Congo remains under Belgian colonial rule and Belgium continues to operate the Katanga mines.
(Archives Royal Palace, Albums AE 213/B)

mandator, and Great Britain would come forward to take this role. After the failure at Tabora, poor little Belgium once again seemed unable to compete. Could Belgium still hope to have a voice?

The First World War also rages in Africa. The Belgian Congo *Force publique* participates in the campaign against German East Africa. The *Souvenir congolais* monument honouring the victims of this operation is unveiled in Leopoldville on 2 July 1927.

(Archives Royal Palace, Albums AE 433/B)

The situation was critical. Aware of their weak position on the international scene, Belgium decided to take what was within its reach – Ruanda and Urundi. They had won them on their own and they could not be taken away. Territories on the Portuguese bank of the Congo River could be obtained at a later date, if necessary – better one bird in the hand than two in the bush.

A NEW WORLD

Between discussions and negotiations

In March 1919, the interim Secretary General for Foreign Affairs, Pierre Orts, in his capacity as an international law specialist, plenipotentiary minister and ex-adviser during the German East Africa military campaigns to the Minister for the Colonies, Jules Renkin, travelled to Paris for informal discussions with Alfred Milner, the British Secretary of State for the Colonies and wartime civil administration specialist in the British cabinet. Together, they were to draft the outlines of the Anglo-Belgian Entente regarding the administration of the occupied territories for subsequent submission to the League of Nations for approval. But all was in vain. No arrangements had been finalised by the end of their last interview on the 20th of March. Was little Belgium, dwarfed by the great nations, to be definitively excluded from this imperial struggle for the ex-German colonies?

In May, Germany was forced to renounce its overseas territories. Its African colonies became mandates administered on behalf of the League of Nations by mandated powers. At this point, nothing seemed to guarantee Belgium a mandate over the territories it occupied, but then again, nothing seemed to indicate the contrary. Yet, on the 6th of May 1919, the Supreme Council of the Allied Powers officially gave Great Britain mandate over all the German East African territories, thus enshrining the decision it had taken following the handover of the cession treaty to the Germans. Warned by the French press, the Belgian government declared itself categorically opposed to the Council's decision, and pointed out the important part played by Belgian colonial troops in the military operations in Africa, the sacrifices, and the rights entailed by the conquest.

As he was called before the Supreme Council of the Allied Powers, Paul Hymans, the Minister of Foreign Affairs, encounters incomprehension. The members told him they were ignorant about the matter; the President of the United States, Woodrow Wilson, even went so far as to express surprise that Belgium occupied territories in German East Africa. When the matter was referred to David Lloyd George, the British Prime Minister, he as well said he was oblivious about the Belgian military campaigns in Africa, about the talks between the two governments, or discussions between Pierre Orts and Alfred Milner for that matter. He declared that he could not discuss the matter in the absence of the latter, who was the only person who could give a fully informed opinion.

As no ministers seemed to be have a clear view on the situation in Africa, Pierre Orts and Alfred Milner launched into acrimonious talks in Paris.[18] On the 11th of May, their discussions started by clearing up the many misunderstandings. Following the decision of the Supreme Council of the Allied Powers on the 6th of May, Milner had concluded that Belgium gave up German East Africa. But this was not the case; the last notes exchanged on this subject between the two governments in April 1916 made the occupa-

Queen Elisabeth walks along the railroad near Bukama. In 1928 the royal couple travels to the Belgian Congo for the inauguration of the new railway line between Bukama and Port Francqui built by the *Compagnie du chemin de fer du Bas-Congo au Katanga*. The trip is essentially designed to put the colony in the limelight in Belgium, but also confirms Belgian sovereignty over the colony. However, the King also is confronted with labour challenges as a result of rapid industrialization after the First World War. (Archives Royal Palace, Albums AE 201/A)

tion of the German East African territories provisional until the end of the hostilities. In addition, nothing – not even the financial reparation obtained for the war damages suffered by Belgium – had been granted to it in return for giving up its right to compensation for its sacrifices in Africa and the harm suffered by its colony.[19]

Once these details had been set out, the tough negotiations continued in order to find an agreement to submit to the Supreme Council of the Allied Powers, which would authorise Great Britain and Belgium to determine their future rule over the German territories. Orts and Milner were obstinate. Initially, Milner offered Orts two deals. In the first one, Ruanda would be ceded to Belgium, with limits farther west than had previously been provided for, on the condition that no further talks with Portugal would be considered. In the second one, the territories occupied by the Belgians would be exchanged for a small territory on the left bank of the Congo River (not the one hoped for), while the British government would retain Urundi and the Kagera Valley in Ruanda.[20]

Pierre Orts, partly satisfied by the second deal, then negotiated the acquisition of Urundi, which was vital to allow Ruanda to be in communication with Lake Tangany-

A NEW WORLD

ika and allow it to develop. Alfred Milner conceded this. After these discussions Belgium was provisionally allocated the territory formed by Ruanda-Urundi, but lost all British support for its future talks with Portugal. But was this a good deal? The Belgian government was sceptical. This proposal, which left Belgium only the administration of Ruanda-Urundi while providing Great Britain with regions of much greater value, was considered to be unbalanced and should be offset by the boundaries of Ruanda being redrawn to its advantage and financial compensation to be agreed by experts.[21] A few days later, the British government refused the financial compensation demanded by the Belgians. It did, however, acknowledge Belgium's unsettled accounts from the German East African campaigns, if the latter does the same with the British. While Orts accepted this acknowledgement, he again disputed the British deal under which Belgium would have to give up the territory consisting of Ruanda-Urundi in exchange for territories of a much lower value. Although time was running out, the talks seemed far from closed.

In order to avoid a failure, Milner then proposed that the first deal, which granted Ruanda-Urundi to Belgium, should be retained for the moment and submitted to the Supreme Council of the Allied Powers, while the second proposal should be studied when circumstances permitted. Following this preliminary agreement, if bargaining were to take place with Portugal, Belgium should in return cede Ruanda-Urundi to the British, with the exception of a small territorial area. Otherwise, the share-out of the territories in German East Africa, as organised by Great Britain and Belgium, once approved by the Supreme Council of the Allied Powers, would be upheld. This solution was not enough for Pierre Orts. Given the refusal to complete the agreement with financial compensation and the uncertainty as to the outcome of talks with Portugal, he declared that he could not make the Belgian government accept a solution which would reduce the advantages gained by Belgium to the absolute minimum. Neither the concessions in the ports of Kigoma and Dar es Salaam, nor the area on the left bank of the Congo River, would offset the loss of the rich regions of Ruanda and Urundi. Ruanda-Urundi should remain Belgian.

Belgium as mandatory

On the 30th of May 1919, the talks finally ended. A two-part compromise was signed. In the first part, the two nations undertook to ask the Supreme Council of the Allied Powers to grant Belgium administration of the territories of Ruanda and Urundi, and for Great Britain to govern the remaining ex-German colonies as well as Eastern Ruanda (the Kisaka region).[22] In the second part, the two nations agreed on a series of transit and transport arrangements to be settled by mutual agreement. In addition, Great Britain undertook to acknowledge Belgium's unsettled accounts for the German East African campaigns, and Belgium did the same in favour of the British, covering the accounts arising from both the military operations and the administration of the territories it had conquered and transferred to Great Britain.

On the 28th of June 1919, the Treaty of Versailles was signed. In Article 119 of the Treaty, Germany definitively relinquishes, in favour of the main allied and associated powers, all its rights and titles on its overseas holdings.[23] On the 17th of July, the Mandates Commission declared that the Orts-Milner agreement was virtually ratified. Then, on the 21st of August, the Supreme Council of the Allied Powers unanimously ratified the agreement. So the fate of the ex-German colonial possessions was settled; they would become mandates, one part of which would be governed in the name of the League of Nations by Belgium, and the other by Great Britain. As from this ratification, Belgium would govern Ruanda-Urundi under a Class B Mandate, which was granted to it by the Allied Powers and confirmed by the League of Nations. But it took another two stressful years to obtain satisfactory economic agreements with the British and another year to obtain satisfaction regarding the borders of Ruanda.

THE END
OF THE EMPIRES?

Manuel Duran and Kevin Gony

The end of the First World War is often equated with the end of the empires and the emergence of the Western democracies throughout Europe.[24] In this historiographic tradition, the peace treaties that followed the war mean not only the punishment of the Central Powers, but also the demise of a number of empires and the start of a new democratic era. This *mythistoire* became commonplace after the Second World War as a result of the construction of a new European identity structure and the politico-cultural influence of the United States on Western Europe. As a result of a series of treaties and decisions by the Allied victors, four great empires in the Euro-Mediterranean area disappeared from the stage between 1917 and 1923. Their territories were divided among various new political "national" entities.

The first empire imploded under the weight of successive revolts that would bring increasingly radical groups to power. The death sentence for the Russian Empire was signed with the abdication of Tsar Nicholas II on the 15th of March 1917. The provisional government that followed was itself ousted in November, ushering in five years of civil war. Despite diplomatic and military aid from the Allies, the enemies of the Bolsheviks lost this war. A new empire was to rise from the remnants of the old: the Soviet Union.

The Second German Empire, the youngest of all the empires, succumbed to revolution. On the 9th of November 1918, the empire ceased to exist, a victim of mutiny, the abdication of *Kaiser* Wilhelm II and the declaration of the republic. It was this new Weimar Republic that signed the armistice, after which the attempts by the German communists to seize power were bloodily nipped in the bud. The Treaty of Versailles (1919–1920) also put an end to German colonial ambitions forever.

1918. Japanese troops attack Bolshevists in Siberia. As a new super power, Japan tries to gain control over parts of the disintegrated Russian Empire. The 70,000-strong Japanese army is followed in its wake by numerous entrepreneurs and merchants looking to do business in Siberia. Japan does not, however, succeed in creating a buffer state in Siberia and has to give in to the Bolshevist armies in 1922.
(National Archives and Records Administration, Washington, 165-WW-157D-12)

In contrast to both its neighbours, the Austro-Hungarian Dual Monarchy did not succumb to revolutionary uprisings, but to nationalistic centrifugal forces. On 28 October 1918 Czechoslovakia declared its independence, followed the day after by the State of the Slovenes, Croats and Serbs. On 11 November 1918 it was Poland's turn to lay claim to Austro-Hungarian territories. That happened the moment Charles I, Emperor of Austria, King of Hungary and Bohemia, renounced the throne. The rest of the empire quickly collapsed in the days that followed, and its final division was ratified in the Treaties of Saint-Germain-en-Laye (1919) and Trianon (1920).

On the periphery of Europe, the collapse of the Ottoman Empire led to a long civil war. The Treaty of Sèvres (1920) was the result of the negotiations that had been conducted since 1916 by the victors, based on the Sykes-Picot Agreement (Asia Minor Agreement). It reduced the territory of the Empire to a fraction of its pre-war expanse. The immediate consequences were a weakening of the already controversial Sultan Mehmet VI and an eruption of Turkish nationalism. Under the leadership of Mustafa Kemal Pasja, the Turkish nationalists secured important victories over France, Great Britain, Greece and Italy, but also over Armenian and Kurdish nationalist troops. They succeeded in abolishing the sultanate and declaring the republic. A new treaty with the Allies, the Treaty of Lausanne (1923), was more advantageous for Turkey and led to forced immigration in order to safeguard the religious homogeneity of the new state. Yet the Middle East remained under the West's control, which either managed to placate the local population with promises of independence (e.g., the Balfour Declaration for the Jewish *Yishuv* in Palestine), or simply stamped their authority over them with occupying troops.

The empire dissected

The term "empire" is often associated with a contiguous group of people or states under one centralised administration, mostly an emperor or *imperator*. Classic examples of this type of empire are those that collapsed in the aftermath of the First World War: the German Empire, the Austro-Hungarian Dual Monarchy, the Ottoman Empire, and Tsarist Russia. However, this is just one type of empire. The concept and the political reality are much more multi-layered. We can distinguish between different types of empires, and each underwent significant changes as a result of the First World War.

The first category is the classic empire, which included the German, Russian, Habsburg and Ottoman Empires already mentioned. In Europe it had its roots in classical antiquity, more particularly the Roman Empire, which was characterised by a tight centralised authority of an imperator, who for five hundred years controlled a huge territorial area around the Mediterranean Sea in Europe, Asia and Africa, from Rome. The idea of the *Pax Romana*, the cohesion of calm and peace with a strict military social structure, formed the ideological substructure for this central authority. During the Middle Ages it would remain a source of inspiration for the idea of the recovery of the Roman Empire, in particular in the Holy Roman Empire of the German Nation, but also in France, England and Byzantium. The German emperors presented themselves as the rightful heirs of the Roman emperors, and the area over which they ruled as the successor to the Roman Empire. At the same time, it was a universalist empire, because at a religious level the Empire was equated with the whole of Christendom. However, it was neither Roman nor German, and certainly not holy, hence the *translatio imperii* was primarily an ideal. The imperial title and the idea of the *imperium christianum* were adopted in the sixteenth century by the Habsburg dynasty.

The colonisation of America, Africa and Asia resulted in modern imperialism, the second category of empires. In contrast to the classical empire, which was a contiguous or closed entirety of areas under a single ruler, modern imperialism was a series of out-lying areas that were conquered and exploited. Having begun with the Spanish and Portuguese conquests and division of America, modern imperialism enjoyed its zenith with nineteen-century colonialism, its high point being the colonial Conference of Berlin (1884–1885), where the European powers proceeded with a territorial partition-ing of the African continent. This crude version of the empire had a long, slow deterio-ration during the twentieth century in the form of decolonisation, with the former European colonies in Africa and Asia fighting for their independence from the "moth-erland". In this period, a new empire was born, the ideological or post-modern empire.

The ideological empire has its origins in the two successors to the old European powers after the First World War: the communist Soviet Union and the United States, which had shaken off its isolationism during the war. From the start, the Soviet Union had universalist ambitions: the overthrow of the Tsarist regime in Russia was, from the perspective of its Marxist inspiration, only the first step to achieving a worldwide class-less and nationless society. To realise this ideal society, in addition to the traditional hard power (military, political and economic) a whole arsenal of soft power instru-ments were also developed, in the form of propaganda, as well as public diplomacy and support for friendly political parties and movements abroad.

The United States also developed after the First World War (but even more so after the Second World War) as a very adept practitioner of soft power, to bring other coun-tries and regions into its political and economic sphere of influence. After the First World War it succeeded – more so than the Soviet Union – in exerting its cultural and material influence on a large part of the world in the form of the ideas of the American Dream and the American Way of Life, as expressed in jazz, private cars, refrigerators, Walt Disney and the Hollywood film industry.

The end of the empires?

So, 1918 was certainly not the end of the empires. On the contrary, the colonial empires that came out of the First World War as the victors reached their territorial peak as a result of the peace treaties after the war. Their ambitions appeared boundless.

The Kingdom of Belgium, for example, acquired the East Cantons and a "mandate" from the League of Nations to govern Ruanda-Urundi. Nationalist circles saw this as their opportunity and staked imperialist claims: the annexation of Dutch Limburg and both banks of the Scheldt, as well as demands in the Rhineland, and even the wish to grant King Albert I the title "King of Jerusalem". Their territorial hunger set the colonial empires against each other, a battle that Great Britain would ultimately win. Despite the loss of Ireland, the British Empire governed a quarter of the world's population and more than a fifth of the earth's surface. Yet at the same time this peak proved to be the precursor to its decline. The ambitions of the new empires (Italy, Japan, and the United States among them) accelerated a downfall that was simultaneously compensated by the fact that the British Empire was slowly evolving into an influence imperialism through the Commonwealth.

Not all colonial empires profited to the same extent from colonial imperialism's swansong. The Spanish colonies in America had already become independent in the nineteenth century, and the final blow had been dealt during the Spanish-American war in 1898, which can also be seen as the warning shot of emerging American imperialism. The Portuguese empire also remained limited in size. Both versions of Iberian imperialism thus exemplified the distress of a still triumphant system, whose decline was already imminent. Nevertheless, the Portuguese empire would stay standing until the Carnation Revolution of April 1974. With the exception of the Italian conquest of Ethiopia in 1935 and the emergence of Japanese imperialism in Asia, the balance of power would tilt towards the ideological empires.

The United States and the Soviet Union put themselves firmly on the international map as the true successors to the old empires. There were two opposing models: the passive soft power of the United States, characterised by a return to protectionism and a temporary fall back to its own nationalism, and the active soft power of the Soviet Union, working particularly via the *Komintern*, the organisation that united representatives from all the European communist parties under the auspices of Russian Bolshevism. In addition to this "soft" approach, the new empires – just like their predecessors – did not shy away from using hard power (demographic, economic, and especially military power) to extend their influence.

German Spartacists man a machinegun at the *Schlesischer Bahnhof* in Berlin, January 1919. When Emperor Wilhelm II abdicates, riots erupt all over Germany. A power struggle between the social-democrat party of Germany and the German communist party leads to a revolt by the communist Spartacists. Between January 4 and 15, 1919 the Spartacists occupy parts of Berlin, but the upraise is bloodily repressed by both government troops and *Freikorps*.
(National Archives and Records Administration, Washington, 165-WW-159A-15)

Historical evolutionism?

Some empires swiftly disappeared after the First World War, while for others a slow deterioration began that would continue until the end of the twentieth century. In essence, it amounted to a power shift to new forms of governance. After all, the idea of the empire did not disappear, it was reinvented wherever familiar imperialist forms clashed with nationalist inclinations or with the social, political and economic reality. New forms of domination appeared under the heading of "historical evolutionism", which gave the ideologies of these new empires a philosophical basis and made it possible to introduce this evolution as an historical law.

Why did some empires disappear after the First World War? Why did other, new empires appear on the scene? And what allowed other empires to increase their power? There are many causes of rise, fall and consolidation. In the case of the German Empire, the classic rationale of the loss of the war came into play: Germany was seen by those who won the war as the main culprit, who should therefore be heavily punished with the loss of territories, the dismantling of its military power and astronomically high reparations. On the other hand, the First World War accelerated, rather than caused,

The Arab Commission at the Versailles peace talks. T.E. Lawrence (third from the right),
a.k.a. Lawrence of Arabia, plays an important part in the Arabic Peninsula during the war, as he succeeds
in convincing the Arabs of rebelling against the Ottoman Empire. After the war the British and the French
divide the Ottoman Empire, but the Arabs only receive small pieces of land instead of the promised empire.
Faisal (front) becomes king of Syria in 1920, but the French quickly put an end to his reign. In 1921
the British place him on the throne in Iraq.
(National Archives and Records Administration, Washington, 111-SC-44854)

the fall of the Russian, Ottoman and Austro-Hungarian Empires. The three empires
had, after all, been subject to internal disintegration for decades, caused by an economic malaise, socio-political and ethnic tensions and a sclerotic governmental apparatus.
The Ottoman Empire, for example, had been regarded as "the sick man of Europe"
since the nineteenth century, the Habsburg Empire had been groaning under the growing tensions between the Austrian and Hungarian elites and the increasingly outspo-
ken Pan-Slavism, and the Russian Revolution of 1917 had already witnessed its bloody
prelude in a series of riots and revolts in 1905. The war proved to be a catalyst rather
than a genuine cause of the collapse of these empires. When the Allies redrew the maps
after the war, strategic objectives were often at play. This was the case with the new
states of Czechoslovakia and the Kingdom of the Serbs, Croats and Slovenes, which
were carved out of the former Habsburg Empire and which were primarily intended to
act as a buffer against Germany or a repeat of the Dual Monarchy.

Right from the beginning, these strategic objectives undermined the principle of the right of self-determination of the peoples, on which the new territorial division of Europe (there was no talk of the colonies) was ostensibly based. Large groups of Hungarians, Germans, Bulgarians and other peoples were suddenly displaced and were living as foreigners in a new fatherland. The growth of other colonial empires – primarily the British, French and Belgian – was the result of old-fashioned spoils of war, with the colony of the vanquished being incorporated into the colonial empires of the victors, sometimes camouflaged as a League of Nations mandate, as was the case with Ruanda-Urundi. The new empires, such as the Japanese, also succeeded in filling the vacuum left by the old empires. It was not difficult for Japan to bring the very fragile Chinese republic, which had succeeded the imperial Qing Dynasty in 1912, to its knees, and gain control of large parts of China.

The First World War at the very least sounded the alarm when it came to the empires. Hegelian thinking, which presumes that the European twentieth century followed the path of a growing democratisation of the West, does not take into account the rest of the world. For there was new fervour for the idea and the practice of the empire after the war, and it was not until after the Second World War that people gradually began to question the principles. This is shown by the steady decline of the post-modern Soviet-Russian and American empires, running parallel to the disappearance of the colonial empires or their shift to ersatz ideological empire. So the idea of the Empire, the Imperium, is not dead – quite the contrary. For more and more countries, it remained a source of inspiration for their ideas about regional domination at the beginning of the twenty-first century, and it keeps changing appearance.

THE PROTRACTED SEARCH FOR A NEW PLACE IN THE CONCERT OF NATIONS

Rik Coolsaet

Four years of war had dramatically changed the face of the country.[25] For decades, Belgium had been one of the top five industrial powers, and its industrial products had been able to compete globally thanks to their low cost. The country was the first to experiment with a new form of enterprise: the financial trust or holding company. Global expansion followed, with Belgian investments in the electricity industry, the tramways and the railways. Belgium was the largest foreign investor in Russia, and was present in the Middle East, Eastern Europe and Latin America. Leopold II's endeavours pushed Belgium to fully participate in the race for China. Furthermore, with the acquisition of the Congo Free State in 1908, it had become a colonial power.

But the war and the occupation put a stop to Belgian global expansion: by 1918 the country was devastated, its industrial heritage dismantled. West Flanders was a desolate wasteland. The Belgian state was facing a rapidly growing government debt to mortgage the reconstruction. The pre-war illusion that neutrality would protect the land forever had evaporated.

In 1923-1924 Belgian and French troops occupy the German Ruhr area. The harsh occupation regime elicits both German and international outrage. On 30 June 1923 a train transporting soldiers going on leave in Belgium explodes on the railway bridge at Duisburg-Hochfeld. Twelve soldiers die, and many others are wounded. Belgian authorities claim a timebomb was set, whereas the Germans speak of a gas explosion. The Belgian occupier immediately takes measures: the bridge is closed to traffic. German citizens can only cross it on foot, in a single line along the tracks.
(War Heritage Institute, Brussels, EST-1-804/49)

In June 1919 American President Woodrow Wilson visits Belgium. He tours the devastated areas in the company of the royal couple. Visits to ruined infrastructure, such as the blast furnaces at Marchienne-au-Pont near Charleroi, are included in the program. (Archives Royal Palace, Albums AE 101/B)

The Belgian government in Le Havre had already realised during the war that the recovery of the country's political independence would have to go hand in hand with the recovery of its economic independence. If not, the country once again risked becoming the puppet in the power politics among its larger neighbours. It was that insight that formed the core of the Belgian objectives at the peace conference that opened in Versailles on 18 January 1919. There, Belgium proposed the lifting of the obligatory neutrality and the payment of reparations by Germany and sought guarantees against the economic and political predominance of both France and Germany.

To prevent France gaining too great an influence over Belgium, Belgian diplomacy was committed to a customs union with the Grand Duchy of Luxembourg, the crucial hub for Belgian's trade with Southern Germany, Alsace-Lorraine, Switzerland and Italy. After all, French control over Luxembourg would hand Paris a means of applying commercial and economic pressure on Belgium.

As for Germany, Belgium felt it should be subjected to commercial and economic discrimination at least for the duration of the reconstruction of Belgian industry and the recovery of its former markets. But above all, the Belgian delegation in Versailles was committed to obtaining reparations, as being the only way to finance the country's reconstruction, repay American war loans and compensate its people for the losses they had suffered. The Versailles Treaty declared Germany to be solely responsible for the outbreak of the war and therefore had to compensate all war damage that had been suffered.

But the Versailles conference did not become what Belgian diplomacy had hoped, though Belgium did acquire a priority right to the German reparations and saw the intended discrimination against the German economy embedded in the Treaty. It also obtained psychological compensation from the major powers in the form of an upgrade to their legations in Belgium to embassies, the very first presidency of the Assembly of the League of Nations (in the person of Louis Hymans) and their non-permanent membership of the Council of the League of Nations. Belgium was also given territorial expansion with the former German cantons of Eupen, Sankt-Vith and Malmédy and a League of Nations mandate over the German colonies of Ruanda-Urundi.

Yet Belgium had hoped for more. Obligatory neutrality may already have been lifted, but international guarantees for the security of the country were not forthcoming. After all, the collective security pledge in the context of the new League of Nations seemed utterly implausible. But it was mainly the lack of results in terms of economic independence that raised concerns as far as the Belgian government and diplomacy were concerned. Paris had successfully objected to the Belgian claims to Luxembourg, and access to the French and British markets was similarly not in the offing. The Belgian share of the German reparations was under severe pressure. Not only did the other victors, such as France, also want as big a slice of the pie as possible, but because economic and commercial restrictions had been placed on Germany, it soon became clear that the country was not actually in a position to make the hefty payments.

Belgium, liege of France?

After Versailles, Belgian diplomacy launched an intensive diplomatic campaign to retain the Belgian priority of payment and as big a share in the German reparations as possible. However, that campaign did not go as expected, and Belgium ended up in a diplomatic impasse.

To ensure its political independence in post-war Europe, Belgium had intended to conduct a policy of strict balance in respect of all its major neighbours. But by prioritising economic independence, Belgian foreign policy unwittingly got tangled up in the French strategy of anti-German block formation.

To appease France with regard to its claims to Luxembourg, Belgium showed that it was willing to take part in the French occupation of several cities in the Rhineland in April 1920. In exchange, France renounced its own claims. However, the occupation soured diplomatic relations with London. Officially, Belgium was still seeking economic and military cooperation with Great Britain, but the Belgian participation in the Ruhr operation confirmed – in British eyes – precisely what London was apprehensive about, namely being dragged into a French anti-German policy through an alliance with Belgium.

To maintain French goodwill, Belgium then declared itself prepared to conclude a military accord. France did, indeed, give the green light to a Belgo-Luxembourg customs union, which was set up in May 1921. But while Belgium regarded the Franco-Belgian military agreement as the first step in its intended balance of power diplomacy, London saw it as additional proof that Belgium was behaving as a vassal of France.

The third and final stage in the Belgo-French diplomatic ballet was the Belgian willingness, in January 1923, to take part in a new French military operation, the occupation of the Ruhr. Again, Paris reacted positively to this Belgian gesture. Four months later, France therefore agreed to a trade treaty that ultimately gave Belgium access to the French market. But it was more than that: it amounted to a genuine economic alliance between both countries, aimed at creating a long-term reorganisation of the economic power relations in Europe, to the detriment of Germany.

Belgium's reputation throughout the world lay in tatters. The country had already alienated itself from the Netherlands with its plans for possible territorial expansion into its northern neighbour and it had angered Luxembourg, which would have preferred a customs union with France. Belgium's military crackdown during the Ruhr occupation, and the strict punitive measures that it took in respect of Germany, earned the country the reputation as a small, brutal major power. At home, Belgian public opinion saw the action as a justified defence of the country's interests, but London and Washington saw Belgium as no more than a pawn in France's power politics.

However, the Belgian diplomatic position soon began to tip. The economic strangling of Germany had the opposite effect from the one intended. The Belgian government came to the realisation that France and Belgium alone could not solve the German question and that they still needed the support of the United States and Great Britain. Ultimately, the alliance with France particularly benefited French business, not Belgian.

A European *détente*

Elections in France, followed by elections in Belgium, cleared the way for a review of the policy towards Germany: rapprochement instead of power politics would be needed to break the diplomatic impasse. In August 1924 an international committee led by the American banker Charles G. Dawes reached a compromise on the German reparations based on a plan set out by the Belgian financier Emile Francqui. The level of the amounts

German *Reichsbank* employees witness the first delivery of American gold at the *Lehrter Bahnhof* in Berlin on the 23rd of December. In the framework of the Dawes Plan, named after American economist and politician Charles G. Dawes, the American bank J.P. Morgan & Company grants Germany a two million dollar loan. Germany has to use the money to settle its debts with the Allies. (Bundesarchiv, Koblenz, Bild 102-00924/foto: Georg Pahl)

was in fact less important than the philosophy behind the Dawes Plan. So that Germany could pay, its economy and trade would need to be rebuilt. To that end, its economic and financial unity would need to be reinstated, and the Franco-Belgian occupation was thus to end. At the same time, Germany was given the opportunity to finance its reconstruction with large foreign loans, chiefly of American origin.

In turn, the Dawes Plan paved the way for a *détente* in European relations. At the beginning of February 1925, the German Foreign Minister Gustav Stresemann proposed a pact, to France and Great Britain, between all the countries "with interests in the Rhine". The participating countries would commit to renounce ware against each other and to guarantee the post-war territorial *status quo*.

On the 5th of October 1925, five countries met in Locarno, Switzerland. Belgium was one of them. After two weeks of negotiation, a series of treaties was signed, the most important of which was the Rhine Pact. In the spirit of the principles of the League of Nations, this laid down the inviolability of the post-war borders in Western Europe, guaranteed by all participating states. Belgium thus ultimately acquired the security guarantees it had been fruitlessly pursuing since Versailles.

International economic relations were another area where Belgium again found its place in the concert of nations. By 1925 the war damage had been largely repaired, and global trade grew strongly from 1924 onwards. Trade flows were back to pre-war levels, and Belgium began to diversify its markets, leading to an economic boom for the country and a substantial expansion of its industrial production and export.

Belgium, advocate of free trade

The nation emerged as a committed free trade advocate: the lower the customs tariffs, the more even the playing field for small countries. When the League of Nations convened at a World Economic Conference in Geneva in May 1927, Belgium therefore played an active role. Under the presidency of former Prime Minister Georges Theunis, the conference was to definitively end the era of economic warfare, by means of a systematic abolition of customs tariffs. It was the beginning of the multi-lateralisation of economic relations on the European continent.

When protectionism reared its head again outside Europe, Belgium reinforced its newly discovered pioneering role. In July/August 1929, Foreign Minister Paul Hymans

Committee opening session chaired by American banker and entrepreneur Owen D. Young in Basle (Switzerland), 1929. In 1929 the temporary Dawes Plan is replaced by the Young Plan. Reparations are set at 112 billion gold mark.
(akg/Isopix AKG2850095)

called for an international "customs truce", which was supposed to culminate in a worldwide collective commercial free trade convention.

But it never came to that... In October 1929 the stock market crashed on Wall Street, setting off a chain reaction, with the major states reverting to a policy of economic nationalism. Not so Belgium. During the 1930s, Belgium continued to pursue its now familiar role of free trade advocate to the full. In doing so, it discovered the benefits of strong economic relations with its immediate neighbours. This was the beginning of a diplomatic journey that would turn Belgium after the Second World War into the architect of European unification.

A NEW WORLD

4

RISING FROM THE ASHES

THE ECONOMIC BALANCE SHEET OF THE FIRST WORLD WAR

Erik Buyst

On 11 November 1918 the guns finally fell silent. The damage could be assessed. The devastation in the trench zones defied depiction: a strip several kilometres wide had been transformed into a lunar landscape. In the rest of Belgium, too, the war left deep scars.

Traditionally, our country imported a lot of food from overseas, but the Allied blockade of trade with Germany and the occupied zones severely disrupted the supply of food in wartime. It was only thanks to the good work of the Commission for Relief in Belgium that a humanitarian crisis was averted. Livestock, however, was in a very serious condition: hundreds of thousands of cattle and pigs had to be slaughtered be-

January 1919. Belgian citizens queue in Brussels to exchange their German marks against Belgian francs. In order to re-launch money circulation Belgian authorities exchange all German marks emitted during occupation. The advantageous foreign exchange rate for the mark creates a lucrative trade in German money. Out of the 5.5 billion francs resulting from the exchange of marks, some 2.5 billion are indeed produced by fraudulent practices. Germany categorically refuses to reimburse these marks. Belgian Treasury is severely affected. (Australian War Memorial, Canberra, A00753)

1926–1927. A security agent, keys in hand, guards a shipping of gold arriving at the Brussels National Bank. Once the Belgian currency is stabilized in 1926 the National Bank systematically buys gold. When Great Britain withdraws from the Gold Standard in 1931, the National Bank is strong enough to absorb this shock to the system. (Germaineimage, 23665346-007)

cause of a lack of animal feed, and it would be the mid-1920s before meat and dairy production returned to pre-war levels.[1]

Estimating the economic damage

Due to similar problems with stocks of raw materials, industrial activity sank even deeper than livestock production. A lack of ores and raw cotton, for example, meant that more and more businesses were closing their doors, leading to mass unemployment among industrial workers. Initially, the occupier left the dormant factories alone, but in 1915 that changed. Machines and installations that could be used immediately in the German war industry, such as blast furnaces and cranes, were transported to Germany. Other equipment, such as the copper kettles from breweries, were reduced to scrap to make bullets, among other things. Towards the end of the war, equipment that could not be used for the weapons industry fell prey to blind destructiveness. With this scorched earth tactic, the occupier would be able to shut down a country for a long time when a ceasefire came.

The coal mines were an important exception to the demolition; they were not affected because the Germans could sell some of the mined coal to neutral countries for hard foreign currency. Yet, in this industry too, production shrank by a third during the war as a result of passive resistance and malnutrition among the miners. After the armistice, however, the mining sector would play a leading role in the reconstruction.

The transport infrastructure also emerged battered from the fight: hundreds of bridges had been blown up and almost half the railway and branch lines network had been destroyed. Added to which, the occupier took a great number of locomotives and other rolling stock to Germany. The ports of Zeebruges and Ghent were badly hit during the hostilities, but fortunately the port of Antwerp emerged from the melee virtually intact.

The number of available homes did not escape the consequences of the warring madness either: 84,000 houses were fully or partially destroyed and more than 200,000 badly damaged, and for four years, new development was at a standstill. The housing situation for the lower income groups had already been far from rosy before the war, partly due to the cheerless workers' quarters in the towns and cities. After the war, Belgium was confronted with a complete lack of housing: thousands of families spent years living in barracks.

According to Fernand Baudhuin, witness and leading economist, the damage caused amounted in total to around 3.5 billion Belgian francs, or almost half the country's pre-war gross domestic product.[2] This estimate does not even take into account the so-called "consequential loss". War cut Belgian exporters off from their foreign customers, and international competitors such as the Americans took advantage of this to grab our overseas sales markets. Furthermore, the difficulties with supplies for some importers of Belgian products were the signal to start introducing alternative activities. The Netherlands, for example, traditionally an important sales area for Belgian steel, started to build its own steelworks during the war: *Hoogovens IJmuiden*. For a country like Belgium, which lived off the export of manufactured goods, this was a sizeable blow. Unsurprisingly, the recovery of the pre-war export markets took a long time.

Given the years of isolation during the Occupation, the dramatic changes on the economic world stage largely escaped the attention of many business leaders, and the pre-war industrial structure was rebuilt with great enthusiasm. Even an influential man like Jean Jadot, governor of the Belgian bank *Société Générale/Generale Maatschappij*, was powerless in the face of the nostalgia for the *Belle Époque*. At the start of 1919 he sought to take advantage of the reconstruction in order to comprehensively restructure the fractured steel industry; upscaling and specialisation were key, to allow modern American mass production techniques to be applied. But the particularism of the steel barons was too strong, and a unique opportunity for exhaustive renewal and reinforcement of competitiveness was lost.[3]

During the First World War, Belgian economic activity hits rock-bottom. Harbours are either damaged or blocked off. Sunken ships in Ghent Harbour hinder maritime traffic. The first American steam ship can only dock in March 1919.
(National Archives of Belgium, Brussels, F 1546, 2357)

A critical financial situation

The heavy loss of foreign investments was another drain. Since the 1890s Belgian investors had been participating en masse in the development of Russian coalmines, iron- and steelworks, railways and tram networks. But the October Revolution of 1917 literally slashed those assets: they were nationalised by the new Soviet regime without any compensation being forthcoming. The investments in Central Europe also lost much of their value due to the collapse of the Habsburg Empire.

Belgium thus came out of the war badly depleted in many domains, just as the workers' movement – partly as a result of Bolshevik uprisings in Russia and Central Europe – was becoming radicalised. To avoid widespread unrest, the Belgian government pushed through a number of social reforms, such as the 8-hour day and 48-hour week.

In this context the existing tax system, primarily based on excises and other indirect taxes, was hastily overhauled. The outdated tax system hit the lower income groups harder than the higher income groups in relative terms, an unfair situation that was no longer acceptable. So, in the reconstruction period, Belgium switched over to a modern income tax. Given the chaotic circumstances and the tax authorities' lack of experience with the new system, tax revenue was initially very disappointing. This coincided with an explosive increase in public expenditure linked to the reconstruction and the start of expensive social programmes; as a result, the government deficit shot up to almost 20% of GDP.[4] Yet the government was not terribly worried, as it blithely issued one government loan after another. They were convinced that the German reparations would soon roll in and then the budget deficit and the rising government debt would disappear.

RISING FROM THE ASHES

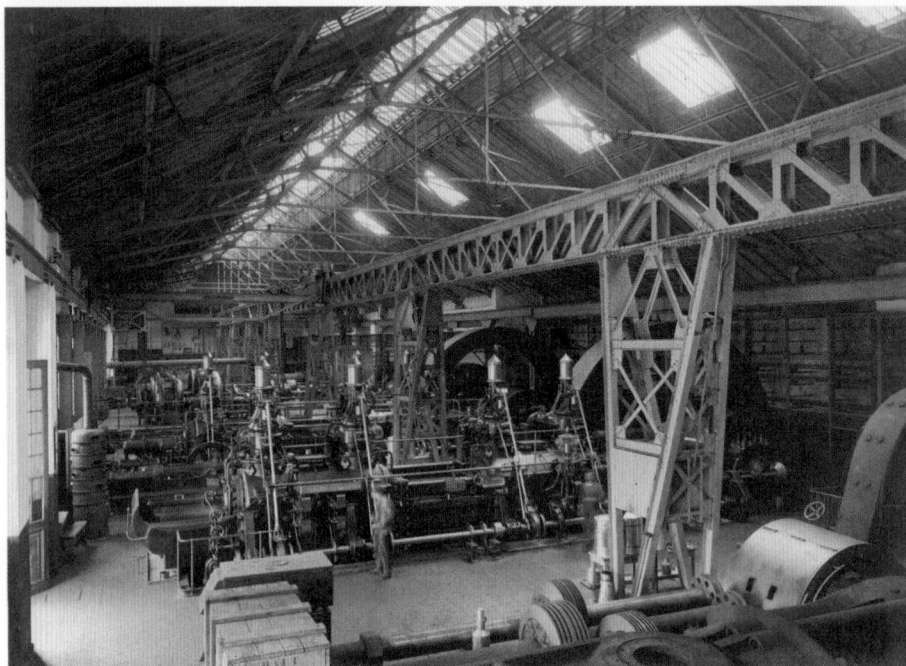

View of the electricity generators at the *Société Anonyme d'Ougrée-Marihaye*, one of the twenty-odd companies linked to the *Union des Centrales Électriques*. This cooperative, created in 1919, groups companies in order to function more efficiently and more cost-effectively. (Archives Royal Palace, Albums AE 430/B)

Government finances were not the only economic indicator that was derailed; consumer prices also went through the roof. The sharp increase in the money supply played an important part in this. Different factors explain the relative abundance of banknotes: firstly, the occupier imposed heavy war assessments that the Belgian administration mostly paid for by printing money, and secondly, everyone in occupied territory was forced to accept payments in German marks. Given that the occupier was making bulk purchases of goods, the amount of German marks in circulation quickly increased. In total, the quantity of the banknotes in circulation during the war increased sixfold. The huge increase in the money supply contrasted sharply with the prevailing scarcity of goods. The oversupply of money inevitably led to price hikes, particularly for groceries and other basic essentials.

The German marks in circulation were a thorn in the side of the exiled Belgian government. Even before the armistice, a plan was devised to organise a large-scale conversion operation immediately after liberation. Holders of marks would be able to fully convert their notes into francs. The unification of the currency in circulation was doubtless necessary to restore public confidence in banknotes, yet opportunities were missed. For example, the government failed to identify war profiteers via the conversion operation, which meant that the tax authorities lost out on a huge amount of war profits. Furthermore, the specific execution of the plan came up against numerous difficulties, so the operation lasted much longer than planned. Smugglers made good use of the opportunity to set up a large-scale illegal import of German marks. Meanwhile, the exchange rate of the German mark against the franc halved compared to the ratio used in the conversion operation. The illegal importation of marks into Belgium thus created extensive profit opportunities. The government was aware of the problem but condoned it in the naive conviction that Germany would pay back, in gold, all the marks that had been collected.

The policymakers also appeared blind to the consequences of that reckless approach on inflation and, hence, on the franc exchange rate. The fraudulent importation of an estimated 2.4 billion marks once again pushed up the money supply in Belgium considerably.[5] Few realised that the amateurish handling of the mark issue had dashed all hopes of a return to pre-war price levels once and for all. At the same time, recovery of the franc's pre-war gold rate became impossible. The major powers admonished Belgium and refused to include the repayment of the marks in gold in the Treaty of Versailles. Our country would have to settle the matter itself with the Weimar Republic.

In spite of all the negotiations and intentions, Germany would never come up with the gold. The collected marks were ultimately pulped for the paper industry. German reparations followed the same path; in the 1920s they came in fits and starts, but at the beginning of the 1930s these obligations were wiped out.

REBUILDING.
A NATIONAL ORDER

———

Delphine Lauwers

At the end of the Great War, Belgium naturally mourned its dead, but on top of this, the scale of the destruction it had suffered brought it up against an extremely tough task – rebuilding. The Belgian damage was of a material nature, above all.[6] The losses were catastrophic: "Bridges had been blown up, railway tracks had been taken up and removed to Germany. In the area of the front alone, a strip sixty kilometres long by twenty kilometres wide had been completely wiped out – three towns and sixty-two villages."[7] Further from the front, other areas had also been largely destroyed, including Dinant, Termonde, Spontin and Visé. The centres of Malines, Louvain, and Namur were devastated. On the 1st of May 1916, no fewer than 600 councils reported damage.[8]

The material losses were colossal – transport infrastructures and other structures damaged, agricultural land ravaged, forests destroyed, etc.[9] – not to mention the unquantifiable losses causing long-term problems for the country's economic recovery, such as on its foreign markets.[10]

The lack of housing was certainly one of the most acute and most urgent problems the Belgian authorities had to cope with after 1918.[11] No houses had been built since 1914, and an estimate of at least 75,000 homes made uninhabitable or destroyed by the war was mentioned. Some went even so far as a calculation that 72,000 buildings had been totally destroyed, 12,000 partially destroyed, and 200,000 damaged. The total came to 284,000 buildings.[12] While the numbers varied, the region most seriously affected was, not surprisingly, Western Flanders, where the front line had been located. The balance drawn up in 1920 showed that in this province alone 41,301 houses had been totally destroyed and 4,245 made uninhabitable out of a total of 79,900 in the

In order to meet the huge needs on the housing market, the government creates the National Society for Affordable Housing. This erects cheap houses all over the country, usually in so-called garden-cities. The Schaerbeek garden city, the *Foyer Schaerbeekois*, is inaugurated on 19 September 1926 by the Minister of Industry, Labour and Social Security, the Socialist Joseph Wauters, and the Minister of Justice, the Liberal Paul Hymans. (Archives Royal Palace, Albums AE 428/A)

country as a whole.[13] It was estimated that approximately 20% of the Belgian housing stock was destroyed during the First World War.[14]

A planned, well-designed reconstruction

After the armistice, the Belgian authorities found themselves facing an immense task. However, they had not awaited the end of the War to consider the matter of "reconstruction work which, even in 1915, was obviously going to be unavoidable and complicated."[15] A series of official bodies and measures had been set up by the Belgian Government in exile. The Belgian legislation on reconstruction, largely inspired by the French laws, was partially drawn up during the conflict. The first Decree Law was adopted on the 25th of August 1915. This required ruined communities to produce general alignment plans which could be used to guide the rebuilding work, and set up the first attempt by the Belgian State to intervene in local planning policies.[16] In September 1916, the Minister for the Interior created the *Fonds Roi Albert* – the King Albert Foundation. It was designed to build temporary homes in unoccupied Belgium and neighbouring countries to house refugees. This housing would then be dismantled and rebuilt in Belgium.[17] The work of the Foundation, by enabling refugees to return, was to encourage the resumption of the social and economic lives of the devastated regions and so speed up the reconstruction process.[18]

According to Sven Carnel, 1917 was to be "the most prolific year in terms of resolutions regarding the rebuilding of the country. This was when the Ministry for National Reconstruction, a War Damage Office, an Economic Council, etc. were set up."[19] These structures were sometimes short-lived, and it was not until the end of 1918 that the Government laid the legal foundations for compensation legislation. Two Decree Laws dated October 1918 recognised the entitlement of victims of war damage to compensation by the State and set up a war damage court in each judicial district.[20] These laws were vague and complex but recognised "for the first time in history, the right to war damage compensation for all Belgian victims."[21] The Law of the 10th of May 1919 set up the scheme for the calculation of compensation payments.[22]

The Law of the 8th of April 1919 set up the system of "adoption by the State" for the worst-affected communities. This stipulated in particular that the State had "an obligation to cover the expenditure required for the restoration of the land and the public services of the commune."[23] The Office for the Devastated Regions was created on the 9th of April 1919.[24] The main remit of this authority, which was in charge of organising and directing the rebuilding work, was to implement the State adoption system, and at the same time to promote the work of the *Fonds Roi Albert*, assess the granting and allocation of loans, etc. These were major tasks, for which it was given wide-ranging powers.[25]

Reconstruction starts immediately after the war, but the task at hand is enormous. Various initiatives make it possible to build emergency housing. In Het Hooghe near Ypres two different kinds stand side by side in 1919. From left to right: two Nissen Huts, a shelter provided by the King Albert Fund and another Nissen Hut probably used for storage. Clear guidelines regulating reconstruction are issued in 1919. (Imperial War Museum, London, Q100379, Ivan L. Bawtree)

The measures taken during the war are testimony to the optimism of the Belgian authorities in exile, who were convinced that "Poor little Belgium", backed by its allies, would receive major reparations. There were many negative effects of the propaganda. When it came to the peace talks, Belgium, until then "wearing a halo due to its status of massacred innocent, was suddenly seen as a greedy troublemaker."[26] So it could no longer count on the financial aid it had taken for granted, which partly explains why the reconstruction process was so slow.

The contemporaries of the Great War were also faced with moral and aesthetic questions – what should the basis for the reconstruction be? Would this be an opportunity to revolutionise the architecture of Belgium's destroyed towns and villages? Should everything be rebuilt? For the question was not only of how rebuilding should be done, but whether it should be done at all. In the eyes of the world, the ruins caused by a new kind of war embodied the modern destructive power and barbarism of the Germans.[27] Voices were quickly raised for at least some of these ruins to be preserved: "For many reasons, in spite of the painful sadness of these ruins, it is important that some should be religiously preserved (...). And these ruins should be left "in situ", to show the world all the suffering, all the martyrdom endured by a small nation (...)! And finally, these ruins should remain, as a permanent reproach to the German race."[28]

RISING FROM THE ASHES

From 29 March till 30 April 1923, Belgium participates in the temporary exhibition about family dwellings, organised in a large exhibition hall in Lille (France). Belgian focus is on the reconstruction of the Devastated Areas. Through information panels, blueprints, scale-models and pictures the visitors can discover how reconstruction evolves. The top piece in the Belgian presentation is a worker's cottage especially built for the occasion. Visitors can even meet three lace-makers at work on the doorstep.

(In Flanders Fields Museum, Ypres, IFFFA070)

Three options were considered for the ruined communities: rebuilding them exactly as they were, preserving the ruins, and/or the building of new modern towns. Some voiced their enthusiasm about the opportunity to start again from scratch and give free rein to architectural creativity.[29] These opinions were discussed behind the scenes in occupied Belgium, and much more openly abroad, especially in places where there were many Belgian refugees.[30]

The Belgian government itself seemed to have doubts about the appropriateness and feasibility of the rebuilding of certain communities, and declared in 1919 that Ypres, Nieuport and Dixmude would not be rebuilt, but that "new towns would be built near the ruins."[31]

A slow, costly process

The heavy task of reconstruction was taken up, as best as possible, by the national authorities. Its pace was lamentably slow, due to financial problems, lack of labour and materials, overworked War Compensation Courts, lack of coherence due to changes of government, etc. For refugees returning from exile, this meant enduring dreadful living conditions for a long time.[32] And the victims did not fail to make their dissatisfaction known.

In addition, the Belgian State, which had no tradition of intervention in town planning, came up against strong local prejudice. In general, little space was given to the modernist ideas developed during the conflict.[33] In fact, most of the victims simply wanted to get their homes back just as they had left them before the War.[34]

Of all the ruined towns, Ypres was the most problematic, and not only because of the scale of the damage it had suffered. After announcing that the town would not be rebuilt, the Belgian government, under pressure from the local authorities, accepted the principle of rebuilding homes, but declared that a "Zone of Silence" – the ruins of the Cloth Hall and Saint Martin's Cathedral – should be left untouched. Intense discussions about these monuments went on for years, involving local, national, and even British authorities. However, in the end, the outstanding perseverance of the local population won the day. After six years of work, the Cloth Hall Belfry was formally reopened in July 1934 with a magnificent ceremony. It was not until 1967 that the near-identical reconstruction of the city of Ypres and, with it, that of the entire country, was completed.[35]

3-2-26

THE RECONSTRUCTION OF INFRASTRUCTURE AND PUBLIC BUILDINGS

Jeroen Cornilly

After four years of war, significant parts of Belgium literally lay in ruins. From Nieuport to Ploegsteert, a long strip, almost five kilometres wide, had been completely destroyed. In the towns on the Belgian frontline – Nieuport, Dixmude and Ypres – the occasional vague impression of the street pattern still remained, while villages like Passchendaele and Poelkapelle had been reduced to piles of rubble and were only identifiable by a place name on a sign. In "Martyr Towns" – like Louvain, Dendermonde, Aarschot, Lier, Dinant and Visé – streets, squares and sometimes entire neighbourhoods had been burned down or badly damaged. In other municipalities the German army or the Allied troops had dynamited church towers and other orientation points for strategic reasons. In many places the transport infrastructure had not fared much better.

A huge challenge

It had already become clear during the war that the reconstruction of Belgium would be a huge challenge. The government in exile made efforts to create an appropriate legal framework, and international specialists in architecture and urban development devoted their attention to the *tabula rasa* that large parts of West Flanders were at the time, coming up with innovative visions for rebuilding a society fit for the twentieth century. The Ypres municipal architect Jules Coomans, for example, flew to Wimereux in 1915 with his entire archive of plans and began to prepare the recon-

View of the building site of Saint Martin's Cathedral in Ypres on 3 February 1926. Reconstruction not only concerns housing. Public infrastructure, such as town halls, schools, railway stations and churches, also need to be rebuilt. Many projects are finalized by 1926, but tradesmen nevertheless continue to be fully booked. (Erfgoedbibliotheek Westflandrica/Stad Kortrijk)

Louvain, 11 September 1922. American donations make it possible to rebuild the university library destroyed in 1914. Peace conditions stipulate that Germany has to supply books, but quite some literature also comes from the United States. The phrase *Furore Teutonico Diruta, Dono Americano Restituta* (Destroyed by German violence, reconstituted through American gifts), initially to appear on the building's frontage, is cancelled after heated debates. (Stadsarchief Leuven, collectie Sprengers)

struction in consultation with Mayor Collaert. He worked out a building line plan, wrote down his vision for the reconstruction in essays, and took part in exhibitions.

In October 1918 – several weeks before the armistice became fact – a law governing compensation for the war damage was enacted. The local government was often so badly destabilised that the higher authorities were forced to intervene. Hence, in April 1919, the "adoption act" was introduced. This created the possibility for municipalities that had been destroyed by more than ten percent to be adopted by the Belgian state. In doing so, they gave away far-reaching powers, to allow the state to supervise the reconstruction in their place. Together with the adoption act, the *Dienst der Verwoeste Gewesten* (Devastated Regions Office) was created, an effective administration for the reconstruction. In the front region, virtually all the municipalities had themselves adopted.

Back on track

The repair of the road infrastructure was a priority. This is clearly visible in the repair of the railway network, of which almost a third had become unusable. Railway bridges had been demolished, and stations such as Ghent Sint-Pieters had become inaccessible due to the lack of tracks. Repairs were done in two stages. The first stage was to make the entire railway network usable again, often with the construction of emergency bridges and temporary stations. The biggest problem soon proved to be the delivery of wood for the sleepers and steel for the tracks; the solution was bulk import. By the end of 1920 the railway network was near-enough fully operational. The building of the final railway bridges and stations became a reality during the years that followed.

The railways were vital for the transportation of both building materials and labour for the reconstruction. The huge demand for building materials gave an important boost to brick production. Hence brick and roof tile factories in the region of Kortrijk were running at full capacity. The factories of the *Briqueteries Mécaniques de Nieuport* in Oostduinkerke, which had been destroyed, were rebuilt as quickly as possible. They supplied *Nieuwpoortse baksteen* (Nieuwpoort brick), an item frequently quoted in building specifications. New brickworks were founded in Rumbeke and Westende around 1920, and in 1920 Joseph Dumoulin began the production of drainpipes in Wijtschate.

Starting a building line plan

In addition to the repair of the road infrastructure, 1919 mainly involved making preparatory plans. If a municipality got adopted, that entailed a number of obligations: drafting a general building line plan, an overall development plan and general police regulations regarding the building. The *Hoog Koninklijk Commissaris* (Royal Commissioner) coordinating the reconstruction often assigned an architect to the municipalities, to draw up the development plans and design the most important buildings. The elaboration of the development plans took a long time and was the subject of frequent discussion. Many plans – for example the plan for the heavily damaged town of Lo – only came to fruition during the course of 1921. Architect Henry Lacoste had to rework his plan time after time and adjust his ambitions. As in almost all historical towns, attempts to make comprehensive changes to the layout of the historical town centre foundered. The final building line plans were merely copies of the pre-war street pattern, with only a few minor interventions: the straightening or widening of streets to accentuate perspectives in the townscape and to improve traffic flow. Planners saw the reconstruction in Dendermonde as an opportunity to partially straighten

and improve the course of the River Dender, even though the numerous discussions jeopardised a quick start to the reconstruction. In Leuven, the remediation of the *Slachthuiswijk* on the River Dyle, which had already started before the outbreak of the war, was optimised and completed. The idea to visually close off the *Bondgenotenlaan* with a monumental "screen block" got no further than the drawing board, a fate that

Infrastructure largely needs to be rebuilt. Many railway stations require interventions, as railway infrastructure was destroyed in the last weeks of war. Starting in April 1919, some 1,200 labourers clear rubble at the Ghent Saint Peter's railway station before restoring it to its pre-war glory. The station is operational on the 1ˢᵗ of July.

(National Archives and Records Administration, Washington, 165-WW-181D-003)

also befell Raphaël Verwilghen's dream of a modern, functionally conceived Louvain town centre.

In the development plans for the villages, where the designers were sometimes able to start with a blank sheet of paper, a central square was an important element. Logically, the most important buildings – church, rectory, town hall, primary school – would

RISING FROM THE ASHES

be situated around it. In the eyes of the architects involved, the reconstruction should lead to an improvement in the comfort, hygiene and aesthetic character of village centres. Georges Hendrickx's design for *Sint-Joris* near Nieuport is illustrative of this.

Pending the actual start of the reconstruction, not only was rubble cleared, but temporary housing, town halls, schools and churches were all erected so that civic life could get underway and local governments could reorganise themselves. Other amenities were also developed fairly quickly because they were vital. These included the drinking water supply, which was a key issue, particularly in the front region. What is also remarkable is that the electricity network saw an accelerated development thanks to the reconstruction.

Inspiration from history

The reconstruction went hand in hand with animated discussions among architects: was this the ideal moment to realise a "modern" project or should they mainly look to the past for inspiration? The supporters of an architecture inspired by regional history won the argument. A pronounced modernistic reconstruction remained the exception to the rule, with Huib Hoste's designs for Zonnebeke village centre being the most important example. The remaining reconstruction architecture in towns and villages can be divided into two major groups. The most important historical monuments were constructed according to the pre-war model, although a number of comments can be made here. Historical "errors" were preferably corrected, as clearly expressed in Jules Coomans' designs for the Gothic town churches of Ypres, for example. For him, the reconstruction was the perfect moment to see his ideal of the mediaeval monuments become a reality, something which had not been feasible during the pre-war restoration. The reconstruction of the Church of Our Lady in Dinant involved the question of whether the characteristic pear-shaped tower pinnacle, regarded as an historical mistake, should be retained in the reconstruction. For the reconstruction of the town hall in Visé, Paul Jaspar also chose to accurately reconstruct the destroyed building, even though he did add a new wing in Mosan-Renaissance style so that the building could meet the needs of the expanded municipality.

In other places, architects chose new buildings in a style that, in their eyes, better aligned with the history of the devastated town. This was powerfully expressed in Nieuport, where the central function of the market square was reinforced with the construction of a new town hall in Gothic style. The reconstructed belfry, the Church of Our Lady and the neo-Gothic college completed the "historical image" of Nieuport. In Dixmude, Jozef Viérin and Valentin Vaerwijck chose to rebuild the town hall in a personal interpretation of the regional architecture and not to reconstruct the demolished neo-Gothic building. On the *Grote Markt* in Leuven the destroyed neoclassical *Tafel-rond* was rebuilt in Gothic style, illustrating how "new" historical monuments reinforced the historical townscape during the reconstruction. A similar scenario played out in the countryside. In West Flanders, village churches were either rebuilt in the pre-war Roman or Gothic style, or the architects chose a new build in Gothic style unique to the area. When it came to the design of town halls, primary schools and guest houses, regional architectural history was the most important source of inspiration. When the reconstruction was complete, the area had greater cohesion than it did before the war.

A long process

On 4 July 1928 the Louvain university library was officially re-opened. The monumental building, designed by American architect Whitney Warren and financed with international funds, is one of the best-known symbols of Belgian reconstruction. Barely 10 years after the armistice, the reconstruction of Louvain, like many other places in the country, was largely complete. In August 1926 the Devastated Regions Office was disbanded, not so much because the work was fully complete, but because from then on, towns and municipalities could stand on their own two feet and complete the work. Nonetheless, work on a number of major sites would take many years to complete. These included the complex of the Ypres Cloth Hall and belfry, possibly the most important symbol of Belgian reconstruction. The belfry was officially unveiled on Sunday the 29th of July 1934 in the presence of the royal couple. For the local press, the belfry was "the symbol that Flanders, devastated by war and despite all its difficulties, wishes to live again with diligence, persistence and courage."[36] The reconstruction of Ypres was deemed complete, although it would take until 1962 before the reconstruction works on the Cloth Hall were fully finished.

CLEARING AND RESTORING THE LANDSCAPE AT THE YPRES FRONT

Franky Bostyn

Just before the First World War, despite massive deforestation, the Ypres area is a green oasis, with woods, orchards, tree-lined drives and hedgerows. The war not only wipes entire villages and towns off the map, it also turns the lush green landscape into a desolate steppe. "What strikes as odd here, is that one doesn't see a single tree, not for as far as the eye can see. Only a few dead trunks emerge from the ground", writes an early front area visitor.

Fields are pockmarked with millions of explosion craters, a.k.a. shell craters, strewn not next to one another, but rather inside and on top of one another. Unexploded ammunition and war scrap are scattered everywhere, alongside the remains of trenches, bunkers or small-gauge lines. South of Ypres mine craters even measure up to 80 metres across. The British start clearing the landscape even before the armistice. The aim is to salvage abandoned war equipment and to repair main roads and railway lines. The task is accomplished by both military engineering auxiliary troops and labour units such as the Chinese Labour Corps. In the spring of 1919, some twelve thousand Chinese work in the area, employed by the military. The _Tchings_ are rather ill-reputed and stay in special camps.

A sheep farmer, holding his trophy, poses with his flock. Livestock competitions are organised in order to stimulate post-war agricultural policy and to improve livestock quality. The idea emanates from the influential professor from Louvain University and _Boerenbond_ vice-president Leopold Frateur. His approach is very scientific and technical, especially with regard to new breeding methods. (Stadsarchief Brugge, BRU001023427)

After the armistice, clearance is also undertaken by punished soldiers; up till the signing of the Versailles Treaty, German prisoners of war are put to work as well. That is exactly when the first inhabitants return from their French exile. They mainly look for reference points enabling them to determine the locations of their former dwellings. However, when surveying the extent of damages, many feel the region has simply become uninhabitable and prefer to settle in France. Others decide to make do and to start a new life in the wasteland.

Sources indicate that the total acreage of destroyed arable land ranges between 80,000 and 125,000 hectares (about 200,000 to 300,000 acres). Restoration costs are estimated at 1.4 billion Belgian francs, i.e. 5% of the then gross domestic product. In some zones, restoration costs do not cover the estimated intrinsic value of the land.

In early 1919 the Belgian association of forest engineers visits Ypres during its annual field trip. They conclude the area has to be thoroughly cleaned before agriculture can even be envisaged and that restoration costs will spiral out of control. A plea is held to afforest the central front area. Similar debates take place in France, leading to the creation of immense *zones rouges* turning entire villages into woodland.

Others, among them Albert Ruzette, West Flanders native and Minister of Agriculture, do believe in restoration. He nevertheless also feels that some 15,000 hectares (37,000 acres) of the Devastated Regions are completely lost for agricultural purposes. However, plans for large-scale afforesting are thwarted by dynamic returnees. They are determined to rebuild and to quickly repossess their land.[37]

Levelling

The Service of Devastated Regions is created in the wake of the law on town adoption dated 8 April 1919. The service supersedes local authorities in matters of reconstruction. In West Flanders, adopted towns are eventually integrated in one of three regions (coast, north and south), each headed by a Royal High Commissioner. The service operates up till the summer of 1926.

A separate administration for restoration of arable land is created within the Office of Devastated Regions. It functions quite efficiently, but coordination with other authorities involved in reconstruction is often lacking. The Ministry of Agriculture, for example, creates an in-house service for the reorganization of agriculture. The afflicted farmers eventually have three ways of rebuilding their estates.

A first possibility resides in restoration by the State, through tenders by the Office of Devastated Regions. In the Westhoek ten heavily devastated areas with complex infrastructure are designated to be levelled in this way. This possibility is also largely selected by local authorities and landowners living outside the front zone. It is quite an expensive matter for the State, with costs often exceeding the restored property's value. For the afflicted people the system is not ideal either, as works progress very slowly and moreover cancel all war damages claims.

A second possibility is provided by contracts for agricultural rehabilitation drawn up by the Ministry of Agriculture from November 1919 onwards, in which owners personally undertake the necessary steps. The pieces of land treated in this way often immediately return to full productivity. The costs equal about half the value of the restored land.

A third and last alternative is presented by the advances on war damages, usually monitored by third parties such as the Belgian *Boerenbond's Heidemaatschappij*. This organization for the development of wastelands had been created in 1913 and is now merged with the *Boerenbond's* newly constituted Service for the Restoration of West Flanders. Local cooperative partnerships, through which afflicted people can claim war damages, contract repairs. For many this is the quickest, most efficient and cheapest option.

By May 1921 some 69,000 hectares (170,000 acres) have already been levelled: 17,000 hectares (42,000 acres) (by the end of 1922: 18,700 hectares or 46,000 acres) by the State; 12,000 hectares (29,000 acres) (by the end of 1922: 17,000 hectares or 42,000 acres) through the contracts for agricultural rehabilitation and 40,000 hectares (100,000 acres) through third parties such as the Heidemaatschappij (by early 1922: 9,375 hectares or 23,000 acres).

In 1920–1921 up to thirty thousand front labourers daily make the trip to the Westhoek to perform the task at hand. Levelling involves removal of war equipment, barbed wire or weeds, and filling of trenches and shell craters. Shell crater draining proves particularly difficult, because ditches and streams have not yet been restored. As explosions compressed the bottoms of the craters, the soil needs to be loosened for water to be able to drain away. Labourers often are up to the waste in water.

Working in the devastated fields is very unhealthy. The smelly goo in the craters is a hotbed of diseases spread by thousands of rats twice the size of peace-time rodents. The first returnees therefore always carry clubs. The summer of 1920 is extremely hot and when the craters dry out vermin of every kind spreads massively.

Levelling is paid by the square meter, and as a result, jobs are often performed rather shoddily. Particularly State assignments lack supervision and control. Shell craters often are merely filled with waste, and accesses to underground constructions are poorly obstructed, resulting in subsidence for years on end.

One hectare (2.5 acres) typically spews up to 5,000 kilos of shell debris. Buried metal and unexploded bombs or shells (up to five per square meter) are to be added to that amount. Moreover, the retrieved items only represent the tip of the iceberg, with loads still present under the surface. Scrap is often evacuated by means of the existing small-gauge lines.

Till the end of October 1919, the British are entitled to all findings; after this date the Belgian State can claim discoveries. As metal prices soar, front labourers often collect all the copper they find to sell it come evening. This totally uncontrollable trade soon becomes an important source of income. As it affects reconstruction, it is eventually officiously authorized. Armed with mallets and chisels, the returnees finally take to the wastelands themselves. Manipulation of loaded projectiles remains forbidden, but the lure of their copper parts often proves too strong, with countless accidents as a result.[38]

In order to re-launch agriculture, King Albert donates 25,000 francs to be used as prize money in a contest: inventors have to come up with ways in which to restore agriculture. The winner is the American engineer Knox, who designs a field levelling machine. The 250 ton contraption, however, comes too late and proves too heavy to be actually used. On 19 March 1921 King Albert discovers the invention in Mesen.

(Archives Royal Palace, Albums AE 139/A)

Restoring the landscape

Returnees want to restore the landscape to its pre-war condition as soon as possible. The old parcel structure is re-instated. The land registry records in Bruges indeed survived the war, and surveyors can therefore be sent out to re-establish plots. This is quite an undertaking, as reference points are completely wiped out.

Environment reconstruction is also hastened by the fact that war damages are granted based on pre-war conditions. Towns and villages are required to establish development plans. While some roads are straightened and a few village squares are extended, the former landscape's overall pattern is recreated. The completely redesigned village of Wijtschate is one of the exceptions confirming the rule.

By late 1920 some 90,000 inhabitants are re-established in the Westhoek, on a total population of 150,000. As many landowners and tenants choose to stay in France, and most war damage grants do not cover the cost of rebuilding, numerous properties come on the market. Owners prepared to start anew are often forced to settle for less. The sale of houses and land without damage compensation induces a social reconfiguration. Those prepared to take on the work can obtain cheap pieces of land.

Numerous farms and estates therefore change hands in the twenties. In many villages tensions smoulder for years on end, opposing returned natives and newly arrived "easterners" who acquired interesting pieces of land. Newcomers also often are more open to modernity, whereas the natives essentially want to re-establish the pre-war situation. Many farms are never rebuilt.

The new landscape largely mirrors the old one, because the former plot structure is re-instated, and most rural buildings are erected in the regional style. Some major differences, however, arise, since typical elements such as windmills and castles are not systematically rebuilt. The loss of dozens of castles and manor houses also engenders the disappearance of their surrounding parks; the link with the surroundings is severed.

Another visual change is the appearance of barbed wire used to fence in pastures. Barbed wire is abundantly present on the former battlefields and replaces the traditional hawthorn hedgerows. Some other small elements in the landscape vanish as well, leading to a partial loss of the traditional Flemish setup. Today, some pre-war landscape elements are nevertheless still recognizable, with even a few hedgerows that have re-budded after the war.

The war and the post-war years also have an impact on the diversity in plants and trees. Some varieties have almost completely vanished, while others have, on the contrary, appeared. Real forests have eventually materialized, particularly in public administration areas, such as the state forests in Houthulst or Zonnebeke and the Gasthuisbossen in Zillebeke. The inferior planting material used then and there still engenders management problems to this day.[39]

Restoration of agriculture

When fields are first ploughed, the acid substrate is enriched with 400 kg of lime per hectare, which under normal circumstances would scorch the soil. Salinization at the Yser front is also corrected with lime. The year 1920 proves quite disastrous, as an infestation of field mice who make up to 50 holes per square meter ruin the meagre harvest on the limited treated acreage. The following years are plagued by wire worms, field mice and rats; agricultural production is insufficient because of deficient topsoil quality.

Many horses from the British and Belgian armies are used to plough the fields. The relaunch of cattle farming is obtained through donations, acquisitions and massive claims made on Germany, deducted from the war reparations. In 1921 it is established that large numbers of supplied animals do not come from Germany but are bought abroad.

Germany is also forced to supply large amounts of agricultural equipment, and mechanized farming is pursued. The Ministry of Agriculture, for example, supplies 130 Fordson tractors, used for ploughing 20,000 levelled hectares (50,000 acres) annually. Both the Ministry and the *Boerenbond* see the afflicted farmers as entrepreneurs and support the organization of farming exhibitions and contests.

As already indicated, the Belgian *Boerenbond* quickly develops into one of the forerunners of rural revival. In Roeselare the Service for the Recovery of West Flanders groups four separate units: an information bureau answering all the questions farmers might have, the already mentioned *Heidemaatschappij* very active in the field of soil improvement, a mediation service managing advances on war damages, and a building service.

In 1919–1922 the *Boerenbond*'s *Middenkredietkas* lends 51 million Belgian francs for the restoration of devastated regions. This is mainly achieved through local savings and loan guilds, the later *Raiffeisenkas*. In that way, the *Boerenbond* – and by extension the Catholic wing – quickly regains control over rural society.

Some 30 building service employees draw up the plans for the rebuilding of farms, dairies, farmsteads, churches, etc. In 1922 the service is merged into the *West-Vlaamsche Bouwvereeniging*.

Despite all efforts, the quality of arable land leaves something to be desired. Problems are only structurally solved when the most severely affected parcels are decompacted. Decompaction consists of ploughing the fields two to three spades deep, bringing quality soil to the surface, and removing war debris. As metal prices soar to 0.10 cents per kilo for iron and 2.50 francs per kilo for (red) copper, countless volunteers report for duty in exchange for the collected metals. Decompaction is launched in 1922 and activities peak over the next three years. Simultaneously, soggy fields are drained with clay pipes. By 1930 fields have been re-fertilised and as prices for metal plummet, decompaction grinds to a halt. Most fields have by then been decompacted and postwar levelling has erased the majority of microreliefs.

Despite sanitization in the twenties most former frontline soils still presented heightened concentrations in copper and especially in lead in 2008. Moreover, the decompacted ploughing layer continues to hide an immense battlefield archive.[40]

The iron harvest

The number of projectiles shot in the *Westhoek* over the course of the First World War is not to be estimated – not even approximated. In 1917 some fifty million are fired during the sole Battle of Passchendaele. Different reasons cause 30% of them not to explode: many percussion fuse projectiles are simply swallowed by the muddy terrain, without exploding. Large quantities of unused ammunition are moreover to be found all over Belgium. This makes for a high-risk situation. For instance, 140 train carriages containing old ammunition explode in Grimde near Tienen on March 21, 1919.

Shortly after the war, the British military start clearing ammo in several places, amongst others at a camp near Houthulst forest. Chinese labourers and German prisoners of war are also deployed to assist in clearance up till mid-1919. The British teach the first returnees that not all projectiles present a similar danger and that one firm blow suffices to defuse a shell. As they need money for entertainment, the soldiers also sell illegally defused shells to the first scrap dealers.

In 1920 the Office of Devastated Regions supplies every West Flanders High Commissary with a unit responsible for the collection of ammunition found during levelling works. A document dated 1 July 1920 tells us that some 13,000 projectiles awaited collection in the sole town of Poelkapelle. The service also has its own destruction yard, such as the one created in the present-day Polygon wood in Zonnebeke in the spring of 1921. Civilians strip projectiles of their copper components and set off the remains. Countless accidents occur, such as the one on 24 June 1922 in Wijtschate, when a couple of small-gauge carriages loaded with ammunition explode, killing 11 people.

The British Pickett company handles the lion's share in ammunition clearing, with 11 branches in France and one in Belgium near Houthulst forest. Some three hundred labourers work on both explosives and toxic ammunition. Projectiles, even toxic ones, are emptied manually. Chemical substances are either burned, neutralized and/or just left in the ground. Between 1 June 1920 and 1 September 1922 Pickett receives 32,000 tonnes of ammunition, 86% of which already is dismantled, including 5,000 tonnes of gas ammunition. The company probably ceases its activities shortly afterwards.

The army, particularly the *Commission de la Récupération*, also analyses dismantlement of old ammunition. Chemical ammunition is the focus of attention by late 1919

On 19 March 1921 King Albert, accompanied by Minister of Agriculture Albéric Ruzette, analyses some initiatives meant to promote agricultural re-launch along the former front line. The clearing of scrap and ammunition is very time-consuming. Most innovations, such as this metal detector, are not widely used. (Archives Royal Palace, Albums AE 139/A)

and early 1920. It is eventually decided to dump some 35,000 tonnes of ammo on the *Paardenmarkt*, a sandbar off the Knokke-Heist coast. The situation is monitored to this day.

In 1920 a *Service de Destructions des Munitions* is adjoined to each provincial section of the *Commission de Récupération*, active over the entire territory, except for the Westhoek, which is treated by the High Commissary services. The military service has grounds in Houthulst, Meerdaal and Leopoldsburg. Up till 1923 loads of collected ammunition are shipped off to Pickett, particularly toxic ammunition. The *Service de Destruction des Munitions* employs both servicemen and civilians.

When both Pickett and the High Commissary services close down, the *Service de Destruction des Munitions* remains the only one active in Houthulst forest. In 1923 it is fully integrated into the army and in 1941, during German occupation, it is renamed *Service d'enlèvement et de destruction d'engins explosifs* (SEDEE). Today, SEDEE annually still collects and destroys some 200 tonnes of First World War ammunition in the Westhoek. The Poelkapelle section still works in Houthulst forest, where both conventional and chemical ammunition is treated.

RISING FROM THE ASHES

Few figures are available about ammunition finds in the post-war years, but the figures relating to accidents indicate a clear trend. In 1919, 1920 and 1921 accidents are on the increase, mirroring the major levelling works. Figures decrease in 1922, only to once again peak in 1923 and 1924, when decompaction is the order of the day. Figures then steadily decline until 1930.

A lot of accidents involve *"koppenkappers"* (literally: head cutters) who, lured by high metal prices, do not hesitate to dismantle ammunition. Dozens of scrap dealers thrive on this lucrative trade, supplying countless people in the area with an income for years on end. At Ypres station alone some 10.2 million kilos of iron are loaded on train carriages in 1926.

A total of 599 accidents related to ammunition are recorded in the southern Westhoek over the period between 1918 and 2008, claiming 358 deadly casualties and 535 wounded. Projectiles are still illegally dismantled to this day, mainly by collectors. Casualties are also to be deplored, despite all sensitizing campaigns.[41]

Caring for the dead

After the war it becomes pressing to locate, register and group tens of thousands of casualties who have not yet been or were temporarily buried. As the southern Westhoek is mainly located in the British front sector, the British take action in this field. Headed by Fabian Ware, the Directorate of War Graves Registration and Enquiries recruits discharged servicemen, employing some 8,559 of them by early 1920. In the Westhoek the exhumation companies use Remy Siding (Lijssenthoek) in the city of Poperinge as a base camp. Casualties are systematically traced. London-based services first divide the former battlefields in 5,000 square meter parcels, and all available data about earlier recorded graves are entered. The units then tour the wasteland with these maps, picketing their plots and studying them carefully.

Locating human remains requires quite some experience, as graves indicated by a cross are few and far between. Rat holes, often found near remains, are important indicators, as are abandoned equipment, sudden concentrations of wild grass (large and dark blades) and differences in soil colours (blue, grey, black).

The survey is followed by exhumation. This is done in the presence of a burial officer who collects personal possessions in ration bags and who has the bodies wrapped in cresol-soaked tarps. A double form is established, one remaining with the body and one with the personal items. All objects are sent to London, where they are analysed in view of identification, and compared to military files.

The exhumation units not only locate British casualties but also German ones. Article 225 of the Versailles Treaty, however, stipulates that only Allied commissions have the right to organise cemeteries. The German war dead are therefore re-buried in the British sector. When Belgian or French servicemen are found, the concerned country's services intervene.

The last British servicemen are withdrawn from the Westhoek as of 1 September 1921; the exhumation companies are concerned by this measure as well. In a timespan of two years they managed to provide a grave for more than 200,000 war dead in Belgium and in the north of France.

Cemeteries are designed by the Imperial (today: Commonwealth) War Graves Commission. Existing battlefield cemeteries are flanked by large concentration cemeteries, counting huge numbers of soldiers "Known unto God" only. The German cemeteries, created from the twenties till the fifties, are gradually concentrated into the four large cemeteries still existing today. Once organised research is rounded up, the Imperial War Graves Commission constitutes mobile units monitoring the last steps of the levelling works executed on behalf of the Office of Devastated Regions.

Locals are repeatedly told that findings of human remains are to be reported either to the Imperial War Graves Commission or to local authorities. By the end of 1919 a two-franc allowance is granted for each find, an amount rising first to five and later to ten francs. This however only applies to the remains of British casualties. Consequently, the number of officially located German soldiers is limited. Bodies not considered for allowances are often robbed and put back in the ground by the men decompacting the area. By 1930 most military cemeteries in the Westhoek are established but some 200,000 soldiers of all nationalities remain missing. Half of them received an unmarked grave in a cemetery, the other half are still buried somewhere afield. As battlefield archaeology has developed into a full-fledged discipline over the past few years, the number of finds of human remains is much larger now than 20 or so years ago. Bodies can still be identified after a century, often through a combination of historical research and comparative DNA testing.[42]

Removal of war constructions

Bunkers differ from all other war constructions through the use of reinforced concrete, a combination of anchored steel and concrete. They were mainly built by the Germans, and in the southern Westhoek an estimated 10,000 were erected, ranging in size from small one-man constructions to large command bunkers.

Immediately after the war, many bunkers are used as emergency dwellings, but a few years down the road they are destroyed everywhere. The clearing of bunkers hindering reconstruction can indeed be claimed in war damage files. Their destruction is also hastened because of the valuable metal they contain. Moreover, bunker rubble is an ideal building supply for road construction.

In 1929 the State takes matters in hand and offers to clear bunkers free of charge in a one-time opportunity. Specialized companies massively destroy them up till 1932. They are usually wrecked with explosives; metal and rubble are then separated. Bunkers in the vicinity of already reconstructed houses are brought down manually, with mallets and chisels.

Two decades later, during the war in Korea, money is once again to be made with metal scrap, which leads to the dismantlement of dozens of bunkers. Interest in the First World War is then at an all-time low. Today, most remaining bunkers are listed as immobile heritage, but some still do disappear.

The British Mark V tanks stuck in the 1917 mud are important landmarks in the post-war landscape as well. They are to be found along three main roads leaving Ypres in the direction of Sint-Juliaan and Poelkapelle, Zonnebeke (Frezenberg) and Geluveld (Meenseweg). Concentration of tanks are called "tank cemeteries". The huge contraptions remain untouched until the Office of Devastated Regions publishes a tender for their removal. A mere two tanks remain: one is placed in the centre of Poelkapelle and another positioned at the railway station in Ypres. In 1941, both tanks are wrecked by the Germans and melted into new guns.[43]

Front tourism

As soon as the armistice is signed, former battlefields are flooded by tourists wishing to see the destructions with their own eyes. Budding front tourism therefore focuses on venues with bunkers, trenches and abandoned equipment such as tank cemeteries. Servicemen still present in the area profile themselves as the first travel guides. As levelling works progress, visiting veterans complain about the fact that the old front is hardly recognizable anymore.

Organizations such as the Belgian Touring Club, British Legion and Ypres League lobby to safeguard items recalling the war. Eventually, the Belgian Ministry of Defence decides to list 25 war sites along both the Yser front and the coast in 1921. At the Ypres front the Ypres League manages to save 180 historically significant bunkers from destruction. In 1933 a booklet is published with a map indicating all rescued constructions. From 1922 onwards, once levelling is largely completed, front tourism focuses on museums and newly erected monuments or cemeteries. A battlefield visit is, in that way, imbued with remembrance.[44]

Three men at work in a field in the vicinity of Vijfwegen near Poelkapelle. It is one of the many fields and pastures requiring levelling after the war. Centrally located is the grave of Camille De Cloedt – erroneously designated as Louis – who fell on 28 September 1918. His body is exhumed in June 1923 and transferred to the newly created military cemetery in Houthulst.
(Stadsarchief Brugge, BRU001023419, Brusselle-Traen collection)

A new landscape?

In conclusion, we could say that clearing and restoring the landscape after the First World War was as consequential as reconstruction. The clearing phase of 1919–1921 concurs with the return of inhabitants and the creation of emergency dwellings. By late 1921, when levelling works are largely completed, the organised search for human remains comes to a halt and the number of ammunition-related accidents sharply decreases. The first phase of front tourism, focusing on destruction, has then come to a close.

From 1922 onwards, restoration and reconstruction according to the local vernacular with numerous references to the past seem to go hand in hand. Decompaction of levelled fields brings about a second peak in ammunition victims. As many relics disappear, tourism focuses on newly created museums and cemeteries.

When reconstruction nears completion by 1930, the landscape is largely restored as well. Today, healing seems perfect. War nevertheless deeply affected the landscape: large amounts of hedgerows, small woods, tree rows and castle parks have disappeared.

RISING FROM THE ASHES

Other elements, characterizing the Westhoek, appeared: the very visible and often spectacular relics such as the dozens of cemeteries, the monuments and the large 1917 mine craters. Recuperation of bunkers as cattle shelter or screw pickets used to fix barbed wire is subtler in nature.

The landscape of the former Ypres front, therefore, is defined by both natural and historic elements, referring to the eras before, during and after the First World War. This conjunction of elements exactly produces the unique ensemble we are to cherish today.[45]

Belgian Van Deuren mortar, ca. 1915–1918. The Belgian army introduces this trench mortar named after its inventor Pierre Van Deuren in 1915. It is light-weight, mobile and sturdy. During the final offensive the weapon also proves deadly accurate. (Collection War Heritage Institute, 800219)

Bronze statuette *La Brabançonne*, designed by Charles Samuel, ca. 1918. A large version of this statuette is temporarily displayed on the Brussels Grand-Place, in honour of the royal family's Joyous Entry on 22 November 1918. A permanent version of *La Brabançonne* is erected on the Surlet de Chokier square in November 1930.

(Collection War Heritage Institute, 200600412)

Pickelhaube with case for the *1. Garde Infanterie* belonging to German Emperor Wilhelm II.
(Collection Huis Doorn, 07102)

Coat for a *generalfeldmarschall* belonging
to German Emperor Wilhelm II.
(Collection Huis Doorn, 04013)

Tapestry representing the royal family's Joyous Entry in Brussels on 22 November 1918. Anto Carte designed the piece in 1934, at the request of the Belgian Senate in response to the passing of King Albert I.

(Collection Belgian senate)

GASPARD-DE WIT. FEC.   ANTO-CARTE. DEL.

Satiric song text, ca. 1919. Songs like these mock the so-called soap barons: Belgians who profiteered on the black market, e.g., by selling soap at exorbitant prices. (Collection War Heritage Institute, Fonds A32)

Scale-model of steam locomotive 81.256 with coal-car 17.033, scale 1/87. The armistice agreements dictate that Germany has to cede thousands of pieces of railway equipment to Belgium. Type G8.1 is built by Orenstein in 1919. Belgium receives 583 copies of this model and registers it as type 81.

(NMBS/SNCB collection – Trainworld Heritage, 8522)

Series of postcards, 1919. Private August Bruyndonckx serves with the Belgian occupation army in Germany and sends his wife in Aalst a German postcard every other day.

(Private collection Simone Bruyndonckx)

Dangers of explosive devices, ca. 1918–1919. Bills drawn by famous artists inform both adults and children about the dangers of abandoned explosives, not only on former battlefields, but all over the country.
(Collection War Heritage Institute, 30500683)

Oak coffin, model n° 3, as used for the repatriation of Belgian war casualties from 1921 onwards. This type of coffin is acquired after a public tender in October 1921. (Collection War Heritage Institute, 201800137)

"Honour". Embellished Belgian helmet commemorating the First World War. (Private collection Willy Wilmotte)

Hinged artificial limb in leather, ca. 1920. The Irish company *Pringle & Kirk* is created to meet the large demand in protheses. The company specializes in the production of modern protheses.
(Collection War Heritage Institute, 200300204)

Flag of the Socialist veterans and their families, Wevelgem, 1918–1938, with flagpole tip "The Broken Gun". The various veterans' associations count a lot of pacifist movements.
(AMSAB collection, VL.00672 and VLT.000074)

Black *crêpe georgette* dress embellished with beading and rhinestones, ca. 1925.

(Collection Modemuseum Hasselt, 2002.0352)

5

A NEW BELGIUM

A SOCIETY IN TURMOIL

Serge Jaumain

Belgium emerged from the First World War battered and bruised. The invasion of August 1914 had initially come as an emotional shock. Germany was greatly admired for its economic, social, cultural and intellectual achievements. When this nation violated the neutrality of Belgium, which it had guaranteed, the population was shaken, and a large patriotic movement originated which benefited from a surge of international sympathy, skilfully nurtured by the Allied powers.

Once they had recovered from the shock of the declaration of war, the Belgians were confronted with the horror of the conflict. The entry of the German troops into Belgium was accompanied by widespread destruction, executions, and abuses of all kinds, images of which quickly went around the world. This violence of the opening months of the war was followed by the cruel hardship of a harsh occupation, the first since Belgium had become independent in 1830.

For four years, the day-to-day lot of the population had been one of deprivation. In occupied Belgium, the requisitions and contributions demanded by the Germans added to the already hard consequences of a blockade that was disastrous for the economy of this

View of the as yet uncompleted Yser Tower erected in Dixmude from 1928 onward. In the twenties, the sober meeting at the graveside of artist soldier Joe English in Steenkerke becomes a way of remembering the ideals of the Yser soldier. As time goes by, the pilgrimage is increasingly engulfed in the views of the Flemish movement. English designed the tombstone for the Flemish soldiers who gave their lives on the battlefield.
(Archives Joris Lannoo, Tielt)

small country, which was very dependent on international trade. Cut off from their international markets, businesses had closed down one after another, unemployment had increased at a dizzying speed, and the situation had been made even worse by food shortages (the Germans refused to provide rations) and deportations of workers.

On the Yser Front, the situation was even more dramatic. While the Belgian army was not as badly affected as the Allied troops, soldiers were to spend four interminable years dug into muddy trenches, living in dreadful conditions at mere survival level.

When Germany capitulated on the 11th of November 1918, it left behind a country bled dry, with a population physically and mentally exhausted by the conflict. After this "total war", characterised by a climate of extreme violence, nothing would ever be the same again, and historians are right in thinking that the "long 19th century" only ended in 1914. The first world conflict was the dividing line. The war had shaken the society that emerged in 1918 to its very roots.[1]

A constructive dialogue

The rise of patriotism which awoke in response to the German invasion, followed by the movements of solidarity developed over those four years, broke down the traditional social and political boundaries. A new, constructive dialogue came into being between groups which had been totally opposed until then, and now had no choice but to cross the divides inherited from the 19th century and work together to organise relief.

An exemplary action was set up in October 1914 by the *Comité National de Secours et d'Alimentation* (CNSA), a national rescue and supply committee, created to organise supplies for the country with the support of an American organisation (the Commission for Relief in Belgium). Politicians of every colour met within the CNSA and worked together in perfect harmony with employers, trade union members, and senior officials. Within this "shadow government", they came to know and understand each other and to establish links which were to be decisive in post-War society.

The attitude of the Socialists was a decisive factor in this process. From the start of the conflict, the *Parti Ouvrier Belge* (POB), the Belgian Workers' Party, had prioritised defence of the country over international pacifist solidarity. It was in this context that, in January 1916, its leader, Émile Vandervelde, who had been appointed Minister of State, joined the Catholic Government which had fled to Le Havre. He was joined by Liberals Paul Hymans and Eugene Goblet d'Alviella. For the first time in the history of Belgium a Socialist became a member of the executive power!

The presence and work of the Socialists within the government and the CNSA and, subsequently, when liberation came, their commitment to defending the Belgian institutions (at a time when a wind of revolution, raised by the events of 1917 in Moscow, was blowing through Europe), were to have a considerable impact on the image of the POB. Seen as pariahs by employers in 1914, at the end of the War the POB became essential partners in the rebuilding of the country.

Adapting the institutions

After those four years of intense suffering there was no point in attempting to restore Belgium to what it had been in 1914. The institutions needed to be adapted as quickly as possible to reflect the changes in society. In this respect, even before his triumphant entry into Brussels, King Albert had brought together various representatives of the country's most lively forces in Lophem (a village near Bruges, where he had set up his headquarters) to sketch out with them the first outlines of post-war Belgium. They came to an understanding in order to boost the social and political reforms and maintain a policy of national unity. An agreement was presented in anticipation of a government led by the Catholic Léon Delacroix and made up of Catholic, Liberal and Socialist ministers, a situation unimaginable before the war. The urgency and importance of these choices were, needless to say, linked with the scale of the suffering endured by the population, and it also answered a current of insurrection running through Europe.

To launch the reforms faster and ensure the vital support of the POB, the constitutional rules were set aside; universal male suffrage was established before it had even been enshrined in the basic law. It was obviously impossible to maintain the old voting system of 1893, which gave two additional votes to the most conservative, wealthiest Belgians, when those who died for their country at the front in the trenches of the Yser only had had one vote.

In addition, on the 24th of May 1921, the Socialists were to achieve the abrogation of the infamous Article 310 of the Penal Code which restricted the right to strike. This recognition of the unions was to contribute to the beginning of a new kind of dialogue, the guarantee of a social stability which would be vital for the economic recovery of the country.

In this unique end-of-war atmosphere, promises of vocal equality were reiterated, and also of higher education in Dutch – a point which was all the more sensitive as the Germans had turned the then French-language University of Ghent into a Flemish-speaking institution. These fine promises, however, took a very long time to produce results; it wasn't until 1923 that the University of Ghent became bilingual, and it only became definitively established as Flemish-speaking in 1930.

When King Albert made his triumphal entry into Brussels on the 22nd of November 1918, he brought with him not only his troops from the Yser but also an agreement on a

In 1921 war veteran and Socialist Julien Lahaut organises a large strike at the Ougrée-Marihaye steel factory in Seraing near Liège. The strike lasts for nearly ten months, wiping out the union financially. Lahaut, kneeling in front between the children, organises shelter all over the country for the strikers' children. The strikers eventually have to give in. Lahaut is, however, excluded from the Belgian Workers' Party. This pushes him straight into the arms of the newly constituted Belgian Communist Party.

(AMSAB-ISG, FO.011486)

series of major reforms which the subsequent governments strove to implement under the eagle eye of the sovereign (he was to chair no fewer than 23 Councils of Ministers between 1918 and 1921).[2]

The thorny question of compensations

The Belgian authorities found an exhausted country: businesses had closed down, machines had been dismantled, communications infrastructures had been damaged, and tens of thousands of buildings had been destroyed… In this respect, they put their hope in the financial reparations imposed on Germany. The Belgians were convinced that they could benefit from their status as a "martyred country", which had been evoked so

A NEW BELGIUM

many times during the conflict, to obtain considerable reparations and territorial compensation. The Belgian leaders therefore went to the Paris Conference with a firm resolve to make Germany pay. The illusion would soon be shattered, however, as the Americans thought that this policy would strangle Germany's economy and might sow the seeds of a revolutionary movement. Under the Versailles Treaty signed on the 28th of June 1919, Belgium could hope for a share-out of part of the funds (2.5 billion gold francs) at best, linked with the first part of the German reparations... but it gradually became clear that this sum would never be paid in full.

A few Belgian nationalists, linked together in a "national policy committee" created in December 1918, also nurtured the wildest dreams of expansion – re-establishing Belgium with its 1830–1839 frontiers. They wanted to gain nothing less than the annexation of Dutch Luxembourg, the Grand Duchy of Luxembourg, *Zeeland* Flanders, certain parts of the Rhineland, and the German possessions in East Africa. These hopes were also doused by the Paris Conference. Finally, the Belgians had to make do with the annexation of the Eastern cantons and some promises regarding Africa (in 1921 Belgium was granted a mandate to Ruanda-Urundi in the name of the League of Nations). While the result was very far from the great projects of the expansionists, on the 25th of July 1921, Belgium nevertheless obtained the creation of the Belgo-Luxembourg Economic Union (a first step on the road towards the future Benelux), in spite of the fact that in September 1919 the people of Luxembourg had voted in a referendum for an economic alliance with France.

In spite of the low level of the German reparations, the overall economic recovery was quicker than expected. The coal mines which had not been too severely damaged returned to full activity quickly, as did the port of Antwerp and the rail network. The iron and steel industry, which had been more severely affected, took two years to get back to full capacity. So within a few years, the country returned to its pre-war industrial dynamism and then, in the second half of the 1920s, benefited from worldwide growth.[3]

A hesitant democratisation of Belgian society

In social terms, the Belgian situation is quite different from the well-known images of *garçonnes*, the Frenchwomen of independent spirit who had replaced the absent men in numerous French factories. Due to the closure of most businesses, Belgian female labour was never called for during the war. The liberation was thus not followed by a rise in women's rights in Belgium. In electoral terms, universal suffrage with voting rights for women was discussed at length, but always with an eye to election gains. The Catholic Party, which had never distinguished itself in the feminist struggle, declared itself greatly in favour of this extension of voting rights, convinced that this would strengthen its electoral potential. And the Liberal Party opposed it vehemently on the same basis! The compromise outcome was the Law of the 15th of April 1920, allowing women to vote in local authority elections only. Only war heroines were invited to vote in the legislative elections, as were war widows, although in the latter case this was a kind of vote by proxy which they lost if they remarried!

The Constitution of 1920–1921 permitted a simple law, voted in by special majority, to extend the right of women to vote in the legislative elections, but it was not adopted until 1948. The institutions were also very slow to admit the new reality that women could stand as candidates at any level at all. In 1921, the POB put the first woman into the Senate (Marie Spaak-Janson) by co-opting her, and it was only in 1929 that the Chamber would, in its turn, welcome its first member, the Socialist Lucie Dejardin. As for the local elections in which women were able to vote for the first time on the 24th of April 1921, these did not cause a landslide – two million women voted, but only 196, a mere 1% of those elected, gained places on local councils.

However, at parliament level, the first elections with universal suffrage for men, held on the 16th of November 1919, overturned the political balance. The Catholic Party which had dominated the parliament since 1884, lost its absolute majority. With 38% of the votes and 73 seats in the Chamber, it was followed closely by the *Parti Ouvrier Belge*, which gained a spectacular victory (36% of the votes and 70 seats) and eclipsed the Liberal Party (17% of the votes and 34 seats). Alongside these three major political parties, a new, small party appeared – the *Frontpartij*, a descendant of the *Frontbeweging*, a Flemish movement which had developed in the trenches – and gained 5 seats. Over the coming years, it was to take its place as the political stimulus of the Flemish movement. These elections were also a major turning point in that they ushered in the era of the coalition governments. Henceforth, it would be almost impossible for any single party to gain an absolute majority. Talks had to be held to achieve compromises between the parties before governments could be formed. They created the position of Prime Minister. Replacing the previous Head of Cabinet, the Prime Minister would now act like an orchestral conductor to ensuring the stability of his coalition.[4]

A revolution in social relations

The presence of the Socialists in the government until 1921 also allowed an implementation of a set of reforms which benefited from the support of a section of the middle classes which was sensitive to social questions. In addition to establishing universal male suffrage and abolishing Article 310 of the Penal Code, these reforms included the creation of a system of taxation based on income, the adjusting of salaries to bring them into line with price changes, the extension of benefits for the insured unemployed to 12 months, the increase in costs reimbursed by health insurance, the creation of the *Œuvre Nationale de l'Enfance* child welfare system, the setting up of restrictions on the sale of alcohol, the establishment of an eight-hour working day (and a six-day week), the creation of the *Société Nationale des Habitations à Bon Marché* for the development of welfare housing, and the development of compulsory free primary education.

Belgium also inaugurated a new era of industrial relations. In 1919, dialogue began between management and workers, with the setting up of sector-based joint committees. These led to collective labour agreements which paved the way for salary scales and improved working conditions while avoiding any major disputes. Managements which had been totally opposed to recognising trade union organisations before the war now understood that direct talks with the workers' representatives were the best way of avoiding wildcat strikes. So industrial relations became an increasingly important feature of the Belgian social and institutional landscape. The unions were further strengthened by the fact that the State entrusted them with a range of responsibilities. In particular, it financed the union funds which paid out unemployment benefits. Success was not long in coming – the unions soon had more than half a million members.

Slow language policy reform

Finally, the 1920s were marked by upheavals in linguistic policy, although the fine promises made in this context at the time of the liberation took a very long time to materialise. In December 1918, the Flemish movement had already set the tone by publishing its "minimum programme" of claims demanding the use of Flemish in the courts and government and at all levels of education in Flanders, plus, at central level, administrative handling of matters relating to Flanders in the Flemish language. It also demanded the reorganisation of the army into separate Flemish and French-speaking units. The success of the *Frontpartij* in the 1919 elections further illustrated the development of a more radical wing of the Flemish movement, supported by a new generation which demanded immediate, far-reaching reforms of the very structure of the Belgian State.

It was not until 1921 that Flemish was imposed as the language of the local and provincial authorities in Flanders. This regional unilingualism, in fact, defined the boundaries of a future country with three linguistic regions, while the Belgian political world became increasingly divided on a basis of identity.

The creation of the *Vlaams Economisch Verbond* in 1926 also gave the Flemish movement a more economic profile. This was the expression of a major change in the country, where coal mining in Campine and the development of vehicle manufacturing and the chemicals industry enabled Flanders to attract more and more businesses and increased its economic weight within the country.

Laying the foundations of modern Belgium

On a political level, the agreement on the revision of the Constitution which enshrined some of the major reforms also symbolically marked the end of the period of national union. The day after the king's signature in October 1921, Minister Anseele took part in a Socialist demonstration at La Louvière, in the course of which he was handed a banner portraying a broken rifle, the symbol of antimilitarism, which caused a protest by the Minister of Defence, backed by the Prime Minister. The Socialists drew their own conclusions from this and left the government. The main social and political reforms, had, however, been achieved. They were no longer an issue, and were even strengthened (by the establishment of an obligatory pension system, for example).

Within a few years, Belgian society had been turned inside out. On social, political, economic, and institutional levels, the foundations of modern Belgium had been laid. They would be decisive for the development of the country during the 20th century.

ANCIENS PRISONNIERS POLI[TIQUES]

1914 1918

FLANDRE ORIENTALE

THE BELGIAN VETERANS IN THE AFTERMATH OF THE FIRST WORLD WAR

Martin Schoups and Antoon Vrints

O n the 11th of November 1918, the day of the Armistice, the Belgian soldiers made their triumphant entry into Ghent. It was the culmination of the grueling liberation offensive that, after years of trench warfare, had brought them in a few weeks from the Yser to the gates of the East Flemish capital. After 52 months of being separated from family and friends in the occupied country, the Belgian soldiers could now gradually liberate Belgium in the footsteps of the retreating German army. The population welcomed the Belgian soldiers as true folk heroes, acting – as they were – as liberators of their own country. Thus, during those days of November 1918, they held a unique position among the other soldiers. That special position further heightened the soldiers' self-awareness. After all, they had already been well aware of all the sacrifices that they would have to make for the liberation of the country, when they were in the trenches.[5] On the strength of those sacrifices they now wanted not only recognition for themselves, but they also wanted to have a greater bearing on the socio-political order of post-war Belgian society.

After the demobilisation, former soldiers therefore felt a great need to join together. From December 1918 onwards, ex-service associations sprang up throughout the country. In 1920 only 20% of former soldiers stated that they were *not* members of a veterans' association,[6] making the coverage of the Belgian veterans' organisations probably the highest in the whole of Europe. Three factors can explain this drive to unite. To begin with, there were pragmatic considerations. The veterans' associations were represented in the body that allocated the Fighters' Grant to ex-soldiers, the *Fonds du Combattant/*

The *Ligue Patriotique des Anciens Prisonniers Politiques de la Flandre Orientale* presents its flag
on 28 December 1920. Evarist De Geyter, a former spy who had been sentenced to death,
acts as standard-bearer. Former intelligence agents are keen on integrating veterans' associations:
the secret missions they carried out during the war can, in that way, finally be acknowledged.
(Stadsarchief Oudenaarde, De Geyter collection)

Numerous veterans' associations are created after the First World War. Local sections are constituted within national or regional organizations, such as the *Vlaamsche Oud-Strijdersbond* in Duffel.
De Vlaamsche Oud-Strijdersbond is created by Jozef Verdyn in May 1919, in defence of veteran interests.
(Gemeentearchief Duffel, F3-0044)

Strijdersfonds (Fighters' Fund). Therefore, there may have been a financial incentive for membership. The fact that Belgium was the most densely populated country in the world – with a very well-connected railway network – also boosted the creation of organisations on a national scale. The minority position of the ex-servicemen may have been important, too. Given that, in Belgium, only 20% of able-bodied men were mobilised, the needs of the veterans were of a less universal nature than in countries like France and Germany, which had a much higher level of mobilisation. The minority position strengthened their will to form their own interest groups. This was particularly so because the Belgian soldiers did not have the monopoly on the suffering caused by war, given the civilian population's experience of occupation. This increased the need to highlight the specific experience of the soldiers even more.

Chiefly apolitical

The minority position that the Belgian ex-servicemen held in society did not mean, incidentally, that these veterans' associations formed a unit. There were numerous competing organisations, which differed due to very divergent criteria. There were associations whose existence was founded on war wounds *(Nationaal Verbond der Verminkte en Invalide Soldaten van den Oorlog)*, religion *(Confédération Catholique des Combattants)*, military rank *(l'Amicale des Officiers)*, language and regional identity *(Verbond van Vlaamsche Oud-Strijders)*, ideology (the *Socialistische Oud-Strijders* and the radical right *Association Nationale des Combattants*) or regiment (the so-called *Fraternelles*). In the 1930s an organisation would emerge with the aim of uniting all the soldiers that had received the medal known as the *Vuurkruis* (Fire Cross), awarded in 1933 to all soldiers who had been part of a fighting unit for twelve months. By highlighting the fact that they had faced real danger at the front, they sought to distinguish themselves from those groups that had spent the war well away from it. There was only one organisation that had the explicit ambition of gathering all ex-servicemen into its fold, namely the *Nationale Strijdersbond van België*. Although the NSB was actually the biggest veterans' organisation, it is clear from the number of members that it could never have had the monopoly. It is also important to remember that the heart of the veterans' associations also beat at the local level. The ambition of the countless local associations was primarily to unite all the former soldiers of a municipality or town.

In spite of that diversity, there were some similarities in the discourse of all those different organisations. With the exception of the *Socialistische Oud-Strijders,* all the associations defined themselves as "apolitical". Though it was indisputably civil organisations that made political demands, they specifically presented themselves as the antithesis of the "career politicians", i.e., the government, parliament and the political parties, whom the ex-servicemen accused of electoral games, corruption, inefficiency and sterile squabbling. The ex-servicemen portrayed themselves, on the other hand, as representatives of sincere "straightforward politics", which transcended classic party political and ideological divisions. As such, they thought of themselves as better interpreters of the wishes of the Belgian little man than the political elites. This contrast can be traced directly back to the Belgian war experience. The elites were suspected of having shirked their responsibilities, while the overwhelming majority of the population – the "common people" – had done their duty during the war. The veterans' associations could therefore be regarded as a social movement with a strong populist base. They saw themselves as men of action, honouring the principle of "deeds, not words". To reinforce their demands, the veterans did not hesitate to take to the streets. They, along with the middle class, were therefore the only group to demonstrate in such large numbers in the interwar period.[7] That finding is at odds with the influential thesis that the Belgian veterans brought much less weight to bear, societally, than their French or German counterparts. However, there was no head-on confrontation with the political system, given that the veterans – ambiguously enough – turned to precisely those same accursed institutions to realise their demands.

Not satisfied with a "handout"

What were the veterans' demands that rang out on the streets of Belgium in the inter-war period? First and foremost, ex-servicemen were seeking material and symbolic recognition of the sacrifice that they and their fallen comrades had made for the country. In the early post-war years the splintered world of the veterans was able to unite strongly around this demand. The former combatants found the concession proposed by the government in the spring of 1919 far too lean. They rejected it as a "handout", and demanded acknowledgement of their "rights". Mentally, this was a huge leap for the Belgian elites, who until 1914 had governed a liberal night watchman state, a state in which social politics were restricted to local charity. Within the government there was grumbling about the veterans being too "materialistic"; it was felt that they should put the salvation of the country (and that of the Exchequer) first.[8] However, the ex-servicemen turned a deaf ear, and in 1919 and 1920 responded to the government's reluctance with a huge wave of action. Many thousands of veterans from different organisations marched repeatedly, and were cheered on by masses of spectators. The campaign had a dramatic culmination: on the 29th of July 1920 former combatants stormed Parliament, a first in Belgian history. The turbulent wave of protest was wrongly seen as evidence that the Belgian soldiers had come out of the war "brutalised". The hypothesis was that the violent experience of war had caused them to develop a violent political style. Although the ex-servicemen were indeed militant, and skirmishes were not unheard of, there was no systematic violence as there was with Eastern European paramilitary groups. The absence of militias, uniforms and weapons clearly distinguished them from the fascist groups in Germany and Italy and their actions. Despite all the commotion over the "storming" of Parliament, the veterans' campaign did bear fruit: the concessions provided in the law of 25 August 1920 "given as a sign of gratitude to the soldiers of the 1914–1918 war," went a long way towards soothing the complaints of those who had fought.

The veterans' material demands, however, were not limited to concessions. The issue of rents also caused a great deal of discontent: after four years away, ex-servicemen refused to cough up the rent arrears on their homes and demanded that the government take measures against excessive rents.[9] On the 23rd of June 1919, for example, after one of the first meetings of the NSB, indignant veterans paid "a visit" to a landlord who had

After the war, numerous veterans become members of a veterans' organization. On several occasions the veterans take to the streets, demanding both material and symbolic acknowledgment. As they feel their demands are insufficiently met, they march on Parliament on 29 July 1920. Parliament is since then fenced off.
(Brussels City Archives, 2528)

thrown a former soldier out on the street to make him change his mind. The government reacted quickly to the issue of rents by freezing them in the summer of 1919. The Rent Act of the 30th of April 1919 made it possible for the justice of the peace to write off the rent arrears of ex-soldiers in certain cases. The demand for recognition of ex-servicemen was not purely material, either. They also led a campaign for military amnesty, feeling – after the victory – that it was inappropriate for soldiers to remain in prison for insubordination or to have to suffer the consequences of military courts in other ways.

Different "fatherlands"

The great authority that the war veterans had acquired was evidenced by the fact that they tried to bring their weight to bear on issues that concerned those other than themselves. Their sphere of action was very diverse. For example, in the mid-1920s they put heavy pressure on politics and justice to tighten up the prosecution of war profiteers. Anyone who had profited from the war should, in the eyes of the veterans, now pay their fair share. Those who had fought could not be allowed to languish while the *nouveaux riche* drove jauntily through the streets in their shiny cars. The presence of German citizens in Belgium also caused bad blood. War veterans staged anti-German demonstrations with the aim of putting pressure on the authorities to deport German citizens and sequester their assets. They also tried to influence socio-economic policy: in 1924, at the time of a dramatic worsening of the Belgian franc exchange rate, the NSB unleashed a widespread campaign against the high cost of living.[10] At markets in Malines and Brussels hundreds of veterans imposed maximum prices for butter. These demonstrations were accompanied by a press campaign in *Het Strijdersblad*, in which the finance capital came in for criticism. NSB's aim, with this action, was to put pressure on the government to call a halt to the currency devaluation and falling purchasing power.

War veterans also regularly came out in full-blown opposition to each other in such protests. The pacifist and internationally inspired protests of the *Socialistische Oud-Strijders*, in particular, provoked the opposition of other veterans. The flag of the Socialist veterans bore the drawing of a soldier breaking his own weapon, which was seen as defamation of the flag of the fatherland. The "incident with the flag of the broken gun" in La Louvière, at which Socialist Minister Edward Anseele was present, would even provoke the fall of the third and last National Union government in 1921. The Flemish radical nationalist *Verbond der Vlaamse Oud-strijders'* protests for amnesty for penalised activists in turn triggered the anger of right-wing and Belgian nationalist organisations. This illustrates how all the war veterans proudly set themselves up as the true guardians of the fatherland, but shows that the interpretation of that fatherland clearly differed depending on who was speaking. As the interwar period advanced, those different fatherlands, Belgium and Flanders, would exclude each other more and more. These different ideas about the fatherland also explain why those who had fought in the war adopted highly conflicting positions with regard to a Franco-Belgian military agreement.

The former Yser soldiers therefore played an important societal role in the liberated Belgium, a role that they commanded by means of their veterans' associations, which the ex-soldiers joined en masse after the war. Despite the fact that they had all served in the same army, the diversity of associations mainly reflects the fault lines within postwar Belgium: Flanders vs. Belgium, left vs. right, and pacifist vs. militarist. Although the dynamic between these different associations was often adversarial, the war veterans did manage to figure prominently in the political climate. In itself, that is a significant finding, given that these were people who had often come from working-class environments and who would have had a much lower presence were it not for their war experience. That they were able to carry political weight had everything to do with the incredible prestige that they enjoyed as liberators of the occupied nation. The veterans themselves bounced back and forth between disappointment and pride. On the one hand, they felt that their demands had still not been met sufficiently, but on the other they never missed an opportunity to emphasise their successes. The men of the Yser retained their pride.

UNSUNG HEROES.
THE REHABILITATION
OF WOUNDED SOLDIERS

———

Christine Van Everbroeck

Many studies have dealt with the return of the veterans, the reunion with their families, their reintegration in society, and their importance as a political force.[11] Some of these, especially in the English-speaking world, have dealt more specifically with the subject of wounded soldiers.[12] None of the veterans escaped unscathed from the violence of war on an industrial scale, but the minds and bodies of those who were disabled, mutilated or suffered psychiatric disorders all bore even greater, indelible scars caused by the horrors they had undergone.

Some 6,000 physical and mental patients had to find their way back to their former lives. Their families, who had often had no news of them for several years, had no idea what had happened to them. They were suddenly faced with the return of husbands, sons, or fathers who had been permanently changed by the war and were no longer the same people who had left four years earlier. Reintegration in families, jobs and society was difficult. The period of separation and the difference of their experiences at the front, in exile, or in occupied Belgium, affected and weighed on all the family reunions. But the wounded suffered the added traumas of incurably damaged body or spirit, lost health, or permanent injury. As a result, their return to private life and their reintegration in society are a special case.

To highlight its work, the Asylum for War Blinds in Boitsfort regularly participates in exhibitions, such as this one in the Brussels Jubilee Park. The exhibition presents its working methods and the items it produces, such as carpets and baskets. The makers are also put in the limelight. Central in the picture is August Lombaerts, one of the war blinds.
(Collection War Heritage Institute, EST-1-922-3-63)

The gradual return

Wounded soldiers gradually returned to Belgium once the war was over. The occupational retraining college which the Belgian government had set up at Port-Villez (Normandy) sent all its students back to their homes and to new working lives.

The Belgian psychiatric institutions temporarily installed in France during the war gathered their patients together and sent them to the *Sint-Johannes de Doper-instituut* in Zelzate, where the new military neuropsychiatry centre (CNPM) was opened. Between March and September 1919, more than 500 Belgian soldiers suffering from psy-

In December 1918 the Belgian army counts more than 77,000 wounded and 123,000 soldiers affected by gas. More than 5,000 soldiers have a permanent disability, and 1,700 of them have been amputated. Through protheses or adapted wheelchairs, such as these tricycles pushed by dogs, war invalids maintain some kind of mobility. When Prince Charles visits the Provincial Congress of War Invalids in August 1922, they hold a parade on the Bruges city square.

(Stadsarchief Brugge, BRU001000051, Brusselle-Traen collection)

chiatric problems returned from France, as well as from Holland and Germany, where Belgian prisoners and internees had been treated during the war.

From October 1919 onwards, the majority of these soldiers were dispersed through various asylums in Belgium to be reunited with their families. Some of them were restored to family life.[13]

One of the major challenges for the veterans, and even more so for those who had been crippled or affected mentally, was returning to their families, sharing their lives again, and taking up their responsibilities again after four years when all they had known had been survival, obeying orders, and camaraderie within a protecting unit.

The return to family life

Families would learn of the sad fates of their sons or husbands from impersonal forms sent out by the military doctor in charge of the CNPM at Zelzate. For these families, it was the beginning of an uncertain future. Some families were determined to see their sons or husbands again, in spite of the illness, convinced that the love of their families would restore their minds and spirits. Patients who had improved or been cured returned home for good. Some, who had received care but were still suffering from intermittent problems, went back and forth between home and institution. But there were others who, initially seeming to have come out of the violence of the conflict unscathed, cracked when faced with the responsibilities of rebuilding family life, becoming violent in public or in private, and had to be temporarily or permanently confined to asylums.

Some doctors recommended the creation of a single psychiatric institution to treat all these soldiers. This would allow them to be with comrades while receiving treatment for their specific problems. But the psychiatrists did not recognise war-related pathologies, and could not see the point of isolating these soldiers from civilians suffering from apparently identical disorders.

Those with physical injuries usually went back home, and those who had completed their rehabilitation training attempted to find jobs which would provide for their families. The others were dispersed throughout the occupational retraining institutions located across the country. Only the blind were brought together in the institution for the blind at Watermael-Boitsfort.

The reintegration of invalids in society consisted first and foremost of vocational rehabilitation.

Working life

Often invalids were unable to return to their pre-war occupations, and had to make do with low wage jobs due to their disabilities. The State, recognising its debt to these citizens who had left a part of themselves in the conflict, tried to protect them. It issued an initial law (on the 3rd of August 1919) guaranteeing their reintegration by granting the disabled, veterans, those who had been mobilised, etc., admission to public offices and jobs.[14]

In 1919, the State took its rehabilitation work further by acquiring the property of Mr. Parmentier at Woluwé, where functional and occupational retraining workshops had been installed after the war. The workshops offered invalids a wide range of skills, including bookbinding, draughtsmanship, wood carving and modelling, shoemaking, piano playing and tuning, basketry, chair caning and reseating, making orthopaedic

A blind soldier is taught how to use a typewriter at the Institue for the Blind in Boitsfort. This institution, created by Queen Elisabeth in October 1919, caters to soldiers who lost their eyesight during the war. The blind are assisted in several ways in order to facilitate social integration. The institute provides free shelter and food, and patients receive an allowance. They are taught braille and mobility techniques, and they are encouraged to acquire skills enabling them to earn a living, such as brush-makers, basket-weavers or piano-tuners. The institute closes its doors in August 1922. (Archives Royal Palace, Albums AE 121/B)

equipment, industrial design, cutting, electricity, and horticulture. In 1919 there were 300 war wounded at the Woluwé institute.[15]

While the invalids wanted to be reintegrated in society, they also wanted recognition and recompense for the sacrifices they had paid for so dearly. This recompense consisted of the granting of pensions.

Pensions

The Law of the 23rd of November 1919 on military pensions[16] established a single rate for war wounded having the same level of disability, regardless of social status or occupation. This single rate, however, differed according to the rank of the pensioner. The disability must have been caused or aggravated by the circumstances of war (fatigue, accident, or danger in the campaign between the 31st of July 1914 and the 30th of September 1919) and have resulted in an incapacity of at least 10% lasting for at least one year. In order to have their rights recognised, applicants had to set up dossiers containing medical certificates, witness reports, evidence of their attendance at the health care services and hospitals where they had been treated, etc. Once this documentation was complete, the invalid would undergo a medical examination to determine the degree of incapacity and the rate of the pension he would receive.[17] Some invalids had mental disorders and were unable to produce all this paperwork, and their families, who would not have been informed of their loved one's experiences, could not fill in the forms either. These came from the *Dépôt des Invalides*, which was in charge of coordinating applications from invalids and organising medical committees.[18] In these cases the evidence of disability would be questioned.

Throughout the interwar period, invalids put in claims for decent pensions. Belgium's economy was in a desperate position, the country had to rebuild itself and was having great difficulties in attempting to return to the place it had occupied in the world economy before the war, and the government kept a tight rein on its finances. Soldiers who claimed decent pensions to support their families were met by flat refusals from the Minister of Defence, Janson. "These young people, some of whom have gone astray, must be told that they have enjoyed a great honour in being able to serve their country and that apart from the many distinctions which are granted to them in return for their special efforts, it would mean diminishing the greatness of their role if we were to associate its memory with that of the payment of a calculated benefit. ('Hear! Hear!' from various benches)."[19]

It was only a step from here to the perception of the disabled as scroungers who were not even attempting to win back their independence. Under the pretext that there were abuses, some members of the government were prepared to pillory injured veterans as low-life profiteers, and wanted to organise stringent budget cuts affecting their pensions.[20]

The disabled organised themselves in associations to put pressure on the government and defend their rights. The first of these to be created was the *Fédération Nationale des Militaires Mutilés et Invalides de la Guerre* (the National Federation of Wounded Soldiers and Injured Veterans) which arose from a merger of various groups which had appeared during the war. It dealt with distributing cash donations, allocating death benefits, giving practical advice, and organising the sale of flowers for the wounded on the 1st of May. It also acted as a pressure group, lobbying Members of Parliament.[21]

In order not to leave the entire initiative in the private sector, the legislator founded an institution for the war disabled via the Law of the 11th of October 1919, the *Œuvre Nationale des Invalides de Guerre* (O.N.I.G.).[22] This institution paid for medical consultations and care. It provided material assistance for the disabled, creating a loan office which would lend small sums at minimal interest rates or give assistance in kind (clothing, bedding, etc.). Special homes for war disabled provided accommodation and rehabilitation.[23] The *Œuvre* helped the disabled to recover their ability to work via occupational retraining and apprenticeship in trades, thus continuing the action of the Port-Villez training college. While the associations supporting the disabled and the veterans' organisations were aware of the problems the war wounded faced, society was not always open to their claims.

Society and the disabled

The heroism and grandiloquent surge of patriotism celebrated by wartime propaganda, of which the veterans were a symbol, were forgotten after the war, and even decried as exaggerated manifestations of a unity which had been eroded by Flemish demands.[24] Both injured soldiers and veterans, living images of the sacrifice, found it difficult to gain a hearing in a society which wanted to move on, and was facing serious economic problems. Seeking respect, they complained of the lack of consideration evinced by their compatriots. Sometimes, they were even denied decorations, as can be seen from a passage in the margin of the file on a mental patient: "Lieutenant, is it really necessary to send military award certificates to veterans interned in mental hospitals?"[25]

The invalids were sometimes paraded in patriotic ceremonies, such as when the body of the unknown soldier was transferred. But although the Belgian war memorials are many and diverse, their names never appear there. These victims were reminders of the destructive madness of the war – they did not have the status of heroes.[26] They remained on the side.

Malmédy vous salue!

"NEW BELGIANS" LIVING IN ANCIENT BELGIAN SOIL? THE ANNEXATION AND INTEGRATION OF THE EAST CANTONS

Christoph Brüll

"Germany renounces in favour of Belgium all rights and title over the territory comprising the whole of the *Kreise* (region) of Eupen and of Malmedy. During the six months after the coming into force of this Treaty, registers will be opened by the Belgian authority at Eupen and Malmedy in which the inhabitants of the above territory will be entitled to record in writing a desire to see the whole or part of it remain under German sovereignty. The results of this public expression of opinion will be communicated by the Belgian Government to the League of Nations, and Belgium undertakes to accept the decision of the League." Article 34 of the Treaty of Versailles marked the key moment of the 20th century for the residents of this region, now commonly referred to as the "East Cantons".[27]

Belgium gained an area of 1,000 km² with 60,000 inhabitants, almost 50,000 of whom were German speakers. Initially, this was unexpected; Belgium had aspired to a much greater territorial expansion which would have involved Dutch and German regions as well as the Grand Duchy of Luxembourg; the great majority of the residents would never have imagined becoming Belgian citizens at the end of the war, even in the Walloon territories around Malmedy. During the 1920s, there were protests that there had been a misunderstanding or, at the least, that the integration of these territories was turning out to be much more complicated than had been expected. Twice, in 1925–1926

Belgian cavalry entering Malmedy, 12 August 1919. Through the Versailles Treaty, Belgium obtains several German districts. Between 1920 and 1925 the country organises a temporary administration under the authority of a High Commissioner, General Herman Baltia.
(National Archives of Belgium, Brussels, F1546, 2724)

and 1929, the possibility of a retrocession was even discussed at the highest level of government. Clearly, declaring that this land was originally Belgian – having shared until 1815 the fate of the territorial units on which Belgian independence was based – was not sufficient to "assimilate hearts and spirits" as the saying went at the time.

RANGE sur les HAUTES FAGNES
inant de la Belgique) à 1 km. de
Monument inauguré en Avril 1923
Altitude de 700 M. au sommet de
terre à rase de la dalle ou repose
la borne.

Post card, 1924. With the annexation of Eupen, Malmedy and Sankt-Vith, Belgium reaches new heights, literally. The Signal de Botrange, in the present-day village of Waimes, sits at 694 m above sea level. In 1923 an artificial hill is created in honour of High Commissioner Herman Baltia, taking the level up to a symbolic 700 m. (Albert Gehlen collection, Breitfeld)

A curious formulation

In reality, the strange wording of Article 34 of the Treaty, which enabled the population to submit their refusal to change nationality in writing, shows that historic arguments were ignored in the case of the British and American members of the Commission for Belgian Affairs at Versailles, chaired by French national André Tardieu. They also wanted to give the impression that the right to self-determination was being respected. Although the two States concerned were not represented there, the Committee saw as decisive arguments that were strategic – the role of the military camp at Elsenborn, created by Prussia in 1890, was considered vital – and economic. This also explains why the whole German *Kreis* of Malmedy was annexed and not only the Walloon districts. The economic reasons put forward by the Commission partly consisted of the fact that the territory of Moresnet-Neutre, which at that time was known for its mines and had been jointly managed by Belgium and Prussia before 1914, had been annexed to Belgium with no further formalities via Articles 32 and 33 of the Treaty.

Although the Treaty of Versailles had been signed on the 28th of June 1919 and Belgian troops had replaced the French and British occupying troops in the frontier region in the summer of 1919, the Government and Parliament were preparing a Law, which introduced a transitional regime for the regions to be annexed. Taking as a blueprint the Decree of the French Republic creating a High Commission for Alsace-Lorraine, this Law of the 15th of September 1919 granted a High Commissioner executive and legislative power, without restricting the period for transition: "Make sure that everything runs smoothly and the costs remain reasonable. You will be like the governor of a colony, which is in direct contact with the fatherland."[28] The mission given by Prime Minister Léon Delacroix to Lieutenant General Herman Baltia, who became High Commissioner on the 10th of January 1920, was suffused with pragmatism, but also showed a certain nonchalance in preparing the transitional regime that the "New Belgians" were to experience from then on.

A public consultation

The first task of the High Commissioner was to organise a public consultation as provided for in Article 34. This was to take place between January and July 1920. There can be no doubt that its result, only 272 refusals out of 33,726 potential votes, did not reflect the feelings of the population at that time. Today, nobody disputes that restrictive measures and threats to the populace, both real and perceived, such as the seizure of ration cards and even expulsion from the territory, contributed to this result. While it is true that Belgium has been accused of being both judge and jury (some Socialists were to talk of "parody" during the 1919 negotiations[29]) and there was a propaganda war between the two camps, the end result exactly matched the expectations of the Versailles negotiators: they knew that a free and secret plebiscite would not have resulted in a majority for Belgium, but they were aware that territorial compensation for "poor little Belgium" was absolutely inevitable. The consequences were disastrous; the way in which the so-called referendum was organised was to weigh heavily on the process of integration of the "New Belgians", the failure of which would become obvious in 1940.

BELGIAN-GERMAN BORDER
ca. 1920

- - - Border Belgium – Germany before 1920
- - - Border Belgium – Germany after 1920
- - - Germanic-Romanic language and dialect border

NETHERLANDS

Aachen

NEUTRAL MORESNET

Lontzen

Raeren

Gueule

KREIS

Eupen

Vesdre

EUPEN

GERMANY

Monschau

Schleiden

Rur

Verviers

BELGIUM

Spa

KREIS

Elsenborn

Malmedy

Warche

Bütgenbach

Waimes

Büllingen

Stavelot

Amel

Amblève

Kyll

MALMEDY

Vielsalm

St. Vith

Our

Beho

Prüm

Reuland

GRAND DUCHY OF LUXEMBOURG

When the League of Nations endorsed the result of the plebiscite on the 20th of September 1920, the Provisional Government had already commenced the transitional process, which extended to every area of the public and private lives of the "New Belgians". The introduction of Belgian Law was to include special measures, the last of which were only to expire in 1927, after the end of the Baltia Government. Unsurprisingly, the linguistic question, with regard to both the administration and education, was a major issue. Unlike French policy in Alsace-Lorraine, the government did not impose French everywhere; instead, it introduced a bilingual system, which provided in particular for German-language elementary education in German-speaking communities. This also concerned the army, where efforts were made to find officers who could understand German to command the regional recruits doing military service from 1924 onward, even before the 1928 vote on the use of languages in the army. On the other hand, at least during the first three years of its existence, the Baltia Government showed a tendency to want to control everything, in particular public speaking. So the press was subject to close scrutiny verging on censorship. In addition, Baltia maintained somewhat troubled relationships with one of the most important groups in the region – the Catholic clergy. Religion was, in fact, one of the most important challenges of the transition phase. Ecclesiastical rivalries between Belgians and Germans were so great that a specific bishopric was set up between 1921 and 1925, headed by the Bishop of Liège under the regime of personal union. In 1925, the territory was finally attached to the see of Liège.

A disillusionment

In 1923, against the advice of the High Commissioner, who advised assimilation over the long term, the Parliament attempted to put an end to the Provisional Government. The law on integration was finally passed in March 1925 and attached the region to the administrative and electoral district of Verviers and to the Province of Liège. A few weeks later, the "New Belgians" took part in their first parliamentary elections. This first use of the supreme law under a parliamentary system led to disillusionment. Although 66.4% of the votes in the Cantons of Eupen, Malmedy, and Saint-Vith went to the Catholic Party, its German-speaking candidate was not elected, as the "New Belgians" only made up one quarter of the electorate in the district of Verviers, which was dominated by the *Parti Ouvrier Belge* – the Belgian Workers' Party. The latter had, furthermore, successfully brought young Brussels lawyer Marc Somerhausen (1899–1992) into Verviers. Catholic circles refused to allow him to speak on behalf of the "New Belgians", although he wanted to make a major claim – the organisation of a free referendum in the three Cantons.

The *Eupen-Malmedy malaise* worsened when, in 1927, the provincial authorities and the Minister of the Interior refused to appoint Léon Trouet, a former member of the Baltia administration, as mayor of Eupen. He was reproached for his membership of the *Heimatbund*, which was then still an association in the form of a pool of people who wanted better treatment of the population by the Belgian authorities, from those demanding a return to Germany to those who wanted the organisation of a real plebiscite.

As a reaction to the activities of the *Heimatbund*, in 1927, the Catholic political circles who considered that the region was Belgian and should stay that way founded the journal *Grenz-Echo*, which quickly became the voice of the so-called "pro-Belgians". In reality, political life was then forced into a change which, in 1929, was to lead to strong polarisation; in reaction to the Catholic party, the *Christliche Volkspartei* then brought together the revisionists – those supporting a return to Germany and the defenders of a free referendum. It should, however, be noted that, even though polarisation could tear apart whole families, social life did not boil down to mere political conflict.

The policy of integration followed by the Belgian authorities was greatly criticised by contemporaries, in particular in Parliament and in the press; this came even before the Nazis rose to power in Germany and the *Volkstumskampf* was intensified in the region. Finally, it was to be the experience of the 1940–1944 annexation and the end of the Second World War which would confirm the belonging to Belgium, as the German alternative had disappeared.

NEW POLITICAL MOVEMENTS AFTER 1918

Marc Reynebeau

At the outbreak of the First World War, Belgium was far from being a fully fledged democracy. Universal plural suffrage, dating from 1893, gave the wealthy a dispro-portionately heavy electoral weight and further strengthened the absolute major-ity of the Catholic party. New, critical or dissident voices did not get a very sympathetic hearing. But when liberation came in 1918 the principle of universal (single) suffrage was "virtually won".[30] Indeed, it quickly followed, although admittedly only for men. It was al-ready in place for the legislative elections on the 16th of November 1919, even before the constitution had been reformed to take account of it; reform did not follow until 1920–21.

Universal suffrage was an old demand of the social democratic Belgian Workers' Party (POB-BWP). From 1916 they also supplied ministers in governments of nation-al unity with Catholics and Liberals for the first time. As the biggest opposition party, they saw in the broadening of suffrage the condition for social and political democra-tisation. But even in 1918 the country was still far from having a political culture of parliamentary democracy. If all men were to win the right to vote from their 21st birth-day, then that would not only be due to a spirit of patriotic unity and national grati-tude to the soldiers and civilians who helped the country through the war. The bour-geois system tried to keep the widening of political authority under control by channelling it along parliamentary and party-political lines. The broadening of suf-frage, for example, led to a quantitative rather than a qualitative and substantive democratisation of the country's administration.[31]

Alternatives presented themselves, and universal suffrage remained the lesser evil. The Russian Revolution in 1917, in particular, concerned the Belgian powers that be. Immedi-ately, they noticed that it had attracted the attention of the soldiers on the Yser Front.[32] In

A *Frontpartij* member posts election bills in Antwerp. The first post-war elections take place on 16 November 1919 and introduce general uninominal male suffrage. A few new parties, constituted during the war, participate in these elections, e.g., the *Frontpartij* and the Belgian nationalistic *Ligue de la Renaissance nationale.* (Letterenhuis, Antwerp, F 4809)

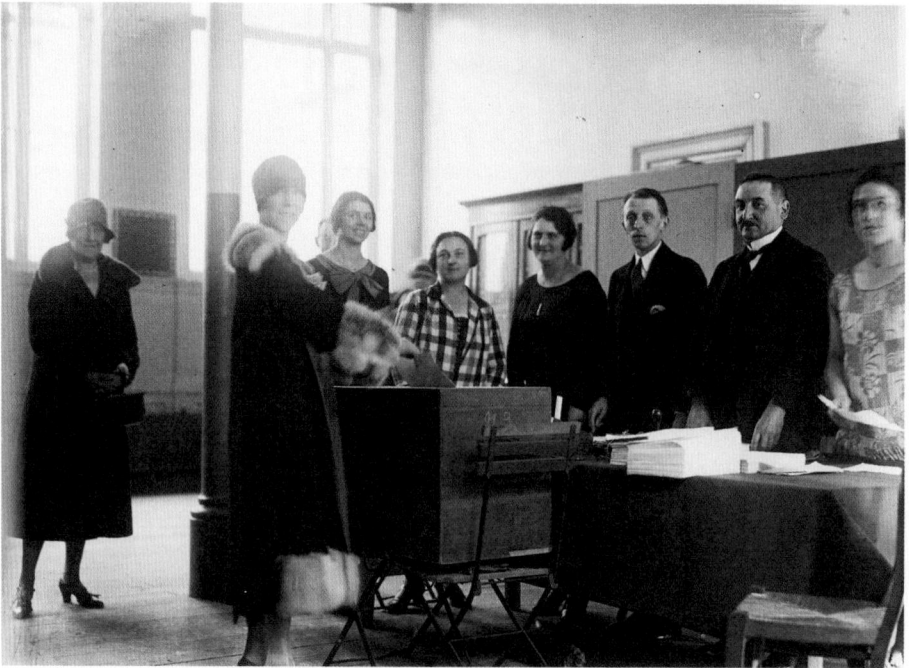

For the local elections of 1926 Queen Elisabeth casts her vote in Brussels. The introduction of general single-vote suffrage for the parliamentary elections of 1919 only concerns men and war widows. Women only obtain parliamentary vote after the Second World War. (Germaineimage, 23299971-01)

1920 Henri Carton de Wiart, who would later become Prime Minister, feared that a Belgian remake of the October Revolution was far from inconceivable.[33] Criminalisation followed in 1923, when fifteen communists were accused of conspiracy against the security of the state.[34] The Court of Assizes acquitted them, but it was just the beginning of a repressive fear of communists that intensified throughout the interwar period.[35] Fear of a change of regime meant that other enemies of the civil state, the Flemish-nationalist activists who fled to Germany in 1918, were suspected of possibly dreamed-of but otherwise unrealistic terrorist and revolutionary plots.[36]

One such activist who fled to Berlin in 1918 was the Antwerp poet Paul van Ostaijen. After a few political detours he openly chose communism at the beginning of 1921 and – because of what he called *de algemeen-stemrechtillusie* (the illusion of universal suffrage) – anti-parliamentarism.[37] By then Belgian already had its first elections with that universal male suffrage under its belt. And they had disappointed radicalised impatient young men like Van Ostaijen: fundamentally, the elections changed little, bringing neither the Flemish nor the proletarian numerical majority to power. There was little room for new political ideas and movements.

From old language demands to anti-Belgian sentiment

Although the elections may have been seen as "an earthquake",[38] it was only in the classical parliamentary context. The big winner was the BWP, which although "new" to government was already a member of the outgoing *Union Sacrée*, which received 81 percent of the vote. Nine parliamentary seats went to new parties, with five for the *Vlaamsche Front* (Flemish Front), which gave the legacy of the Flemish Nationalists' *Frontbeweging* (Front Movement) from the trenches a political dimension. Right-wing radical Belgian nationalism, which was at that time annexationist, won a seat. From that movement, which was initially closely connected with the mainly Brussels French-speaking bourgeoisie, Pierre Nothomb, who would later become a Catholic member of parliament, was the public figurehead throughout the interwar period.

That was the panorama of political renewal after 1918. On the bourgeois right wing, and particularly among the heirs of 19th-century religious fundamentalism (ultramontanism), a radical core developed, who made an anti-democratic and reactionary choice based on a Belgian nationalism, following examples like Charles Maurras' *Action Française* and Benito Mussolini's fascism. A burgeoning Flemish nationalism reformulated the old language demands into a pronounced anti-Belgian sentiment that acquired increasingly authoritarian traits through Catholic integralism and which, in 1933, gave way to the fascism of the *Vlaams Nationaal Verbond* (VNV). And while the traditional reformist social democracy integrated itself into the system, it made compromises that radicalised some of its left flank, chiefly young men and trade unionists. Out of that, in 1921, came the communist party (KPB), emerging as a Belgian division of the Communist International which was being managed increasingly tightly from Moscow.

However, new societal ideas were not just brewing within political parties. In intellectual and artistic circles there was a lot of enthusiasm for the internationalism, pacifism and humanism of the French *Clarté* movement, the "International of the Spirit", which sympathised politically with communism.[39] In French-speaking Belgium, *Clarté* inspired literary circles in the main. In Flanders, the movement attracted activist youths who after the war were creating a subculture for all kinds of progressive political and social experiments. Common to all, especially, was anti-bourgeois non-conformism; their Flemish nationalism also fitted in with this, even though their ideals did not always transcend a noncommittal conviviality. At that point, the political watershed between left and right had not yet occurred; in their spirit of opposition, the mostly young Clarté-ists mainly had radicalism in common. It was not until the thirties, and certainly during the Second World War, that the ideological rift opened up, as former activists collaborated with the Nazi occupier, among them Paul Colin, who was an example of "the ambivalences of a certain literary modernity and a pacifying humanitarianism disconnected from social and political reality."[40]

The Delacroix government is constituted on 21 November 1918, one day before the Joyous Entry in Brussels. It is a national union government, with representatives of the three major parties: six Catholics, three Socialists and three Liberals. Léon Delacroix, a political novice, becomes Prime Minister (a newly created function) and also is in charge of finances. After the November 1919 elections this government is succeeded by a similar one, again led by Léon Delacroix. (AMSAB-ISG, FO.0011400)

Armed defence corps

Many of these new parties and movements held a common skepticism about parliamentarianism, and if they did take part in elections it was primarily for propaganda reasons. Even the KPB placed its emphasis not on the political battle but on the social. It gained a strength that transcended the significance of its number of votes or members, through its militant engagement in social unionism.[41] Liberal democracy needed to consolidate and prove itself, and from the outset there were doubts about it. In small extreme-right groups, certainly in French-speaking Belgium and in veterans' associations, nationalism sufficed as social glue, making further political representation redundant. The latter also applied to a major current within Flemish nationalism, a current that culminated in the VNV. In its earliest political expression in the Front Party, however, it initially proved more subtle. From the late twenties, a small section evolved into social democracy or communism; a segment at the other ideological extreme ended up in an anti-democratic corporatism that found parliamentary representation superfluous in principle. In 1926 Joris Van Severen and Cyriel Verschaeve even argued in favour of a politics with "legions based on military force", and "armed defence corps."[42]

A year later, this also appeared to be an option in a Flemish nationalistic myth that looked back at the First World War and regretted that nothing had come of the dream in which 25,000 Flemish soldiers would desert the army to legitimise activist collaboration in occupied Belgium, as an armed unit.[43]

Yet the criticism of parliamentarianism in the interwar period did not have to be a priori anti-democratic. It found its place just as effectively in the limitations of parliament as an instrument of representative democracy and in its persistently bourgeois nature. And also in its vulnerability, as was evident in 1926 when bankers exercised their financial might to bring down the Poullet-Vandervelde government, which was deemed too progressive, or in the shock of the economic crisis of the thirties. Many new political ideas that emerged in organisations, parties or documents after 1918 were not consolidated until after the Second World War, after the experience with totalitarian Nazism and in the new context of the Cold War.

Site de Guerre — Ingang / Entrance 2?
Oorlogsoord
War Site
Gd REDAN ·:(=):· Gt REDAN
Gte PÜLSCHANS

au profit des ↟ ten voordeele der ↟ to the benefit of the
Invalides de Guerre Oorlogsverminkten disabled Soldiers

6

THE REMEMBRANCE OF WAR

"THIS IS HOLY GROUND." WAR TOURISM IN BELGIUM

Wannes Devos and Piet Veldeman

"Louvain and Liège are names never to be forgotten in history. For centuries they have been lightly traced in its pages, but now by reason of the great war they are imperishably engraved. An automobile journey from Brussels to these two places affords an opportunity for observing three phases of German destruction in Belgium – the purely military, as illustrated in the ruins of Fort Loncin; the barbarous, as typified in the sacking and burning of Louvain and the killing of its citizens; and the criminal, as evidenced in the district of Liège which was maimed industrially, crippled financially, left truly an inanimate *mutilé*."[1] Just one year after the armistice the travel guidebook *Louvain – Liége [sic]* invites English-speaking tourists to come and explore Louvain and Liège, where the traces left by the German army are still clearly visible. Such touristic promotion of war history is common practice in post-war

As early as 1918 the Ministry of War decides to list a number of war sites along the Yser front and to publish travel guides. The *Great Redan* in Nieuwpoort becomes one of these 25 listed venues. The former Belgian position, popular with British tourists, is restored with new supporting beams, steel plates and concrete bags. However, as the public gradually loses interest, the venues decline. When the harbour access channel is dredged after the Second World War, the *Great Redan* is plugged with sludge.
(Nationaal Archief, Collectie Spaarnestad, Den Haag, Het Leven, SFA022803164)

As soon as hostilities cease war, tourism starts up. Former battlefields and military positions
draw lots of visitors. The easily accessible German coastal batteries are also very popular.
On 19 October 1918 two Belgian women, one of whom is holding a German helmet, seated on the barrel
of a German gun at the Eylau Battery in Ostend, triumphantly pose for a British officer.
(Imperial War Museum, London, Q11380, Thomas Keith Aitkin)

Belgium. On the increase since the middle of the 19th century because of improved
means of transportation, higher incomes and extended leisure time, mass tourism after
1918 easily finds its way to the former war sites.

As the introductory quote clearly indicates, tourism not only revolves around the
West Flanders frontline region or iconic cities such as Ypres and Dixmude but also aims
at other former war zones in Belgium. Both the forts in Liège, Namur or Antwerp, and
the martyr cities such as Aarschot, Andenne, Dendermonde, Dinant, Louvain, Tamines
or Visé are included in post-war tourist programmes, with varying success. Execution
grounds, both in Brussels and in the capital towns of the provinces, as well as pillaged
industrial sites, can all potentially become tourist hotspots.

Some of these places already have a definite appeal during the war, but German occupation then bars the public from visiting them. Nevertheless, a travel guidebook listing six walking tours passing through local points of war interest in the Vilvoorde area
is published in the fall of 1914, before the Germans restrict mobility. Ruined villages,
schools, train stations, castles, windmills and even greenhouses are presented, alongside
several abandoned Belgian and German trenches, and countless shallow graves.[2] The

European tourist sector also flourishes. Starting in spring 1915, London-based travel agencies organise trips to battlefields in France, although market leader Thomas Cook remains quite sceptical. "When the war is over, it will be different," the company says.[3] In France, tire producer Michelin adds a new series to its catalogue during the war: *Les Guides illustrés Michelin des Champs de Bataille*. It is no coincidence that the covers sport the *bleu horizon* colour, the characteristic shade of the French military uniforms. The first part is published in September 1917 and over the next few years some thirty titles are added. By the time of the armistice, expectations are quite high: the French *Touring Club* anticipates 1.5 million tourists over the first year. Its Belgian sister organisation is also prepared for a tourist tidal wave.

Difficult beginnings

Belgium, however, has to wait for its massive influx of war tourists. The country is devastated, and railway lines, especially in West Flanders, are very badly damaged. Roads all over the country are also in need of repair. Groups such as the *Touring Club de Belgique* insist on clear road signs and for years on end pressure local authorities into removing the German-language signs on their territories: *"A bas les inscriptions boches!"*[4] Moreover, abandoned ammunition makes moving about quite dangerous, and local facilities are rudimentary and limited. The pre-war tourist infrastructure along the coastline has been damaged by the war as well. Elsewhere, few war sites have a touristic tradition: even the mediaeval town of Ypres, with its numerous historic monuments, only counts one hotel when the war breaks out. Petrol and food are both expensive and hard to come by. Some regions even lack drinking water.

Some lone travellers brave these hazards and difficulties. These early-bird war tourists often travel on their own, usually by car, bicycle or motorcycle and essentially set course to the area around Ypres and Dixmude. Once on site, the curious adventurer is amazed by the abandoned and scarred landscape, littered with military material. The idea that battles of life and death were fought here not so long ago impresses, just as does the image of the first mourning families looking for the last resting places of their loved ones.

Holy ground vs. entertainment

Every visit to a war site is indeed not to be considered a tourist trip. The motivations for visiting such locations vary widely and in some instances lead to heated conflicts. Widows, orphans, family members and friends look for the places where their loved ones fought, died or are buried. They are first and foremost prompted by grief and try to

A Belgian sentinel guards the ruins at Ypres. The panel warns souvenir hunters. As Ypres is seen as holy ground, some feel the ruins are to remain untouched.
(Imperial War Museum, London, Q100485, Ivan L. Bawtree)

obtain closure. This group is closely followed by a second category of travellers: the war veterans come to honour their fallen brothers-in-arms and to revisit the locations in which they fought. The journeys these two groups undertake are not mere tourist trips but rather true pilgrimages. These pilgrims act out of religion and make a ceremonial voyage to holy ground commemorating the dead. A third group of travellers is concerned with educational matters: during school field trips children learn about the war and its devastating consequences for the concerned regions.[5]

Notice.
This is Holy Ground.
Tone of this fabric may be taken away.
A heritage for all civilised peoples.
By order.
Town Major Ypres

These motivations often are in stark contrast with those of regular tourists. The latter visit illustrious places stimulating imagination out of sheer curiosity, as they heard of them in war-time stories, papers, or even movies. Their fascination with war has nothing in common with the respect pilgrims ask for their dead friends or relatives.[6] Pilgrims see the possible conversion of former war sites into tourist attractions as nothing less than sacrilege. In these circles voices are heard in favour of fencing off the Ypres Cloth Hall with barbed wire or, even better, of barricading the city in order to drive back all tourists. In popular French culture this sometimes is the task of the *Diable bleu*, the ghost of the fallen French soldier arising from the grave to chase away tourists showing a lack of respect for the former battlefields.[7] In spite of the enormous differences between the tourist and the pilgrim, there are some resemblances too. They stay at the same hotels, buy the same kitsch souvenirs and have their pictures taken amidst the same ruins…

At cruising speed

Starting in spring 1919 the area around Ypres and Dixmude is swamped with national and international tourists. Touristic facilities have improved: by 1920 some 14 hotels have opened their doors in Ypres alone. Public transportation has also been restored. Starting in September 1919 a tram again connects Ostend to Nieuport, while the national railway system introduces cheap tickets enabling travellers to reach the former front zone by train. The restored tram and train services also bring in more foreign tourists. Ostend is a hub for British pilgrims and tourists arriving in the city not only by boat, but also increasingly by plane. Organisations such as the Salvation Army, the YMCA and in particular the Saint Barnabas Society put together pilgrimages leaving from Britain. Tourists travelling on an individual basis can book arrangements with a travel agent. Belgium is not only visited by the British; the French also cross the border. The first American travellers arrive in October 1919. Very understandably, German tourists still stay away.

However, not all tourist roads automatically lead to the Westhoek. On an imposing bill designed by the Belgian railways in 1919, a soldier on an abandoned German gun invites a tourist to tour the Yser front sites, but trips to Dinant, Louvain or Liège are also advertised. School field trips are not limited to Ypres, Nieuport or its surroundings either. Although perhaps for financial or logistic reasons, martyr cities in the immediate vicinity are often visited as well. The *Touring Club de Belgique*, who organises group trips to the Yser front by bus or train, also invariably includes other national war locations in its programmes. In 1920 and 1921 visits to both martyr cities and the forts at Loncin (Fortified Position Liège) or Marchovelette (Fortified Position Namur) are suggested. With Walem and Sint-Katelijne-Waver, two Antwerp forts are also included. In 1922 the battlefield at Halen and the martyr city of Aarschot are still visited, but later group trips are scheduled according to inaugurations of war monuments. This trend is also established at the Yser front.

This duality between the frontline and the rest of the country is also noticeable in the countless tourist brochures appearing in the years following the armistice. The *Louvain-Liége [sic]* guidebook published in English in 1919 mentioned above exclusively lists venues away from the frontline. That same year the (extremely anti-German) *Guides illustrés Michelin des Champs de Bataille* dedicate a guide to Brussels and Louvain, leading the tourist from the execution grounds at the *Tir national* to the Louvain

Les défenseurs du Fort de Loncin. Not only tourists visit former battlefields and war sites. Veterans also tour the locations they were deployed in. Survivors showing their pennant pose in the rubble of Fort Loncin that exploded on 15 August 1914. Major Victor Naessens, the fort's commander in 1914, is among them.
(War Heritage Institute, Brussels, 201870825)

ruins. A blue Michelin guide is also made for Antwerp in 1921, but the book focuses on the city's history and sightseeing highlights, rather than on the 1914 events. The city's fortification system is not even mentioned. However, two other 1920 Michelin guides exclusively discuss trench warfare. Between 1919 and 1920 the *Touring Club de Belgique* publishes travel guides entitled *Ce qu'il faut voir sur les champs de bataille et dans les villes détruites de Belgique*. A first part combines the military operations of August through October 1914 and the German atrocities committed in that same timeframe, and the second part concentrates on *Le front de Flandre*. Travel guides emanating from other organisations usually put the Westhoek centre stage. The Belgian railways publish *On the Field of Honour: The Belgian Front on the Yser* and in 1922 a Ministry of Defence brochure lists 25 official Yser front venues. Personal initiatives almost exclusively focus on the West Flanders battlefields as well.

Trivialisation of war

Belgian war tourism reaches unknown heights in the first few post-war years because of increased mobility, international interest, renewed accommodation and special travel guides. However, one of the biggest challenges the sector quickly has to face is the disappearance of the conflict's physical evidence. As early as August 1920 the *Touring Club de Belgique* members' magazine issues a warning: "The front is dying."[8] The scars of war moreover fade all over the country. With reconstruction as a main concern, war equipment is scrapped, ruins are removed, battlefields are turned into arable land or woodland areas, houses are rebuilt. Ironically, this reconstruction is partly financed by the tourist sector. Moreover, as forts, coastal fortifications and harbours are recycled by the military, many of these venues lose their public function. The disappearance of immovable military heritage is epitomized in the fact that even the 25 venues officially selected by the Ministry of Defence in its April 1922 listing are not spared: a few years later only a couple of them remain. Both high maintenance costs and diminishing public interest play a part in this evolution.

As time goes by, the tourist's fascination for war indeed wanes. The plummeting number of travel guides or school field trips are there to prove it: from 1925 onwards a visit to a war site seems to become accessory. However, war tourism does not grind to a complete standstill, certainly not in the former frontline area. Belgian pilgrims feel a lesser need for visiting the former battlefields, as many soldiers initially buried in military necropolises have been exhumed and now have their final resting places in local cemeteries. People can also come to terms with their losses at local war monuments or at the grave of the Unknown Soldier in Brussels. This dwindling number of visitors does not concern British venues, however. In spite of a small decrease between 1923 and 1926 British, Australian, Canadian and New Zealand travellers still massively visit the Belgian front area. As its fallen soldiers are not repatriated the British government continues to support pilgrimages to Ypres (and the Menin Gate). By the end of the 1920s a new international visitor appears in Belgium: the German pilgrim and tourist. The *Volksbund Deutsche Kriegsgräberfürsorge* is the main organiser of trips to the former Belgian front zone.

On all remaining war sites the "real" and brutal war has meanwhile been replaced by a sterile, embellished and artificial version of the conflict, a version more suited to the war tourist. The Trench of Death in Dixmude characterizes this: in 1923 and 1924 the authentic sandbags are replaced by hardwearing concrete replicas. As American historian George Mosse puts it, a process of trivialisation has affected the conflict, "cutting the war down to size so that it would become commonplace instead of awesome and frightening."[9] For those who have not witnessed it, the war becomes familiar, easily recognisable, comprehensible and manageable. As the devastated landscape is restructured (with newly created cemeteries and easily identifiable monuments), as daily activities once again follow their course (with tourists and farmers replacing the pilgrims) and as popular remembrance culture grows (with literature, art, theatre, cinema, postcards, pictures, toys, exhibitions, etc.) the image of war becomes far more acceptable. This evolution shocks veterans when they visit their former battlefields: "Our war, the war that seemed the special possession of those of us who are growing middle-aged, is being turned by time and change into something fabulous, misunderstood and made romantic by distance."[10]

WAR MEMORIALS
TO THE BELGIANS
OF THE GREAT WAR

Laurence van Ypersele

The scale of the commemorative movement that gripped Belgium like the rest of Europe bore witness to the urgency felt by the people to safeguard the memory of this event. Communities acted fast, usually without government assistance; most of these monuments were inaugurated between 1920 and 1924. Belgium experienced another, final spurt in 1930, the year of the centenary of Belgian independence. Their urgency, in fact, was a matter of making something of this war, so that none of the deaths had been meaningless, and of forging an identity and a future.

For war memorials are not testimonies to the reality of war, but are rather representations of it which contemporaries have made – or attempted to make – after the event. In fact, analysis of the memorials shows that contemporaries constructed a coherent, but largely fictional, image of the war. It has to be said that the important thing was not to produce an accurate record of the horror and suffering, but to honour the dead and ensure they were not forgotten. Hence the need to choose prominent locations for this memory carved in stone, places where social activities were most frequent, symbolic sites. So stelae, monuments, and obelisks were erected in public places, near churches and town halls.

As soon as the German troops leave Brussels, temporary stucco monuments are erected.
These are often based on scale-models and drawings already created during the war.
The monuments are displayed in key locations for the royal couple's Joyous Entry on 22 November.
(War Heritage Institute, Brussels, PK 14)

On 10 November 1922 the blind veteran Renold Haesebrouck designates the Unknown Soldier amongst five coffins. Shortly afterwards, the Unknown Soldier is buried in Brussels. Haesebrouck stays on in Bruges to attend the funeral of the four other nameless soldiers. A small ceremony is held at the military cemetery. (Stadsarchief Brugge)

Blunders by the Belgian government

In order to cope with the grief and suffering, the loss of life and the task of rebuilding, it was necessary to maintain a sense of the war as it had been experienced or conceived of during the conflict. Heroes had fallen in the field of honour in the name of their country, but they would stay alive in people's memories; they had fought barbarism in the name of civilisation, but the hated enemy would pay for all the evil done. So the dead deserved to be remembered for ever, while reparation should be made for their sacrifice. Now, this desire for remembrance was not only orchestrated by the holders of the official memory, but shared by all the populations involved. In Belgium, it was actually the veterans, the associations of prisoners of war and deportees, and the ordinary civilians who dictated the course to be taken by the national authorities. For in fact the Belgian government had trouble enforcing its decisions. It even had to abandon them, as it was so keen in this immediate post-war period to preserve the memory of the war experienced by the people.

In fact, the Belgian State did not want to encourage the wave of memorial building. After a debate in Parliament in June 1919, the government decided that only monuments of an artistic nature could receive State subsidies, and that these subsidies would cover no more than one third of the total cost. On the other hand, the idea of a great national memorial for the soldiers and civilians who had died for their country was adopted by Parliament on the 14th of July 1919. However, this became bogged down in discussions for more than two years; various sites were proposed, but neither they, nor the identities of the artists, were unanimously agreed on. Finally, the Belgian government followed the practices inaugurated in 1920 by Great Britain and France; under pressure from veterans, supported by public opinion, on the 11th of November 1922, the State Funeral was held of the Unknown Soldier, who was buried at the foot of the Congress Column in Brussels. On the eve of the event, the bodies of five unidentified soldiers from the strongholds of Liège, Namur, and Antwerp, the Yser front, and the zone taken back in the autumn of 1918, had been laid in state at Bruges Station, where the body of the Unknown Soldier was to be chosen by a blind soldier, assisted by the National Defence Minister. In 1924, at the request of the *Anciens Combattants* veterans, a sacred flame was lit at the tomb, and is still burning there to this day. From that moment on, the project for a great national monument affirming the Belgian identity born of the war through the figures of heroes and martyrs, soldiers and civilians, became obsolete. It was never to come to fruition.

The triumph of local memorials

Meanwhile, the great majority of local authorities erected their memorials without State assistance, via local subscriptions. With the exception of Liège, where the provincial identity was stronger, the provincial authorities did not contribute either. In other words, in Belgium, local freedom triumphed and the expression of local identities was not obstructed.

The memory of the war as seen from these innumerable monuments is rather strange. First of all, it should be noted that, while memorials in France were generally erected to those described as having died "for France", in Belgium the phrase used was, almost exclusively, *"pour la Patrie"* – "for the Nation." This Belgian *Patrie* which rose triumphant from the armistice included civilians as well as soldiers, unlike the other countries in the war. In fact, although the ultimate symbol of national heroism continued to be the Belgian soldier, this does not occupy all the space on the memorials. Alongside can be seen the figure of the civilian massacred in August 1914, the patriot who was shot, or the deportee. Depending on local experience, a civilian figure may well take priority over the soldier. At Tamines, for example, the martyrs of August 1914 take pride of place; on the Place Saint-Martin, a gigantic monument inaugurated in 1926 represents the bodies of civilians, fallen but intact, at the foot of a grieving *Patrie*, raising her arms to the heavens. In Hainaut or Eastern Flanders, on the other hand, the deportees stand out remarkably. They are usually represented as martyrs with heads bowed or emaciated bodies. So there is not, as the case of Northern France,[11] a refusal to remember the occupied populations. Only the exiles are excluded from Belgian memory.

However this may be, throughout Belgium, the memory of the heroes and martyrs enhances the greatness of the country they died for (pacifist monuments are, in fact, extremely rare and of later date). The glorification of combatants, in the same way as civilians, gives a meaning to their deaths – the sacrifice freely made for the mother country and its future, in other words for the survivors who owe them their gratitude. And this new *Patrie*, as impassive as eternity, is in turn glorified by her children, who died as heroes. Initially, the Belgian *Patrie* had a variety of faces – the national identity was rooted in local or provincial identities. So national symbols which are a female allegory of the *Patrie* are widespread, with the Belgian lion, sometimes overcoming the German eagle, or the sovereigns representing the Belgium kingdom sitting happily side by side with local saints, town coats of arms, the *perron* symbol of Liège, or sometimes the AVV-VVK in Flanders.

In this immediate post-war period, the Belgian identity looked rather like a Russian matryoshka doll, but the different levels fitted together differently depending on location. The importance of provincial identity was particularly strong in Liège, and also in Luxembourg. Hainaut, however, combined national identity with local identity, without exalting the province. Similarly, in the North of the country, the symbolism on the monuments did not differentiate between Flemish and national identities. In addition, the medieval inspiration so dear to Flemish iconography is hardly to be seen on the war memorials. In addition, the AVV-VVK symbol is not solely nationalist, but also – and perhaps particularly in this period of mourning – a religious symbol.[12] Throughout Belgium, the religious symbols greatly in evidence on the memorials also express the need for consolation and the hope for eternal life. But while in Wallonia these symbols are purely religious, in Flanders they are more ambiguous and open to increasingly divergent interpretations.

All these deaths, so difficult to justify and accept in themselves, could not be represented in all their horror. So, as everywhere in Europe, many monuments represent the soldier as defender or conqueror, while on others, the death throes of the soldier or even the deportee are evoked in a tranquil, gentle climate. Only the victims of the August 1914 massacres provoke a pain that cries out for vengeance. But none of these dead or injured are disfigured, dirty, or ugly. They don't groan, they don't cry, they don't rebel. The soldier dies without fear or suffering, in an impeccable uniform – as on the Châtelet monument, inaugurated in 1921. And the patriot shot by the occupy-

Hundreds of monuments are erected in memory of civilian and military casualties. Next to the innumerable official war monuments, there are monuments created by the initiative of local organisations and societies. On 1 July 1928 Princess Marie-José unveils a monument in memory of Yvonne Vieslet in Marchienne-au-Pont. Yvonne, aged 10, was shot by a German soldier in October 1918 when she gave food to a French prisoner of war.
(Germaineimage, 23300001-003)

ing force advances proudly, bare-chested or carrying the flag, towards an invisible firing squad – as on the Brussels monument to Gabrielle Petit, inaugurated 1923. The heroes of the past never die alone. They always have someone nearby to catch their last breath – brothers in arms, a patriotic allegory, or a divine apparition. And often a woman or a child sculpted at the foot of the moment will bear witness for all eternity to their gratitude and their sorrow.

The war took away the loved ones of many families, and the memorials engraved in stone and bronze turned them into heroes. In fact, these monuments are trying to make the immense disaster of 1914 to 1918 into a "Great War".

The memorial settings from the Great War lasted through the 20th century,[13] so, at the end of the Second World War, the Belgians instinctively had recourse to the imaginary conflict depicted after the First World War. The war dead and victims had to be honoured as heroes (the resistant fighters) and martyrs (the others). Even though the Second War was not a new version of 1914–1918, the *Patrie* was, once again, the standard for attempting to glorify the dead. Needless to say, the details of the Nazi occupation and the genocide of the Jews do not appear. That would only come 20 years later.

THE REMEMBRANCE OF WAR

In short, the names of the 1940–1945 victims were engraved on the First World War memorials. And the eleventh of November and the Unknown Soldier were used to equate the heroes of the Second World War with those of the First. And, while the memory of the Second World War did not take long to supplant the memory and meaning of the First, it is transparently clear to everyone that 1914–1918 was not "the War to end all Wars"...

A Belgian war monument awaits a buyer, around 1921. In order to meet the large demand for war monuments in the first half of the 1920s, some workshops publish catalogues with available creations, ready for order.
(War Heritage Institute, Brussels, B.1.114.43-28497)

SOUVENIRS DE
S.M. LE ROI | GEDENKENISSEN VAN
Z.M. DEN KONING
~ ALBERT ~

PATRIOTISM BEHIND GLASS. THE REBIRTH OF THE ROYAL MILITARY MUSEUM

Wannes Devos

"When the day of the opening of our Museum in the hall of the Cinquantenaire approaches and the public will be invited to view the collections, some may laugh in secret, especially if they have had the chance to view the mementoes of this war in Paris or London ... where all good intentions of these countries concerning patriotic ideas compete with each other to enrich the Military Museums to their fullest, which are, to these countries, monuments of national glory."[14] On 19 September 1919 an irate Théophile Théodore Baron Jamblinne de Meux addressed his grievances in a letter to the Chairman of the *Commission Centrale de la Récuperation*. Almost a year after the end of the First World War, it was clear to Jamblinne de Meux, who in 1919 had been appointed General Manager of the Royal Military Museum in Brussels by Minister of War, Fulgence Masson, that his museum was being systematically disadvantaged in obtaining (German) ordnance that had been left behind. The committee set up by the Ministry of War in December 1918, which was supposed to be responsible for the recovery of any such spoils of war on Belgian territory, would therefore have to pay the price.

The side-swipe by the retired major general was chiefly the result of the curatorial battle for tangible reminders of the war, a battle which flared up after the armistice. Up-and-coming tourism to the Western Front in Belgium led to the establishment of all manner of war museums along the Yser Front, the Ypres Salient and the coastal strip.

The royal family has pride of place in the Royal Military Museum, with fervent patriotism and royalism going hand in hand. King Albert's uniforms, for instance, are displayed in a true shroud in 1934.
(War Heritage Institute, Brussels, PK 7)

Civic museums had "1914–1918" plans and, very early on, exhibitions about the war were held in the forts at Merksem and Loncin. For the Military Museum, curatorial competition regarding the First World War was in fact as old as the war itself: an initial application to set up a new war museum had been sent to the Cabinet of the Minister of War in August 1914, but been rejected. The curatorial race played out at international level, too. In addition to existing museums, like the *Musée de l'Armée* in Paris, which devoted new rooms to the recent conflict, a new generation of war museums was born.

In 1923 the Royal Military Museum displays its German equipment in the "Trophy Gallery". The name clearly illustrates the anti-German feelings prevailing at that time. The term "Trophy" is eventually dropped in favour of the more neutral denomination "German Gallery".

(War Heritage Institute, Brussels, PK 7)

In 1917 alone, the Imperial War Museum was founded in London, Canberra saw the appearance of the War Museum Australia and a *Bibliothèque et Musée de la Guerre* opened in the French town of Vincennes. This increase in museums was part of a "memory boom" that had swelled in Europe and the rest of the world since the 1890s, and which took on unprecedented proportions with the impact of the First World War.[15]

Political support

The words of Jamblinne de Meux give the impression that the Royal Military Museum was left to its fate after the war. However, this does not tally with reality, which in fact testifies to a far-reaching political interest in the institution. In 1919 it became clear that the Military Museum, which had been housed in a number of former buildings of the Military School in the Abbey of La Cambre in Ixelles since its official creation in 1911, would be allowed to make the necessary arrangements for a move to the prestigious *Parc du Cinquantenaire* complex in Brussels. This meant that a political commitment had been given to a major reopening for the public. In contrast to other Belgian museums, which continued to operate relatively normally during the First World War, the Military Museum had actually been closed to the public during the conflict. However, an alternative Belgian Military Museum had been set up on French soil, in Le Havre.[16]

Along with a new spatial context came the creation of a new legal framework. A series of Royal Decrees between 1919 and 1923 laid the foundation for the further development of the museum. The Military Museum was subdivided into an historical and a technical department, plus a library and an archive. The staff also became more professional: General de Meux was appointed General Manager with, alongside him, *Capitaine-commandant* Louis Leconte, one of the founders of the pre-war museum, who was honourably discharged. As a civilian, he was assigned the job of permanent curator.

Political support was at its most tangible when it came to collecting war souvenirs from home and abroad. The reaction of Minister Masson's cabinet when hearing of Jamblinne de Meux's misgivings addressed to the *Commission Centrale de la Récuperation* is illustrative. Immediate steps were taken: the museum received a proposal to appoint someone to be given the privilege of sifting through all the commission's repositories in the search for valuable war souvenirs. This was characteristic of the post-war museum collecting policy: political support – from local level to the royal family – meant the Military Museum enjoyed a privileged position. This unwritten rule also applied internationally. The museum could, without scruple, successfully enlist the services of military attachés in London, Rome, Paris or Washington, or make use of foreign military or diplomatic contacts in Brussels. Relationships with the new or revamped war museums in Europe and beyond were also forged in this way. The Imperial War Museum, especially, attracted considerable attention. A great deal of information was obtained, via the Belgian military attaché in London, about the design, financing, set-up, and collection policy, etc. of the British big brother. Collection exhibits were also regularly exchanged with those major foreign museums. The political credit generated by the reputation of "little Belgium" was fully redeemed in the curatorial quest for objects.

However, in a post-war Belgium in which economic recovery was proving difficult, there was no immediate surplus of money to finance a major national military museum.

Armistice agreements dictate that the German army is to hand over military equipment in good working order. Some 5,000 artillery pieces, 25,000 machineguns and 3,000 trench mortars are to be surrendered to the Allies. Large depots filled with equipment in that way see the light of day. In 1919 Fort Merksem seizes the opportunity to present this equipment to the public. Some of the exhibited items will eventually be included in the Royal Military Museum collections.
(War Heritage Institute, Brussels, PK 77)

This manifested itself, among other things, in the slow relocation and installation plans in the *Parc du Cinquantenaire*, meaning that the opening of the museum had to be postponed several times. This drew the following symbolic words from General Jamblinne de Meux in February 1921: "Belgium needs to at least inspire itself a little by the example of her big neighbours, who do not economise on anything in order to glorify their Military Museums, the sublime sacrifices of their army. It has been too long that we have been persterd by the public to visit ours."[17]

A pantheon for the nation

The development of a major national military museum appeared to play perfectly into the hands of the Belgian government, which wanted to avoid post-war chaos and envisaged unity among its people. The patriotism of the First World War was bound to seal the cracks in the unitary character of the nation. The Military Museum seemed to grow into an instrument of the state, used for the glory of state power and the promotion of national identity. During the interwar period the institution therefore closely resembled the traditional European nineteenth century national museums that had served to legitimise the (new) nations and instruct the public. The museum's aim was to create a national, patriotic (military) pantheon to boost patriotic feelings among the population. In addition, it also had to offer military technical education, which took shape among other things with the creation of a Technical Hall where the evolution of firearms was key.

The legacy of the First World War played a crucial role in the construction of a patriotic museum narrative. The importance of the museum grew "in line with the manifold lessons to be drawn from this great war and with the renowned role that Belgium played in it."[18] The political collective memory of the conflict that was orchestrated in the museum was homogeneous and unified and initially coincided with the cultural collective memory in Belgium which was reflected in, among other things, patriotic monuments or commemoration days and public holidays.[19] While the latter were very quickly challenged by alternative commemorative practices within Flemish nationalist or pacifist circles, the same certainly cannot be said of the Military Museum during the interwar period.

Patriotism in three zones

On 22 July 1923 the museum was officially inaugurated in its new location in the *Parc du Cinquantenaire* by King Albert. Numerous national and international dignitaries – with the exception of a German delegation – were invited to the opening. It was a high day for those kindly disposed towards the Belgian nation, although Jamblinne de Meux was not among them. He stayed away from the inauguration, having stepped down as director for interpersonal reasons just a few months before the opening. From now on, Louis Leconte would put himself forward as the sole voice and advocate of the museum.

The patriotic museum narrative for the First World War translated primarily into a tribute to Belgian victims and heroes: a corner dedicated to fellow countrymen who had been executed was illustrated with photos and souvenirs, and added colour to the Belgian zone relating to the conflict. The hero par excellence was the Belgian army with its "Knight King" Albert, depicted in, among other things, a magnificent painting by Jacques Madyol, several metres high. In addition, the love for the fatherland was also shaped, surprisingly, by a strong international interpretation in what was known as the Hall of the Allies, where the post-war gifts from Allied countries – from France, via Japan, to the United States – were arranged. With those tributes to the victors, the Belgian nation staked an important place on the international stage. Lastly, an anti-German element also played a part: the impressive spoils of war taken from the enemy were displayed in a gigantic German – or rather anti-German – hall, which was also referred to as the Trophy Hall. Patriotism, in fact, transcended the presentation of the First World War, being expressed in, among other things, the presentation of the Brabant Revolution as a starting point of the museum or the glorification of King Leopold II in the exhibition space relating to the nineteenth century.

A museum as memorial

Right up to the eve of the Second World War, a similar patriotic museum narrative was upheld, although the anti-German element of it sometimes made way for an anti-Bolshevik discourse. The latter, for example, was reflected in the inaugurations of new and revamped international sections (in particular for Finland and Latvia) in the Hall of the Allies. In practice, the narrative was further substantiated by thousands of collection exhibits linked to the First World War, which continued to be sent to the museum from all over the world. The patriotism in the museum proved ideal for use in Belgian nationalist circles, which were keen to link the development of domestic policy to the development of national power.

Just like many other national military museums in Europe, at times during the remainder of the interwar period the Royal Military Museum resembled a national political memorial more than a museum. The redesign of the museum following the death of King Albert in 1934 was symbolic: after his death, his uniforms and other memorabilia were transferred to the museum, to be installed in a new room that bore a strong resemblance to a mausoleum for the King.

When the new German occupier entered the museum in the *Parc du Cinquantenaire* in 1940, they may have been surprised: the military might of Belgium on show in the museum's stuffed display cases stood in stark contrast to the real military clout of the newly conquered land...

REPATRIATING THE WAR DEAD. PRIVATE MOURNING OR NATIONAL INTEREST?

Jan Van der Fraenen

After the Great War, the various national governments had to agree on what should become of the many military graveyards and the graves scattered along the Front. Already in September 1917, the Belgian government, which had relocated to Le Havre, assumed responsibility for the creation of cemeteries for the Belgian and Allied servicemen who had been killed during the war. The government wanted in this way to show its respect for the many thousands of men who had made the ultimate sacrifice in defence of their homeland. However, at that time a legal framework existed only for municipal cemeteries and not yet for national cemeteries. In order to expunge national guilt, the government decided to extend the Napoleonic decree that dated from 1804. From that time on, the Belgian government assumed responsibility for the upkeep of cemeteries but was unwilling to revoke the former right of mayors to oversee municipal cemeteries. This was an important legislative initiative, because after the war all around the country hundreds of graveyards were added that did not fall under the authority of mayors, and from then on they became the responsibility of the state.[20]

After the war the British Graves Registration Unit keeps on working in the Westhoek. The former battlefields need to be cleared and thousands of abandoned bodies are to be buried. Men serving with Exhumations Units systematically search the battlefields and dig up casualties in order to identify them.
The soldiers are then laid to rest in new graves. The service counts some 8,600 men.
(Imperial War Museum, London, Q100914, Ivan L. Bawtree)

Belgian servicemen are buried in the Bruges communal cemetery both in 1914 and 1918.
Some of them are exhumed after the First World War, to be reburied in local cemeteries.
War volunteer Florent Ars is one of them. He dies in a German field hospital on 11 November 1914.
In 1921 his body is exhumed in Bruges and reburied in the local cemetery in Silly.
(War Heritage Institute, Brussels, B.1.185.95/14620)

Bury or repatriate?

Even while the war was in progress, in most countries a profound and emotionally charged social debate arose as to whether the remains of fallen soldiers should be repatriated, and the controversy became even more intense after the armistice. Many next of kin felt it was important to have the remains of their fallen family members close to home. After all, in order to come to terms with death and put their minds at ease, people need to see the actual body and be sure that their loved one is actually dead. A body, a grave and the necessary social customs and rituals that accompany death, such as funerals, are all part of the grieving process and help people come to terms with death. However, this process is disrupted if the body or the grave cannot be located and people therefore have no opportunity to say their last goodbyes.[21] Of course, this is impossible for the next of kin of soldiers who are missing in action, as there is no identifiable body and therefore no known grave. For families who live in countries that are far from the Western Front, such as Australia or America, there are certainly practical obstacles (mainly cost and distance) that make it difficult for relatives to visit war graves. However, those who live in France, Belgium and the UK, want the body of their loved one close by.

The repatriation issue was the subject of heated debate for many years, especially in France. Repatriation was impossible and even illegal during the war. The ban, in fact, dated back to November 1914.[22] The war was still raging, and there were many graves along the Front Line. After the war, the situation was completely different, but the French government nonetheless continued to declare for three years that it was illegal to disinter and repatriate war victims irrespective of their nationality. After the war, France was deep in mourning, and it was felt that moving hundreds of thousands of corpses to every corner of the land would only add to the grief. Furthermore, at that time the French government was strapped for cash and could not afford the cost of repatriation.

In the United States, following a fierce debate, the decision was taken to repatriate the bodies of fallen soldiers. The government initially pledged to bring home all American servicemen, including those who had been killed in action, but the reality of the war decided otherwise. In 1917, the US Commander-in-Chief decided that repatriation would not start until after the armistice. However, by the time the armistice was signed he had decided that the task of repatriating the remains of all dead American servicemen would remove every trace of US casualties from the battlefield. Ultimately, the American government decided to take a two-pronged approach: next of kin were told they could decide whether or not they wanted to repatriate the remains of their dead relatives. Only 37% of the bodies of American soldiers who were killed during the war are still buried in the nine American war cemeteries in France and Belgium. This clearly shows that there is general consensus within society that war victims should be repatriated. In France too, it was ultimately decided that the families concerned should be given the choice. Since 1921, between 250,000 and 300,000 French soldiers who died in the war have found a final resting place in their native town or village, a figure that represents 25% to 30% of the total number of French military war dead.[23]

In Belgium, the situation did not differ greatly from that of the Allied countries, but the public debate was less emotionally charged and less intense. For one thing, the number of Belgian soldiers who died in the war (approximately 41,000) was considerably less than in most of the other nations that were swept up in the hostilities. Following the example of France and Great Britain, the Belgian law of the 15th of November 1919 made it illegal to repatriate the remains of Belgian war victims from military or municipal cemeteries. The main reason that was given for this was hygiene, because many of these soldiers had died from the Spanish flu. This point was made in October 1919 by the then Minister of War, Fulgence Masson: "If we were to allow mass exhumation at this time, would the country not be exposed to the most severe epidemic diseases?" However, some bodies were disinterred clandestinely. For example, a gravedigger in the city of Bruges received a conditional prison sentence and a hefty fine for digging up four bodies at the request of the family members. Two of the dead had in fact died of the Spanish flu.[24]

The ban on repatriation lasted for six months but was then extended until the 15th of November 1920. The reason was that the process of identifying all the Belgian war graves had not yet been completed.[25] In the meantime, the Belgian State Journal reported (and newspapers were asked to carry the report) that all fallen soldiers would receive a uniform gravestone. It was felt that graveyards should thus become places of pilgrimage and that they should be places of remembrance of "the bravery of our heroes and their sacrifice for a just cause." This aim could be achieved only by having the fallen soldiers "rest in peace together in full equality in the place where they fell in the same sacred cause." The Ministry of Defense therefore said that all servicemen should be interred together and called on the next of kin not to repatriate their loved ones. On the one hand, the Ministry argued that the ultimate sacrifice made by these brave men would in this way be forgotten. On the other hand, the same Ministry encouraged those families to show solidarity with the relatives of soldiers who did not have a known grave. The Ministry expected "Belgian families to consider it their duty to sacrifice their personal interests to the general good." However, the Ministry also acknowledged the importance of "emotional reasons" and therefore nonetheless left open the possibility of allowing families to repatriate the bodies of fallen soldiers. Families had only three months to submit their request. The actual repatriations began in March 1921. The government paid for the body to be disinterred and transported to the train station of the family's choice; the family then paid for the body to be taken to a cemetery and reburied.[26]

Although the French, American and Belgian governments eventually allowed the bodies of dead servicemen to be repatriated, the British Empire maintained the French ban dating from 1914. Well-off families attempted to bring their sons back to Britain during the war, often with success. In most cases, this involved military officers. Even after the war, there were many requests for bodies to be repatriated to Britain, but the Imperial War Graves Commission was adamant that this would not be allowed. It was mainly rich families that were given authorisation to exhume and repatriate the bodies of loved ones. Moreover, the prospect of disinterring the 400,000 identified graves was a daunting task. At the end of the day, the Commission argued, having common cemeteries in other countries served a higher ideal: all those men would lie together on the battlefield where they had fallen.[27] They lay there, it was said, shoulder to shoulder irrespective of rank or status.

The situation was much more difficult for Germans. For one thing, Germany had lost the war, and the Treaty of Versailles stipulated that Allied governments were responsible for the upkeep of the German graves in their respective countries. Repatriation to Germany was therefore out of the question.

After fierce debate, the American government decides to repatriate American dead upon request of their families. On 25 April 1921 several barges make a stopover in Liège. They carry the bodies of 960 American soldiers. The coffins are transferred to Antwerp harbour by way of the river Meuse and then repatriated to the United States. (War Heritage Institute, Brussels, B.1.84.62-14608)

Military cemeteries

After the war, the former battlefields became places of memorial and commemoration, with many monuments and military cemeteries. These cemeteries would become important sites for commemoration. The government was responsible for their upkeep, and they took on a number of meanings. Cemeteries not only fulfilled a funerary function, but they also became places to express grief. In addition, they became collective places of war remembrance. More than once, the government exploited cemeteries for its own particular aims and objectives. The government thus made it clear that the many thousands of soldiers had not died in vain but that the war had served a higher purpose, for example liberating the country or dying for the new nation state.

In France and Italy, smaller cemeteries were cleared and the bodies were taken to larger national necropolises close to the battlefield. These cemeteries formed a border where an invisible army of dead soldiers kept watch.[28] Despite the fact that many thousands of bodies were repatriated, the cemeteries remained impressively large. In Italy, the process of centralising military graves began in 1930 at the initiative of the Fascist government. All small graveyards were cleared, and the bodies were reburied in new large cemeteries, where the graves took on a new meaning in the commemoration culture. While the dead were previously remembered mainly at a local level and in fairly traditional ways, cemeteries were exploited by the Fascist regime and emphasis was placed on military order and discipline.[29] The dead also took on political significance in Poland. In the late 1920s, a separate section was allocated in military cemeteries to soldiers who had died fighting in the Polish Legion for the independence of Poland. In this way, the Polish government sought to drum up support for its recently regained independence and to draw a distinction between Polish national heroes and other war dead.[30]

In Belgium, the centralising of individual graves and smaller graveyards was organised by the *Dienst der Militaire Grafsteden*. This service was set up in April 1917 as the *Militaire Gravendienst* and began the task of searching for the graves of fallen soldiers, disinterring and identifying bodies and organising reburial. Individual graves and smaller graveyards were cleared, and the bodies were all taken to larger cemeteries. From 1924, uniform tombstones were erected in these cemeteries. However, Belgian tombstones were not to be found at all graves. In late August 1915, the army decided that wooden crosses could be adorned with an inscription, but only in the French language. This monolingual policy prompted considerable agitation among Dutch speakers. This led in 1916 to the establishment of the *Heldenhuldefonds*, a "Heroes' Fund" that collected money to buy more durable gravestones *(Heldenhuldezerkjes)* with inscriptions in the Dutch language. Around seven hundred such gravestones were placed during the war, and after the war families had the option of leaving these commemorations for fallen heroes in place. Today there are still 137 such gravestones, but most of them were removed in 1925.[31]

The *Dienst der Militaire Grafsteden* was also given responsibility for the upkeep of the majority of German graves. It maintained the existing German graveyards but employed a former combatant or a cemetery warden to care for these graves. These final resting places were not generally well cared for. They were usually surrounded by barbed wire and cleared of weeds. The same situation prevailed in the few German cemeteries in the Ypres district that were managed by the Imperial War Graves Commission. In 1925, the IWGC commissioned the Belgian service to maintain the last remaining German cemetery. It was only at that time that the *Volksbund Deutsche Kriegsgräberfürsorge* began to play an important role in this regard. This association was established in 1919 as a citizens' initiative to assist the German government in its efforts. First and foremost, the *Volksbund* assisted the families of the war dead, usually by helping them locate the grave of their lost loved one. In the late 1920s, the *Volksbund* also became active abroad by taking over the upkeep of German graves and creating cemeteries. The *Volksbund* was strongly politically oriented, was very conservative and even became a vehicle for the propaganda of nationalist movements. Cemeteries were organised according to strict rules and were stripped of individual monuments. It therefore came as no surprise that in 1933 the *Volksbund* unhesitatingly latched onto national socialism and helped foster the national-socialist hero cult.[32]

In the early 1920s, *Nos Tombes/Onze Graven* (Our Graves) was assigned the task of maintaining the Belgian war cemeteries. This non-profit association was the result of the merger of two organisations.[33] *Le souvenir belge* also offered its assistance from 1922 onwards. It subsequently became clear that the Ministry of Defense found the task of maintaining the war graves a burden when in 1928 it transferred this responsibility to the Ministry of the Interior and Public Health. The cemeteries were landscaped, and upkeep was regarded as an ongoing task. It was therefore decided that this was not the job of the army and that it was no longer considered appropriate for the Ministry of War to intervene.[34] This transfer was also part of the economy drive of the Jaspar government, because no additional personnel would thus be recruited by the Ministry of the Interior and Public Health. By then, the war cemeteries had largely lost their function as places of mourning and had become merely collective places of remembrance.

THE ROARING TWENTIES

"MUCH SHALL BE FORGIVEN YOU FOR YOU'VE SEEN A LOT OF MOVIES"

Matthijs de Ridder

These are the opening words to Paul van Ostaijen's 1921 masterpiece *Occupied City/Bezette Stad*. It is not immediately clear what should be forgiven. Escapism, perhaps? The "you" being addressed is "Mr Soandso", an everyman who was the model for Van Ostaijen's generation. It is a generation that appears to have spent many hours in the cinema, given that they say they know the adventures of Fantômas, Zigomar and Chéri-Bibi. "Fatalitas!" exclaims Van Ostaijen dramatically, using a catchphrase from the hero Chéri-Bibi.[1]

Hero is perhaps not the right word. In actual fact, the characters that Van Ostaijen quotes are all master crooks, elusive criminal masterminds who exploit reality with childish ease. The world that the poet evokes is one in which injustice prevails and the forces of law and order are rendered powerless. It is an image that is very ap-

Between 1919 and 1926 the American Jack Dempsey is world boxing champion in the heavy-weight category. He not only is a successful boxer but also a movie actor. In the mid-1920s he stars in numerous movies. This turns him into one of the richest sportsmen of his time. (Bundesarchiv, Koblenz, Bild 102-10569/foto: Georg Pahl)

In 1925 Queen Elisabeth and Prince Leopold welcome the actors starring in the silent movie *Ben-Hur: A Tale of the Christ* at the royal palace. The movie is produced by Metro-Goldwyn-Mayer and distributed in Europe by Gaumont-Metro-Goldwyn. The company tries to get a return on investment for one of the most expensive silent movies ever made by means of publicity vehicles and promotion campaigns. (Archives Royal Palace, Albums AE 167/A)

pealing to these restless souls (for which they may be forgiven because they've seen a lot of movies). But it is a fleeting fantasy: even before the end of the page, war breaks out.

A new and provocative medium

That Paul van Ostaijen's *Occupied City* – the modernist text par excellence – begins with an evocation of film, is telling. In 1921, film was still a new and provocative medium, even though it strikes you that the French adventure films to which Van Ostaijen refers were already about 10 years old by then and no new inspirational film oeuvres appear in his meandering report of the First World War. In the "empty cinema" where "weary people" attempt to escape the reality of war, there is only one bright spot: Asta Nielsen. But although she made the hearts of these youths beat faster, she did not manage to change the face of the world as drastically as the pre-war crime films.

Paul van Ostaijen was not alone. For many, the post-war film experience was heavily influenced by the war. Given that Belgium had been subjected to the same trade regime as Germany during the Occupation, many American films didn't reach the public until after the war. Whereas, in large parts of the world, it was the war that made Charlie Chaplin the perfect symbol of the little man rising up against the major powers; Belgium only became familiar with the Little Tramp after the war. Chaplin soon became a darling of the public here as well, but the intelligentsia wavered: was Chaplin really the one delivering on the new medium's great promise?

Nobody actually dared say with certainty what the future of film would be. In its short existence the medium had already changed guise several times. In November 1895 in Brussels, one month before the first commercial film screening in Paris, a select company in the *Palais d'été* were still watching a technical innovation. They were very enthusiastic, but nobody knew at that point what the practical application of the invention would be. Subsequently, film spent around a decade as an attraction at fairs and markets, before finding a home in music halls and theatres specially set up for film, in around 1910. By then, the original enthusiasts were already largely disaffected. The Lumière brothers, for example, sold their rights and pursued colour photography. Film was the domain of information gathering (news, impressions from air shows, motor races, etc.) and of popular entertainment: melodramatic scenes, banal comedies and "apaches", the term used at the time for crime films.

In Belgium, the work of Alfred Machin was an exception. Originally from France, Machin had come to Belgium to shape the as yet undeveloped film industry. His films were surprisingly subtle for the time, and in 1913 he invented, almost by accident, a new genre: the anti-war film. In *Maudite soit la guerre* (Damn the War!) a young officer abroad falls in love with the daughter of his host family. Then a war breaks out and he ends up on the other side. At the dramatic climax, the girl's beloved and her brother kill each other in hand-to-hand combat. With spectacular footage of shellings and aerial dog-fights, Machin appeared to be warning of the war that would hold the world in its grip a few months later.[2]

Suddenly, film was playing the role normally ascribed to literature. Fiction was snapping at the heels of reality. But it was a one-off: the war crippled Belgian film production. Despite several attempts to use the film during the war for Flemish-nationalist propaganda, nothing came of it.

Charlie Chaplin during the filming of *The Gold Rush* in 1924. Released in 1925, the comedy establishes cinema as a true artistic genre. The movie, one of the most successful silent movies ever made, is a worldwide box-office hit. Chaplin wrote the scenario, directed the movie and was one of its main actors. (Isopix, 20185751-001)

No blockbusters, just yet

The first major film productions after the war can certainly be categorised as propaganda, released in this case, however, by the Belgian government. Films like *La Belgique martyr* (1919), *Belgique* (1921) and *La libre Belgique et l'héroïque Gabrielle Petit* (1921) had but one aim: to praise the fatherland. Little new fiction appeared

during those years. When, occasionally, thoughts of making a feature film were enter-tained in Belgium, the script was often drawn from literature, but not determined by the newest voices. During those years, anyone thinking of a good and popular story would automatically think of Hendrik Conscience, whose books *De loteling* and *De arme edelman* were filmed by Armand du Plessy in 1919 and 1921.

These prints were definitely not blockbusters neither were they warmly received by Belgian critics. For the time being popular film was primarily an import product. Pearl White, Mary Pickford, Douglas Fairbanks and Charlie Chaplin were stars of the silver screen here, too. Artists and intellectuals joined the long queues standing outside the "palaces around the corner", but however much they supported the concept of film, they often found it not to their liking. Certainly the avant-garde artists were eager to overcome the lag caused by the war, but other than the pre-war crime films, popular cinema was not entirely living up to its promise. Film raised all sorts of expectations. In the minds of the avant-garde together with the image, this dynamic art form should also have mobilised the masses. But whereas in France people were happy to attribute victory in the First World War to the moral support offered by "Charlot", as they nick-named Chaplin – and the Swiss Yvan Goll saw in him the messenger of a revolutionary form of thinking – in Belgium Chaplin was simply too late to provide revolutionary inspiration. The only major film with broad appeal to raise the hope of a drastic political and social revolution during those years was *The Red Lantern* (1919) with the ravishing Alla Nazimova in the role of the half-British, half-Chinese Mahlee, who played an incendiary role in the Boxer Rebellion. The poet Gaston Burssens saw in Nazimova a "red lantern signal in the night."[3]

Globally, until the mid-twenties, a wait-and-see attitude could be detected among the cultural elites. Despite the fact that film masterpieces like *Das Cabinet des Dr. Caligari* (1922) by Robert Wiene and *Nosferatu* (1922) by Friedrich Wilhelm Murnau had already been released, it wasn't until the Belgian release of Charlie Chaplin's *The Goldrush* (1925) that everyone agreed that film was also a worthy art form. "Whether film can be a work of art is no longer a problem for us," wrote novelist Maurice Roelants in 1926 about this "masterpiece". "Charlie has answered. We have Charlie, the artist."[4]

A domain of loners

That doesn't mean, however, that alongside the newly established film art there is a Belgian film industry to speak of. In 1925, Paul Nougé strongly criticises of cinematography in general and Belgian cinema in particular. He believed filmmakers were "poor anthologists" of the work of true artists. For the time being, film was a watered-down version of something that had been done so much better in literature and painting. Which is odd, because with all its possibilities, cinema should actually have been in a position to develop its own form.[5]

Quite early on, the general public had revealed its preference for the continuous story, and thus the thinking about a new visual language was forced to play out in the margins. In 1920–1921, having moved to Berlin, Paul van Ostaijen wrote the film script

De bankroet jazz (The Bankruptcy Jazz), in which he experimented wildly with associative montage and bird's eye view (and in which Charlie Chaplin ultimately tells Europe that the money has run out). They were paper experiments, because it would take until 2009 before the provocative screenplay was filmed. In Brussels, a short time after the original script was written, Van Ostaijen's future business partner Geert Van Bruaene was drawing attention to innovative cinema during the *Séances cinématographiques du Cabinet Maldoror*, which in 1925 screened films by, among others, Abel Gance, Robert Wiene and D.W. Griffith.

Thinking about innovative cinema, however, remained the domain of loners. In the review *7 Arts,* Pierre Bourgeois and Paul Werrie were among those discussing what they referred to as pure cinema, an avant-garde cinematography they saw as an extension of constructivism. However, they did not seem to be actively intent on having an avant-garde Belgian film industry. When Van Ostaijen surfaced in Brussels at the end of 1925 and spent some time working with Bourgeois and co, his film script, for example, never seemed to be the subject of discussion. Modern film remained primarily an attractive mirage.

That said, the first modern Belgian films were eventually created by the *7 Arts* crowd. In 1927 Charles Dekeukeleire found inspiration in a poem by Paul Werrie for his first short film: *Combat de boxe*. The artistic impression of a boxing fight was followed a year later by *Impatience*, in which the montage technique was even more associative and the classic tale was unleashed even further.

In *7 Arts*, Paul Werrie was enthusiastic about Dekeukeleire's work. His choices may have been a little too obvious in places, but much was forgiven the young filmmaker, because his films constituted "finally, a birth in this land of failed filmmakers."[6]

"THOSE WERE EXHILARATING DAYS." THE EMERGENCE OF AVANT-GARDE IN POST-WAR BELGIUM[7]

———

Sergio Servellón

In the first decades of the twentieth century, visual arts in Europe are thoroughly transformed, with various new artistic currents quickly succeeding one another. However, as indicated by the either indifferent or mocking reactions to the few modernist views expressed in Belgium, this development only truly materializes in the country after the First World War. The 1912 exhibition featuring Italian Futurism at the Brussels' Georges Giroux Gallery, for instance, only gets negative reviews in the French-speaking press, while Flanders remains totally silent on the subject. The *Great Zwans Exhibition*, a 1914 Brussels event ridiculing Futurism and other international innovations, on the other hand, meets with quite some success.[8]

The impaired former order, characterized by a failing political system unable to come to terms with democracy, is rejected even before the war, but paradoxically enough, society simultaneously mourns the old rural settings swept aside by growing materialism. The environment changes drastically everywhere, not only because of a boom in construction along the coastline, but also with the appearance of electrical wiring and billboards maiming the Flemish countryside. The First World War also profoundly scars the landscape and heightens the polarization between old and new. Retrospectively, Leo Picard denounces the economic climate destabilized by "a shower of

Cultural all-rounder Paul-Gustave van Hecke is an author, theatre man, creator of literary magazines and film critic. He moreover is one of Belgium's first fashion designers; he also runs an art gallery. However, van Hecke is best known as an art aficionado. He promotes, for instance, the Flemish Expressionists and the Belgian Surrealists. (Letterenhuis, Antwerp, H3832/P)

dollars in Europe" coming from the United States, as this speculation not only translates into growing materialism, but also brings music hall tango and jazz.[9] The war begets renewal all over Flanders, and artists respond to this innovation by including pornography, cigarettes, boxing or soccer in their art.[10]

The worldwide degeneration or moral disruption caused by the war also creates resistance. The generation straddling the turning point in this evolution reacts against the disappearance of old values by forging an idealistic and "constructive" story. After four years of unfathomable suffering, it is generally felt that the hardships endured surely have to and undoubtedly will result in something worthwhile and that the "Great War" definitely has to be the very last one. The dead are still being mourned but new hope simultaneously arises. Society wants to build a human, "humanitarian", future, in which all people share the spirit of brotherhood.[11] This idea not only emerges as a result of the solidarity created in the trenches where all skin tones and races mingled, but it is also product of innovative impulses engendered by the war industry's technological development. It not only promises an entirely new world, but also generates new "aesthetic" experiences.

An accelerated evolution towards radical art

The most radical avant-garde, particularly abstract art, materializes in our regions in 1917, initially in The Netherlands through the foundation of *De Stijl* (The Style) with Piet Mondriaan, Vilmos Huszár and the Belgian Georges Vantongerloo as its major representatives. Some other Belgian artists are internationally active in this field before 1920: think of the Futurist Jules Schmalzigaug residing in Venice and of Marthe Donas, included in the *Section d'Or*, who rises to fame in Paris.[12] In Belgium, Modernism develops slowly and, as mentioned above, only after the First World War. Its development gives birth to a very unique mix of styles or idiosyncratic variants of international tendencies. The early Expressionist experiments by Constant Permeke or Gustave De Smet can be labelled "constructive" and are indebted to the compositions of Cubism. Belgian artists apply their newly acquired knowledge about Fauvist complementary colours in abstract compositions quite unlike those created by their Dutch colleagues involved in *De Stijl*, and more closely linked to Orphism as produced by Robert Delaunay and František Kupka in Paris. Fritz Van den Berghe, on his part, evolves from Expressionism to a surrealistically coloured imaginary world, whereas all-rounder Floris Jespers merrily switches from one style to the next in a clever mix. Curiously enough, the first pioneers, such as Jozef Peeters, Prosper De Troyer and Felix De Boeck, feel the need to emulate the entire gamut produced by the new styles. In a two-year rollercoaster, roughly from 1918 to 1920, they peruse all developments from (Post-)Impressionism to Abstraction. Knowledge, both technical and theoretical, acquired earlier is transferred to the next period.

Belgian avant-garde is not only displayed in Brussels and Antwerp but also goes international. The pioneers' abstract and pre-abstract works are presented alongside masterpieces by Pablo Picasso, Georges Braque, Fernand Léger, Henri Matisse, René Magritte and Theo van Doesburg at the 1921 Geneva modern art exhibition.

That same Van Doesburg, *De Stijl* co-founder and propagandist, boosts bubbling Modernism by giving a series of lectures in both Antwerp and Brussels. These lectures are crucial in the development of *Zuivere Beelding*, the southern variant of Neoplasticism.[13] Peeters (who takes the initiative in Antwerp), Vantongerloo, Karel Maes, the brothers Pierre and Victor Bourgeois (the organisers in Brussels), Victor Sevranckx, Magritte and Felix De Boeck enthusiastically attend the lectures. The addresses turn the postwar agitation into a plea for total renewal: a *tabula rasa*.

Flemish Expressionism vs. *Zuivere Beelding*: about decadence and ethics

The artists start with a clean slate and wish to achieve more than the mere development of a new visual language: the idea is to create a whole new society. The shape this new society is to take on is the subject of heated debates. After the First World War, Belgium becomes a front-runner in social progress characterized by the breakthrough of mass mobilization.[14] In the artistic world this implies that cultural trendsetters are forced to choose between society and individuality. The epitome of artistic individuality in the late 19th and early 20th centuries is illustrated by Willem Kloos, for whom literature, and by extension art, is "the most individual expression of the most individual emotion."[15] By the end of the century some had suggested that art was in need of an ethical component, and that idea constitutes the core of the cultural battle in Flanders and Belgium after the First World War, with two Modernist teams facing one another: Expressionism vs. *Zuivere Beelding* abstract art.[16]

The team working along the lines of aestheticism consists of the Expressionists defended by *Sélection*, an authoritative magazine forcefully led by Paul Gustave Van Hecke and André de Ridder. A first Latem group, counting Gustave Van de Woestyne, Georges Minne and Albert Servaes, is succeeded halfway through the First World War by a strong generation with, for example, Gustave De Smet, Frits Van den Berghe and creative whirlwind Constant Permeke. Exiled in The Netherlands or in Great Britain, these artists escape the violence of war and acquaint themselves with international tendencies. Van den Berghe and De Smet are in that way influenced by Fauvism and Cubism in The Netherlands. Armed with their personal bleak palette and with their rash compositions, distinguishing them from German kindred spirits in *Die Brücke* and *Der Blaue Reiter*, they unleash their Expressionist fury over Belgium.

Van Hecke publishes his aesthetic "manifesto" even before *Sélection*, particularly with *Fashion*. In that article (appearing both in three instalments in *Het Roode Zeil*[7] and in a separate edition enhanced with three etchings by Gustave Van de Woestyne), Van Hecke takes the stand under the pseudonym of Johan Meylander: "A decadent Flanders. We still may have a long way to go, but the idea is highly seductive. *Mourir en beauté* and be an eternal example for all generations to come. The entire world is indeed still feeding on the nipples of Roman and Greek decadence!"[18]

Een dekadent Vlaanderen? is an article published in the 1920 December issue of the magazine Ruimte and a counter-manifesto by Flemish extremist Herman Vos, a journalist and politician. Vos warns of an "idle, perfumed and aimless vast middle class" infatuated with the idea of "mourir en beauté." Salvation will therefore not come about through an evolution from "Salon to Club", a path obviously unattainable for a "people of plebeians, of fighting democrats, of a few isolated poets".[19] Hyper-individualism is balanced against ethic art.

Immediately after the war, Vos and his Front Party's explicitly social programme meet with some success in the harbour town of Antwerp. At that point in time several young avant-garde artists link their collectivistic artistic aspirations to the Flemish movement. Jozef Peeters, to name just one, extensively calls on this network, in view of the organisation of international exhibitions and lectures by Van Doesburg.[20]

Het Overzicht and 7 Arts

As a pioneer of abstract art in Flanders, Jozef Peeters is a fervent defender of "collective art": the new visual language has a social part to play and has to contribute to the emancipation of the people. He is an artist, but also particularly active as a promoter and manager, the Flemish equivalent of Theo van Doesburg. In 1918 he creates the *Kring Moderne Kunst* and organises three congresses between 1920 and 1922.[21] The second Congress for Modern Art, taking place in Antwerp in 1922, is enhanced by a prestigious international exhibition presenting artists such as Alexander Archipenko, Paul Klee and Kurt Schwitters.

Alongside Fernand Berchelaers, later known as Michel Seuphor, Peeters puts Belgian avant-garde on the international map by means of his extensive network covering the whole of Europe. The magazine *Het Overzicht* plays an important part in this enterprise.[22] The periodical, created as a pro-Flemish mouthpiece in 1921, evolves, from 1922 onwards, into the number-one authoritative artistic publication for the Belgian abstract movement. *Het Overzicht* publishes articles and numerous reproductions of

Marthe Donas poses next to her art work. Donas' work is very popular after the First World War. She exhibits in Geneva, Berlin and Rome, and her work is included in a travelling exhibition in the United States. Donas is a Belgian national, but her international fame is largely engendered by her Paris network counting artists such as Alexander Archipenko and Piet Mondriaan. (Marthe Donas Foundation)

works by both Belgian and famous foreign artists such as Picasso, Wassily Kandinsky, László Moholy-Nagy and Robert Delaunay. In March 1924 the internationally acclaimed periodical *Der Sturm* publishes a Flemish-themed issue, featuring texts by Pierre Bourgeois, Maurice Casteels and Paul van Ostaijen, as well as illustrations by Victor Bourgeois, Felix De Boeck, Jos Léonard, Karel Maes and Jozef Peeters. With this issue, put together by the editors of *Het Overzicht* upon request of director Herwarth Walden, Peeters positions himself as the undisputed leader of Belgian avant-garde.

In Brussels the *Zuivere Beelding* ideals circulate through the avant-garde periodical *7 Arts* that keeps in close contact with its Flemish counterpart. In joint operation with editor *L'Equerre*, *7 Arts* for instance sets up a booth at the *Salon de La Lanterne Sourde,* the *Les arts belges d'esprit nouveau* exhibition in the Brussels Egmont Palace in December 1923. Jozef Peeters represents abstracts painting alongside Pierre-Louis Flouquet, Karel Maes, Felix De Boeck and Victor Servranckx. With the garden city *La Cité Moderne* in Berchem-Sainte-Agathe built in 1922, the booth's designer, architect Victor Bourgeois, realises one of the greatest performances of the Modernist movement in Belgium by concretely connecting a purely aesthetic matter to a societal concern.[23] It is to be noted that the *Cité Moderne*'s build coincides with the return to Belgium of the Flemish Expressionists from their exile in The Netherlands. Shortly afterwards the latter settle in Afsnee, a village along the river Lys, and their magazine *Sélection* increasingly

THE ROARING TWENTIES

Gathering of the Sélection avant-garde group, in response to a visit by French artist Marc Chagall. The group is represented by the Sélection magazine, led by Paul-Gustave van Hecke. The picture shows, amongst others, Gustaaf De Smet, Frits Van den Berghe, André De Ridder and Floris Jespers.
(Letterenhuis, Antwerp, S 5756/P)

objects to urban development.[24] The movement, therefore, directly opposes the Brussels abstract artists, who see their contributions to *La Cité Moderne* as a substantiation of their community ideals.

From Dada to bombshell Surrealism

Antwerp-based Paul Joostens must also be mentioned, who not only single-handedly put experimental collage art on the map, but also treated the world to Dadaist texts and images by means of mechanomorphic copy. In these works, inspired by Francis Picabia, Joostens processes randomly assembled creatures and messages full of sexual and socio-critical innuendos. In doing so he paves the way for the last avant-garde movement to see the light of day in Belgium in the 1920s: Surrealism. The Brussels Surrealists develop an utterly subversive strategy. Their activities start in 1926, when they interrupt a play by the Groupe Libre with a set by Baugniet.[25] Magritte, who had designed the bill, changes sides, and criticizes his former friends. His later fame as the pioneer of Surrealism par excellence could indeed almost make us forget that he started out as a member of the utopic abstract avant-garde. He renounces the demagogy of all things rational in favour of imagination, falsification and reverie. P.G. Van Hecke's eclecticism reaps rewards: as adamantly as he promoted Flemish Expressionism, he strongly defends budding Surrealism.[26]

Surrealism is an antagonism of Expressionism, with a more intellectual approach, averse to individual emotions. It nevertheless is equally removed from the fundamentally visual approach favoured by the Constructivists. The Surrealists, who feel to be the heirs of Dada anti-art, see the "Idealists" as the enemy. Surrealism uses a conventional painter's idiom but nevertheless expresses incongruous associative concepts. Not unlike Frankenstein-monsters, the images want to give ailing Modernism a new lease of life.

The poetic attitude towards "unrealism" adopted by Surrealists is in stark contrast to the ever more loudly proclaimed call for the past. As the 1930s draw nearer, the revolutionary state of mind peters out. This translates into a return to figurative art and to traditional genres such as interior scenes, portraits and still-life. In Flanders this restoration is expressed through intimate realism, a.k.a. Animism, with War van Overstraeten and especially Albert Van Dijck as its protagonists. This tendency will persist through the Second World War, and as a result, the former radical avant-garde is all but forgotten for the next 30 years. Only Expressionism will meet with some kind of acceptance, particularly through a supposed "identity" reflex.

The roaring avant-garde dream with its international aspirations had run its course. The promise encapsulated in the years following the First World War, but never realised, grabs the imagination to this day.

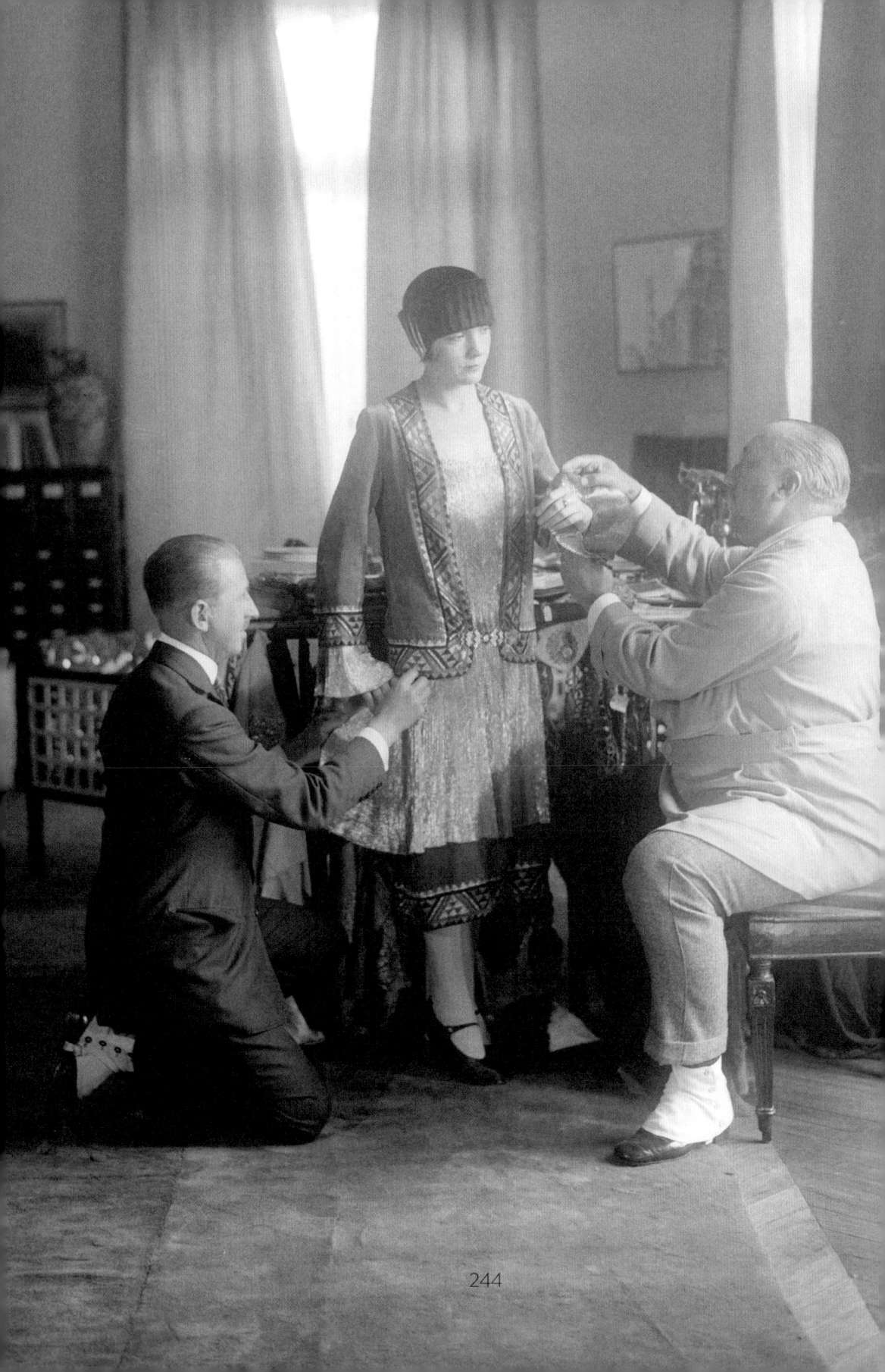

ON FLAPPERS, SPORTSWEAR AND FEMALE EMANCIPATION DURING THE ROARING TWENTIES

Karolien De Clippel

During the twenties, society underwent profound changes, and exuberance reigned. This decade was not labelled the Roaring Twenties for nothing. A crucial factor in this was the First World War, and especially the end of it. That had both positive and negative repercussions: on the negative side was the economic destabilisation that gripped not only the United States but also Europe, with the stock market crash of 1929, culminating in the Great Depression. On the positive side was the relief that arose after the armistice, leading to an unbridled party atmosphere and a desire for change.

For women in particular these post-war years were significant. During the war they had taken over the work of their husbands, sons and fathers, and as a result they had acquired a much more active role. Inevitably, this led to greater self-awareness and feminism. After the war they refused to give up their freedom and independence and meekly take up the old social gender roles once again. In line with this, women's suffrage was introduced in many Western countries: in Germany and Austria in 1918, in the United States in 1920, and in The Netherlands in 1922. In Belgium, however, it would be 1948 before women got the vote.

Fashion designer Paul Poiret (on the right) dresses a model. Poiret rises to fame before the First World War. He is a popular designer acclaimed for his flowing and colourful garments. His fame, however, decreases after the war, when he has to compete with the likes of Coco Chanel. His label runs into financial difficulties, and in 1929 the Maison Paul Poiret has to cease its activities.
(Boris Lipnitzki, Roger-Viollet, Paris, 4325-9)

The flapper girl

It was in that context of feminine emancipation that the famous "flapper girl" was born. This new or modern woman was young, self-aware, liberated and libertine. By working outside the home and therefore moving in a traditionally male domain, she adopted an attitude to match. She listened to jazz, smoked and drank in public, and drove a car. This challenging feminism also left its mark on her appearance and wardrobe. She wore a short bob and heavy make-up, which at the time was associated with prostitutes and other "loose" women because of its excess and artifice. Her clothing was an extension of her life philosophy and new social standing.[27] The binding corset, which had dominated fashion for centuries, was discarded.[28] In its place came practical and comfortable clothing that gave the wearer freedom to move. For the modern woman, fashion was no longer a pure consumer item, but a statement with symbolic value.[29]

One designer who was able to adapt perfectly to these social changes was Frenchman Paul Poiret. Inspired by orientalism and Sergei Diaghilev's *Ballets Russes* (1909), *Le Magnifique* freed women from the tight S curve and long, narrow skirts. Instead, he gave them a linear and therefore instantly more comfortable silhouette that recalled the straight lines and two-dimensional aspect of the Japanese kimono, the Greek chiton and the kaftan from Africa and the Middle East.[30]

Sportswear

In France, flapper girls were also known as *garçonnes* due to their boyish looks. To achieve this androgynous appearance, young ladies would try all sorts: not just binding their breasts to make them look flatter, but also going on diets and playing sport on a grand scale. A healthy body was a priority: physical exercise was glorified in the pages of leading fashion magazines such as *Fémina* and *L'Officiel de la couture et de la mode de Paris*. This led to a high demand for sports clothing for women.[31] But it was more than that: sportswear became a mentality. The French designer Jean Patou understood this way of life better than anyone. What was revolutionary was the fact that he was able to convince his global clientele to wear sports clothing not just during, but also before and after exercise. His creations allowed women to dress both elegantly and comfortably and consequently made an emphatic contribution to the emancipation of women.

However, Patou was not just a great designer, he was also a shrewd businessman. This is evidenced by the fact that he succeeded in convincing sports champions to wear his clothing not just on the sports field, but also off it. The example of Frenchwoman Suzanne Lenglen captured the imagination. She was a flamboyant athlete and the first female ten-

nis player to enjoy international fame. When she won her first Wimbledon title in 1919, her outfit designed by Jean Patou made as much of an impression as the strength of her game. At the age of 20 and wearing neither a corset nor an underskirt, she actually played in a daring silk pleated dress with sleeves as short as her hem, so that the spectators could see her white stockings when she reached for the ball. Lenglen thus became not only the ambassador for Maison Patou, but also a role model for other women. Ultimately, Patou succeeded in transposing technical innovations that were introduced specifically for sports clothing – such as the pleated skirt for greater mobility – into everyday and even couture wear.

Femininisation of fashion in Paris

Patou may have entered the history books as the inventor of sportswear, but he was certainly not the only one to market more female-friendly and sporty attire during the twenties. It is no coincidence that a number of female designers rose to prominence in that period, who today have a place in the canon of fashion history. They include Jeanne Lanvin, the founder of Paris's oldest existing fashion house,[32] and the legendary Gabrielle "Coco" Chanel. She was the epitome of the new woman due to her appearance –

One of the icons of the 1920s is star tennis player Suzanne Lenglen. The Frenchwoman not only wins 34 Grand Slam titles, but is also dressed by French fashion designer Jean Patou. Lenglen's outfits stun the world of tennis: she wears short pleated silk dresses with short sleeves. She in that way revolutionizes female sports equipment. (akg/Isopix, 3970183)

short hair, brown skin, constantly smoking and wearing sporty attire – her lifestyle and her financial independence.

Even before the First World War, Chanel was making comfortable clothing; during the war, she began to experiment with jersey. An elastic material that until that time had only been used for underwear and for sports attire such as bathing costumes, and tennis and golf clothing, jersey was regarded as too "ordinary" for couture clothing. Chanel overcame this prejudice and was resolute in her choice of fabric. Jersey proved successful for two reasons: firstly, it provided a solution to the shortage of fabrics caused by the war, and secondly it met women's demands for simple and practical clothing. Chanel's smooth jersey suits and dresses offered the added advantage that a woman could dress without help from staff. Chanel's professional success and her introduction of comfortable couture clothing for women made her a particularly important figure when it came to gender equality; this was given a boost in the twenties, with fashion playing a prominent role.

Paris in Brussels

At that time, Paris was still the centre of the Western fashion world. The city of light determined the trends that were adopted elsewhere, including Belgium. Belgian department stores in the style of Hirsch & Cie, as well as dressmakers and seamstresses, made reproductions or adaptations of the Paris designs. Compared to couturiers from other countries, those from Belgium – particularly Brussels – held a privileged position in Paris until after the Second World War. They were able to become customers of the big couture houses and reproduce legal designs against payment. Those designs varied slightly from the originals and, in general, the Belgian variations were simpler and easier to wear than their Parisian prototypes.[33]

Houses that made original designs were as good as non-existent in Belgium, with one exception: Maison Norine.[34] Founded in 1916 by Paul-Gustave Van Hecke and his partner Honorine "Norine" Deschryver, the fashion house had its heyday in the interwar period. Just like their Parisian counterparts Poiret and Chanel, the couple associated themselves with the avant-garde art of the time. More than that, for them fashion became art. Norine's trademark was the *robe peinte*: a dress in hand-painted fabric that conformed to the visual language of modernism and of their friend René Magritte. Their original creations were very successful and were especially appreciated by art-loving intelligentsia. But despite their own sense of artistic authenticity, even Maison Norine continued to treat Paris as the gold standard.

In short, the fashion of the twenties played a key role in the western world in the emancipation of women. Fashion became a sort of political statement, a way of giving shape to newly acquired freedoms. For the first time in history comfort and elegance went hand in hand. This emancipatory trend was conveyed not only in consumer behaviour, but also in production. Female designers went on to establish themselves in the competitive fashion landscape of which, today, they are an essential part.

SOUNDS AND VIBRATIONS IN THE ROARING TWENTIES

Géry Dumoulin

I t is always difficult to grasp the whole complexity and diversity of the soundscape of a bygone era, even when it is relatively recent. The modern concept of "sound-scape", so dear to Raymond Murray Schafer,[35] refers to overall noise, whether originating from nature or from the activities of men and machinery, regardless of intensity, purpose, or perception; and music, in all its facets, is clearly an integral part of this vast, vibrating landscape.

A general frenzy

The nineteen-twenties are in strong contrast with the years that came before. Here music claims its dues – the thundering of the bombs is replaced by a musical frenzy, as though to wipe out the memory of the ultimate noise pollution produced by the war. Of course, musical life in Belgium did not come to a complete standstill during the conflict – but was the heart really in it?

After the war, music was to be heard almost everywhere in Brussels. The capital crystallised the essence of the country's musical activity, although the Flemish and Wal-loon towns also recovered their cultural lives, particularly during the summer season when the populations of the coastal resorts and certain French-speaking towns, like Spa and Dinant, grew enormously.[36]

There were many musicians and they were to be found in many places, from the cafés to the concert halls, from small theatres to the Brussels *Théâtre de la Monnaie* opera house, from the dance halls to the cinemas, via the hotels, restaurants, bowling alleys, skating rinks, and chain stores, not to mention the streets, bandstands, and pri-

One of the style icons of the 1920s is the French-American singer and dancer Freda Josephine McDonald, a.k.a. Josephine Baker. (Germaineimage, 22829165-001)

The *Bistrouille Amateur Dance Orchestra* at work in Brussels in 1929. The group gets its inspiration from the hugely popular *Mitchell's Jazz Kings*. The group consists of founders Marcel and René Vinche and talented jazz musicians. The big band will become one of the most famous jazz formations in Belgium.
(Collection Musical Instruments Museum, Robert Pernet Fund, RMAH/MIM, King Baudouin Foundation)

vate homes. In the early 1920s, there were some 2,000 unionised professional musicians in Brussels alone, performing at around 180 different venues.[37] And added to this already considerable body were the non-union musicians, plus military bands, amateurs performing in brass bands and orchestras, choirs and other ensembles, street musicians, etc. And wherever musicians could not be found in the flesh, mechanical organs, orchestrions, and gramophones filled the gap.

The music hall contributed to the euphoria of the post-war years by holding great shows, often in the form of magical, spectacular reviews, which no longer had anything in common with the satirical reviews of the pre-war period.[38] The great variety of entertainment available can be seen from the playbills, which advertised not only reviews, but operettas, ballets, concerts, tea dances, exhibitions of scantily-clad young ladies, stars – all designed to please audiences from every spectrum of society. The most popular venues in Brussels included the Alhambra, run by the owner of the famous *Casino de Paris*, and the *Cirque Royal*, where Josephine Baker created a sensation in 1925 with her *Revue Nègre* following the success of her production in Paris.

Dancing galore

During the Roaring Twenties, entertainment was the order of the day, with dancing at the top of the agenda. The old dances that had first seen the light of day in the 19th century and were still around before the war (such as the quadrille, the polka, the mazurka, the schottische, and so on), now gave way to the fox-trot, the one-step, the two-step, and syncopated variations from America. The romantic waltz was still holding out, but java moved in to breathe new life into the mazurka. The Argentine tango continued the vogue it had started before 1914, and was a great success. Dancing was everywhere – in custom-built dance halls and many other establishments which were happy to hold dances featuring interludes with singers. And where there was dancing, an orchestra, no matter how small, would be playing. The new fashion for American dances saw the arrival of instruments such as the saxophone, the banjo, and the drums. At that time, a typical orchestra for dances of this kind would consist of a dozen musicians on piano, drums, three saxophones, two trumpets, one or two trombones, a sousaphone, a banjo, and a violin.[39] In smaller venues, an orchestrion or pianola would replace the orchestra.[40]

Jazz installs itself

The Roaring Twenties, as they were known on the other side of the Atlantic, marked the arrival in Belgium of an essential musical genre of the 20th century – jazz. Its forerunners had already been in evidence well before the war, with, for example, the arrival at the beginning of the century of the John Philip Sousa Band, which would add some ragtime to its performances, and the minstrel shows, with black or blacked-up white players airing the cake-walk, with its exotic rhythms. Where bands "sparkled with syncopation",[41] dance and jazz were intimately linked. During the Great War, soldiers from the New World would sing their "songs as convoluted as barbed wire",[42] but jazz first made its official appearance in Belgium in 1920, at the Alhambra, with the black American group Mitchell's Jazz Kings. There was no going back.

Belgium made a major contribution to the development of jazz in Europe. Small Belgian jazz bands sprang up, like the Bistrouille Amateurs Jazz Kings,[43] one of the first on a European scale. The first magazine in the world focusing entirely on jazz appeared here in 1924, thanks to Félix-Robert Faecq.[44] The first recording of "Belgian" jazz was by saxophonist Charles Remue & His New Stompers Orchestra in 1927, just 10 years after what is considered to have been the very first jazz record, by the Original Dixieland Jazz Band in New York. Robert Goffin was both witness and player in this period, which he was to describe in the first documented study of jazz published in the early

On 1 November 1926 *Radio Belgique*'s news desk goes on the air. Journalist Théo Fleischmann has the honour of reading the very first radio news bulletin. The written press is worried about its future.
(Germaineimage, 22829159-001)

1930s.[45] Belgian musicians didn't take long to forge a solid reputation abroad, thanks to both their instrumental virtuosity and their improvisation and composition; these included Chas Remue, David Bee, Peter Packay, Clément Doucet, Jean Pâques, and Égide Van Gils. However, this new music wasn't to everyone's taste – some considered it to be just a lot of noise accompanied by outrageous gesticulations. Few representatives of the world of serious music took jazz seriously, although some of the more open-minded foresaw its universal appeal.

Classical music evolves

In the field of opera, the *Théâtre de la Monnaie* was trying to recover after being forced to close throughout the hostilities. While outstanding works were still being performed there, the pace had slowed down considerably, and the operatic scenario as a whole was now no more than "a reflection of the great foreign musical centres".[46] Concerts, on the other hand, flourished throughout the country, especially in the capital, where the *Concerts Populaires* and those organised by Désiré Defauw stood out. The *Palais des Beaux-Arts*, which had been in the pipeline since 1919, was officially opened in 1929.

The musical taste of the day still seemed to be under the influence of post-romanticism and the admirers of César Franck, but more and more modern music was being heard, thanks in particular to its promotion by Paul Collaer in his *Pro Arte* concerts. This was when Erik Satie, Darius Milhaud, and the composers of the *Les Six* group became known in Belgium, as did Igor Stravinsky, who triumphed in 1924 and also took his first steps as conductor there.[47] Belgian composers, disciples of Paul Gilson, met to form the *Synthétistes* group, which offered a compromise by adding modern elements onto an academic base. They enjoyed a certain popularity thanks to the Belgian military music flagship orchestra, the *Musique des Guides*, directed by Arthur Prévost. Paradoxically, during the inter-war period, there was also a major change in the preferences of a disoriented public who were more comfortable with the works of the past than with the contemporary repertoire.[48]

When looking at the cultural landscape of the time as a whole, Belgian Surrealism cannot be overlooked. Marked in particular by the paintings of René Magritte, this movement was not distinguished on the musical side, although a composer like André Souris, who was well aware of modern music and jazz, caused controversy by delivering a determinedly iconoclastic jolt to the musical establishment of the time.

The wireless takes on

In technical terms, the improvements in sound reproduction (recordings became electric) and the standardisation of records at 78 rpm should be highlighted. Musicians, composers and audiences all benefited from the resulting increase in the airing of classical music and jazz. Other forms of mass medium became generally available in the twenties, with wireless telegraphy (WT) and sound broadcasting. From 1923 on, *Radio-Bruxelles* played live classical music, and light and dance music, broadcasting concerts and, occasionally, jazz. Other private radio stations, such as Radio-Schaerbeek and *Nationale Vlaamse Radio*, also broadcast musical shows, and foreign transmissions could be picked up. The official *Institut National Belge de Radiodiffusion* (INR) was established in 1930.[49]

EPILOGUE

EARNING PEACE?

Chantal Kesteloot

As soon as the armistice was signed, Frenchman Georges Clemenceau, President of the Council and "Father of Victory", announced: "We have won the war, but now we will have to earn peace and that could very well be quite another matter." Did Belgium manage to obtain peace 10 years down the road in 1928, and if so, what kind of peace? Or is one rather to speak of a "thirty-year war", as General de Gaulle did on Radio London in 1941?

In 1928 the overall mood indeed is one of appeasement, a new era seems to dawn, the fissured continent's wounds seem to have healed. But still, 10 years later, in September 1939, a new cataclysm is on the cards. The thirties feel like a terrible waste, a missed opportunity. Particularly striking is the democracies' incapacity to resolve the economic crisis, their inability even to merely survive... Changeover seems unavoidable. To this day, both journalists and teachers present the thirties as an absolute anti-model, an utter foil. The Roaring Twenties as opposed to the Gloomy Thirties... And yet, between the eight-hour workday launched in 1921 and paid leave obtained in 1936, nuances abound.[1]

Declaring that the thirties were a dead end could be seen as both an oversimplification and an anachronism, but one simply cannot ignore that Belgium had to address many challenges making it impossible to "earn peace". The logics of interior policy seemed to have been blurred by a noxious international context.

The *Oeuvre des Automobiles pour Invalides de Guerre* is created in 1922. The organisation supplies war invalids with chauffeur-driven cars and organises trips both in the country and abroad. The war invalids can in that way visit venues that are opened especially for them. They are heartily welcomed wherever they go, as here in Namur.

(War Heritage Institute, Brussels, EST-1-688-1)

Masses and democracy

All fighting forces engaged in the Great War had to face the phenomenon of armed masses. The experience is durably imbedded in the history of European societies through veterans' associations. Even if mass groups do exist in the twenties, collective imagination typically associates them with the thirties.[2] Society counts numerous target groups and witnesses mass phenomena: youngsters, the working classes, the unemployed, mass protests, fascists, communists... The red spectre frightens the elite disproportionally. This terror feeds on fantasies, the fear of uncontrolled violence, and increased xenophobia exactly when thousands of refugees come knocking. Masses both seduce and frighten, even more so as they now evolve in an internationalized society characterized by production, communication and movement. The masses define society and its workings. Efficient propaganda fuelled by all kinds of fears is thoroughly professionalized and the masses become its prime target.

Permanent disagreements

The November 1927 Cabinet crisis engendered by debates about the length of military duties puts an end to the second edition of a national union government. The Socialists leave the scene. Beyond the military issue, other disagreements between the partners also smoulder, especially with regard to social reforms and language issues, two permanent challenges in the inter-war period. Quite quickly though, a Catholic-Liberal coalition led by Henri Jaspar is established. In spite of general elections in 1929, the same, just slightly adjusted, government is maintained until 1931. Has Belgium figured out how to obtain political stability?

A centenary both sturdy and fragile

In 1930, Belgium lavishly celebrates its centenary. However, the event is not hailed with equal enthusiasm all over the country. Nevertheless, in the timespan of one century Belgium managed to establish its legitimacy on the European scene, a conclusion not necessarily foregone immediately after the revolution. But is the Belgian nation possibly undermined from within? Is the beautiful patriotic surge of 1914 and its extension in November 1918 already a thing of the past? Does the incomplete democracy introduced by male universal suffrage not suppose both the establishment of a more egalitarian society in which every citizen has his place and the creation of institutions recognising all individual identities?

The language issue, with all it implies in matters of equality between the Flemish and the Walloons – a promise made by King Albert in his speech from the throne on November 22, 1918 – has heavily influenced political debates for several decades. In 1929 a government for the first time considers a global solution it would personally lead and be in charge of. However, when push comes to shove, the process does not follow the expected course. Nevertheless, the 1932 language legislation, introducing regional language homogeneity, can to a certain extent be seen as its result. This is a crucial moment as the then legislative arsenal continues to determine the outlines of present-day federal Belgium. However, although the new laws meet the requests of a large majority, some dream of bigger things. Their political project reaches beyond the Belgian democratic framework. But even regardless of these minorities, the 1932 laws have obviously not managed to settle the conflict. The purely language-related issues become community-related and affect an increasing number of fields. In this framework, amnesty is one of the more emblematic episodes, as it highlights varying sensibilities that, even if they do not necessarily reflect Flemish and Walloon societies in their entireties, translate dominating views leaving little or no room for nuance.

Economic crisis, political crisis?

Although Belgian economy is not immediately affected by the October 1929 stock exchange crash, it nevertheless is not completely insulated and cannot escape the tidal wave. The 4% level of unemployment of 1930 jumps to 20% in 1932. In May 1931 the Jaspar government, exhausted by four years at the helm, throws in the towel. Up till 1940, no less than seven successive Prime Ministers and ten governments try to run Belgium. In other words: the political deadlock is pervasive. Political deciders reveal themselves incapable of finding a durable solution. The regime itself is therefore questioned. Does the very essence of democracy and its parliament, do the principle of the proportional system and the compromises this entails, does the increasing influence exerted by political parties not make it impossible to solve the crisis?

With political and financial scandals making matters even worse, some voters start questioning or rejecting democracy. Belgium is not the only country facing this problem. The very question of the efficiency of democracy haunts countless European nations. On the eve of the second world conflict, eleven European countries still stand by a regime many hold to be very sick. Democracy is weakened in Belgium as well. The 1936 general elections yield landslide results. Up till then 90% of voters favoured the so-called traditional parties, even if part of the elite not yet considers the Belgian Workers' Party as such. In 1936 one voter out of every four supports the newcomers on the political scene (Rex and VNV) or the communist party. The shock to the system is enormous, even more so as the measures adopted by the outgoing government led by the young Paul Van Zeeland have somewhat straightened things out.

The economic crisis and the international tensions put Belgian democracy face to face with hitherto unseen challenges. Even more so as several men in power in the early thirties are products of the pre-1914 society. As the crisis amplifies they have to face completely new challenges, demanding the very redefinition of the State's role in economy. Over the decade's second half, a new generation of men rise to power. Some of these men stand out from the crowd within their own parties: other methods, other political cultures and therefore inevitable confrontations with established methods. This state of affairs will deeply challenge the commitment of some of them.

The year 1914 seemed to constitute a turning point in the 20th century, but 1939 is characterized by an inevitable leap towards a new hellish conflict. Belgium is once again involved against its will, in spite of the reorientation of its foreign policy: the end of the military alliance with France, the establishment of a "policy of independence" before the restoration of neutrality. Both Belgian society and its European counterparts have been unable to earn peace. The economic crisis constituted the young Belgian democracy's first shock to the system; the war will be the second one. Both of them reveal the country's defencelessness. On 10 January 1940 a German plane crashes in Belgium,

A woman poses next to a large 17-cm gun used by the former *Gneisenau* coastal battery in front of the Palace Hotel on the Ostend boardwalk. In 1923 the four guns in this battery are sold off as iron scrap.
(War Heritage Institute, Brussels, EST-1-813/77)

a few kilometres from the German border. Outlines for the invasion of the country are found on board. The idea that Belgium would somehow be able to remain outside the conflict reveals itself to be decidedly illusory. However, political preoccupations are once again elsewhere: the government narrowly escapes a new crisis in late April, when debates focus on the reorganisation of the Ministry of Public Education based on language criteria... Priorities clearly lie elsewhere. Two weeks later, Belgium is invaded.

ENDNOTEϟ

The war year 1918

1   *International Encyclopedia of the First World War* (https://encyclopedia.1914-1918-online.net); David Zabecki, *The German 1918 Offensives*, Abingdon, 2006; David Stevenson, *With our backs to the Wall: Victory and defeat in 1918*, London, 2011.

2   Marcel Weemaes, *Van de IJzer tot Brussel. Het bevrijdingsoffensief van het Belgisch leger 28 september 1918*, Marcinelle, 1969.

Between war and peace

1   A useful source of information regarding King Albert's movement is the diary of his ordnance officer, which can be consulted in digital form on the website of the State Archives of Belgium www.arch.be. See also Marcel Weemaes, *Van de IJzer tot Brussel. Het bevrijdingsoffensief van het Belgisch leger 28 september 1918*, Marcinelle, 1969.

2   Regarding the riots in Brussels: Luc Sieben, "De novemberdagen van 1918 in Brussel: revolutie en ordehandhaving", in Patrick Lefèvre and Piet De Gryse (eds.), *Van Brialmont tot de Westeuropese Unie. Bijdragen in de militaire geschiedenis aangeboden aan Albert Duchesne, Jean Lorette en Jean-Léon Charles*, Brussels, 1988, p. 155–176. A witness account in Louis Gille, Alphonse Ooms and Paul Delandsheere, *Cinquante mois d'occupation allemande*, part IV, Brussels, 1919. Another account from the Mayor's Chef de Cabinet: Auguste Vierset, *Mes souvenirs sur l'occupation allemande en Belgique*, Paris, 1932.

3   This crucial episode is studied at length in several publications by Henri Haag. See in particular Henri Haag, "Le choix du roi Albert à Loppem", in Carlos Wyffels (ed.), *Actes du colloque roi Albert*, Brussels, 1976, p. 169–191.

4   No report of that conversation exists, but its tenor can be inferred from Francqui's announcement on his return to Brussels: "At the *Société Générale*, where the National Committee meets, Mr Francqui gives (...) an account of the King's Joyous Entry (...) in Ghent. (...) He announces that the solemn arrival of the Sovereigns in the capital is pushed back to Friday November 22, mainly for political reasons, in order to allow for government to be reconstituted first." (Gille, Ooms and Delandsheere, p. 429).

5   For the entrance of the King in Brussels: Chantal Kesteloot, "Een nieuwe Blijde Intrede in het bevrijde Brussel", in *Albert & Elisabeth. De film van een koninklijk leven*, Brussels, 2014, p. 86–97. For the actions of the King: Jan Velaers, *Albert I. Koning in tijden van oorlog en crisis 1909–1934*, Tielt, 2009. For broader context: Emmanuel Gerard, *De schaduw van het interbellum. België van euforie tot crisis 1918–1939*, Tielt, 2017.

6   No literature about the OLP exists. Archive documents are the relevant sources. For example, see *Instructions pour les O.L.P.*, War Heritage Institute, Royal Military Museum archives, *Ex-CDH*, O.L.P., 351.

7   The OLP information bulletins are an important source regarding the health situation in Belgium at the time of the liberation. Much of the information in this article is based on these bulletins. See: War Heritage Institute, Royal Military Museum archives, *Ex-CDH*, O.L.P., 3875.

8   Letter from Doctor M. Art to the Chief of the Belgian Mission to the British Army, 10 December 1918, War Heritage Institute, Royal Military Museum archives, *Ex-CDH*, O.L.P., 3875, 18 December 1918, no. 110.

The American Helen John Kirtland poses next to what remains of a sea mine at the Belgian coast, ca. 1919. Kirtland is one of the first female photo journalists. During the war she works in France, for the YMCA, the American Army and Navy, and for *Leslie's Illustrated Weekly*, among others.
(Library of Congress, Washington, 2012646950)

9   The work of sociologist Ernest Mahaim is of exceptional value for research into the consequences of the First World War in Belgium. A great deal of data in this article is taken from his work. Ernest Mahaim, *La Belgique restaurée: étude sociologique*, Brussels, 1926.

10 Bernheim uses a text poster to call on the public to remain calm. This, and many other text posters that are stored in numerous archives, are an interesting source for the study of post-war Belgium. The collection in the Ghent City Archives, available at beeldbank.stad.gent, is a fine example. *Inwoners van Gent, onderofficieren, kaporalen en soldaten*. Poster announcement from Lt. Gen. Bernheim, Ghent City Archives, available for consultation at beeldbank.stad.gent, 14 November 1918.

11 There is a wealth of literature about the repression during the liberation days of October and November 1918. The following is a good start: Xavier Rousseaux and Laurence van Ypersele (eds.), *La patrie crie vengeance! La répression des "inciviques" belges au sortir de la guerre 1914–1918*, Brussels, 2008. The work of Jos Monballyu also gives a lot of fantastic insights: Jos Monballyu, *Slechte Belgen! De repressie van het incivisme na de Eerste Wereldoorlog door het Hof van Assisen van Brabant (1919–1927)*, Brussels, 2011.

12 *De Gentenaar – De Landwacht*, "Drama te Heusden", 25.12.1918, p. 3.

13 Antoon Vrints and Xavier Rousseaux, "La répression étatique d'un phénomène de crise social. Le banditisme pendant et après la Première Guerre mondiale en Belgique", in *Quand les canons se taisent, Actes du colloque international*, Brussels, 2010, p. 303.

14 *De Gentenaar – De Landwacht*, "Drama te Heusden", 25.12.1918, p. 3.

15 The full text of King Albert's address can be consulted via the website of the Belgian Chamber of Representatives: Zitting van 22 November 1918, opening van de wetgevende kamers zittingsjaar 1918–1919 (22 November 1918), http://www.dekamer.be.

16 For the occupation of the Rhineland, see Margaret Pawley's study: *The Watch on the Rhine. The Military Occupation of the Rhineland, 1918–1930*, London, 2007.

17 G.W.L. Nicholson, *Canadian Expeditionary Force, 1914–1919*, Ottawa, 1964, p. 525.

18 There are no mapping studies about the Allied presence in Belgium and France. However, a great deal of information can be gleaned from the official histories of the Allied armies. H. Stewart, *The New Zealand Division 1916–1919: A Popular History Based on Official Records*, Auckland, 1921; Benedict Crowell and Robert Forrest Wilson, *Demobilization. Our Industrial and Military Demobilization After the Armistice, 1918–1920*, New Haven, 1921; Ministère de la Guerre, État-Major de l'Armée, Service Historique, *Les Armées Françaises dans La Grande Guerre*, vol. VII, part II, Paris, 1938; Charles Bean, *The Australian Imperial Force in France during the Allied Offensive, 1918*, Sydney, 1942; G.W.L. Nicholson, *Canadian Expeditionary Force, 1914–1919*, Ottawa, 1964.

19 Charles Bean, *The Australian Imperial Force in France during the Allied Offensive, 1918*, Sydney, 1942, p. 1072.

20 For the presence of foreign troops and workers during the war, the "In Flanders Fields Museum" publication is still relevant. It deals with not only the period 1914–1918, but regularly references the post-war period. The issue of prisoners of war is also discussed. Dominiek Dendooven and Piet Chielens (eds.), *World War One: Five Continents in Flanders*, Tielt, 2009.

21 For the German prisoners of war in Belgium before and during the war, the two unpublished inventories of Erik Janssen are very important, as is the inventory of Hans Vanden Bosch, *Inventaris van het archief van de Belgische Middendienst voor de krijgsgevangenen, 1914–1925*, Brussels, 2009; Erik Janssen, *Inventaris van het archief van de Dienst voor de Duitse Krijgsgevangenen van de Belgische Middendienst voor de Krijgsgevangenen, 1914–1924 (1922–1926)*, unpublished inventory, Brussels, 2011; Erik Janssen, *Inventaris van het archief van het Korps van de Krijgsgevangenen [1914] 1918–1921*, unpublished inventory, Brussels, 2011.

22 Michaël Amara, *Des Belges à l'épreuve de l'Exil. Les réfugiés de la Première Guerre mondiale (France, Grande-Bretagne, Pays-Bas)*, Brussels, 2008, p. 368–373.

23 Michaël Amara, "Des exilés à l'heure du retour. Les réfugiés en Belgique à la fin de la Première Guerre mondiale (1918–1919)", in Pierre-Alain Tallier and Patrick Nefors (eds.), *Quand les canons se taisent – En toen zwegen de kanonnen*, Brussels, 2010, p. 217–218.

24 *Office central belge pour les Prisonniers de Guerre. Quatrième et dernier rapport (Septembre 1917 – Mars 1924)*, Brussels, p. 529–583.

25 National Archives of Belgium (NAB), Minutes of the Council of Ministers, Minutes of 10th December 1918.

A new world

1   Margaret MacMillan, *Paris 1919. Six Months that Changed the World*, New York, 2002; Annie Deperchin, "La conférence de paix" – "Les traités de paix" – "L'application des traités", in Stéphane Audoin-Rouzeau and

Jean-Jacques Becker (eds.), *Encyclopédie de la Grande Guerre 1914–1918: Histoire et culture*, Paris, 2004, p. 993–1030; Bo Manfred Memke, Gerald D. Feldman and Elisabeth Glaser, *The Treaty of Versailles. A Reassessment after 75 Years*, Cambridge, 2006; Jean-Jacques Becker, "Les conséquences des traités de paix", in *Revue historique des armées*, 254, 2009, online 15 March 2009, consulted 3rd of February 2018; Carole Fink, "The Peace Settlement, 1919–1939", in John Horne (ed.), *A Companion to World War I* (Blackwell Companions to World History), Chichester, 2010, p. 544–557; Helmut Konrad, "Bâtir la paix", in Jay Winter (ed.), *La Première Guerre mondiale. Vol. II: Etats* (Cambridge History), coordinated by Annette Becker, Paris, 2014, p. 647–678 (original English edition: Cambridge University Press, 2014); Alan Sharp, "The Paris Peace Conference and its Consequences", in Daniel Ute, Peter Gatrell, et al. (eds.), *1914–1918-online, International Encyclopedia of the First World War*, Berlin, 2014-10-08.

2   See, for example, J.M. Keynes, *The Economic Consequences of the Peace* [1919].

3   Peter Haslinger, "Saint-Germain, Treaty of", in Daniel Ute, et al. (eds.), *1914–1918-online*, Berlin, 2016-12-06.

4   Stefan Marinov Minkov, "Neuilly-sur-Seine, Treaty of", in Daniel Ute, et al. (eds.), *1914–1918-online*, Berlin, 2017-02-20.

5   Miklós Zeidler, "Trianon, Treaty of", in Daniel Ute, et al. (eds.), *1914–1918-online*, Berlin, 2014-10-08.

6   Leonard V. Smith, "Post-war Treaties (Ottoman Empire/ Middle East)", in Daniel Ute, et al. (eds.), *1914–1918-online*, Berlin, 2014-10-08.

7   See Henry Kissinger, *Diplomacy*, Paris, 1996, p. 203 ff.

8   Denise Artaud and André Kaspi, *Histoire des États-Unis*, Paris, 1969, p. 175.

9   Général J. E. Valluy and Pierre Dufourcq, *La Première Guerre mondiale, Vol. 2, 1916–1918*, Paris, 1968, p. 133.

10   Raymond Cartier, *Le Monde entre deux guerres, 1919–1939*, Paris, 1969, p. 15 ff.

11   Quoted in Paul.-F. Smets, *Paul Hymans, un authentique homme d'État*, Brussels, 2015, p. 237–238.

12   Jean Monnet, *Mémoires*, Paris, 1976, p. 98.

13   From 1918 to 1929, its official name was the "Kingdom of Serb, Croats, and Slovenes".

14   The present territories of Rwanda, Burundi and part of Tanzania.

15   See Isidore Ndaywel è Nziem and Pamphile Mabiala Mantuba-Ngoma, *Le Congo belge dans la Première Guerre mondiale (1914–1918)*, RDC, 2015; Guy Vanthemsche (ed.), *Le Congo belge pendant la Première Guerre mondiale. Les rapports du Ministre des Colonies Jules Renkin au roi Albert Ier 1914–1918*, Brussels, 2009; Jan De Waele, *Voor Vorst en Vaderland: de situatie van zwarte soldaten en dragers in dienst van het Belgisch Leger (Force Publique) tijdens de Eerste Wereldoorlog in Centraal-Afrika*, unpublished master's thesis, Vrije Universiteit Brussel, 2000–2001.

16   Frans van Kalken (ed.), *Paul Hymans: mémoires*, Brussels, p. 336–343 and 453–461.

17   The mandate system must be seen as a form of temporary administration meant to stop when the mandated territory has reached self-determination. Under the control of the Permanent Mandates Commission, the mandatory authority has the obligation to guide the populations of the mandated territory towards autonomy first and then complete independence. There are three classes of mandates named by the letters A, B and C. Mandate A applies to a part of the territories of the former Ottoman Empire that were considered almost independent (Syria, Iraq, Lebanon and Palestine). Mandate C concerned South West Africa and the Pacific Islands. The former German colonies of Africa, whose state of development was considered inferior to those of the A mandate, are governed by the mandate B. Susan Pedersen, "The Meaning of the Mandates System: An Argument", in *Geschicht und Gesellschaft*, 32, 2004, p. 560–582.

18   See Roger William Louis, *Ruanda-Urundi 1884–1919*, Oxford, 1963, p. 231 ff.

19   Service Public Fédéral Affaires Etrangères (SPFAE), Archives Diplomatiques (AD), AF 1.4. Report of Orts-Milner's interview, Paris, 12.05.1919.

20   SPFAE, AD, AF 1.4. Compte-rendu de l'entretien Orts-Milner, Paris, 15.05.1919.

21   SPFAE, AD, AF 1.4. Pierre Orts à Octave Louwers, Paris, 19.05.1919.

22   Jean Rumiya, *Le Ruanda sous le régime du mandat belge (1918–1931)*, Paris, 1992, p. 86–88.

23   Pierre Orts, "The Claim for Colonies: A Belgian View", in *Journal of the Royal African Society*, 36, No. 142, Jan. 1937, p. 25; "Belgian Mandate for East Africa", in *The American Journal of International Law*, 17, No. 3, Suppl. Official Documents, 1923, p. 149.

24   This article made use of the following literature: Eric J. Hobsbawn, *Nations and Nationalism since 1780. Programme, Myth, Reality*, Cambridge, 1990; Edward Said, *Culture and Imperialism*, New York, 1998; Michael Hardt and Antonio Negri, *Empire*, Cambridge/London, 2000; Niall Ferguson, *Empire: How Britain Made the Modern World*, London, 2004; Eric Walberg, *Postmodern Imperialism: Geopolitics and the Great Games*, Atlanta, 2011; Claire Delahaye and Serge Ricard, *L'héritage de Théodore Roosevelt: impérialisme et progressisme (1912–2012)*, Paris, 2012.

25 For literature, see: *Documents diplomatiques belges 1920–1940*, Brussels, vol. 1-2, 1964; Guido Provoost, *Vlaanderen en het militair politiek beleid in België tussen de twee wereldoorlogen*, Louvain, vol. 1-2, 1976–1977; Fernand Vanlangenhove, *L'élaboration de la politique étrangère de la Belgique entre les deux guerres mondiales*, Brussels, 1980; Sally Marks, *Innocent Abroad. Belgium at the Paris Peace Conference of 1919*, Chapel Hill, 1981; Eric Bussière, *La France, la Belgique et l'organisation économique de l'Europe, 1918–1935*, Paris, 1992; Rolande Depoortere, *La question des réparations allemandes dans la politique étrangère de la Belgique après la première guerre mondiale 1919–1925*, Brussels, 1997; Rik Coolsaet, *België en zijn buitenlandse politiek 1830–2015*, Louvain, sixth edition, 2014.

Rising from the ashes

1   Jan Blomme, *The Economic Development of Belgian Agriculture, 1880–1980. A Quantitative and Qualitative Analysis*, Brussels, 1992, p. 293.

2   Fernand Baudhuin, *Histoire économique de la Belgique, 1914–1939*, part 1, Brussels, 1946, p. 74.

3   René Brion and Jean-Louis Moreau, *De Generale Maatschappij van België, 1822–1997*, Antwerp, 1998, p. 257.

4   Joseph Pirard, *L'extension du rôle de l'Etat en Belgique aux XIXe et XXe siècles*, Brussels, 1999, p. 839.

5   Valéry Janssens, *De Belgische frank. Anderhalve eeuw geldgeschiedenis*, Antwerp, 1976, p. 173.

6   Rolande Depoortere, "La Belgique et les réparations allemandes: la grande illusion", in *Comment (se) sortir de la Grande Guerre. Regards sur quelques pays "vainqueurs": la Belgique, la France et la Grande-Bretagne*, Paris, 2005, p. 127.

7   Sophie De Schaepdrijver, *La Belgique et la Première Guerre mondiale*, Brussels, 2004, p. 292.

8   *Fonds Roi Albert. Habitations pour les Belges sans-abri*, Paris, 1917, p. 15–16.

9   Pierre-Alain Tallier, "L'annexion des cantons d'Eupen-Malmedy et la reconstitution du patrimoine forestier belge après la Première Guerre mondiale. Le rôle prépondérant de l'administration forestière et de son directeur général Nestor Iris Crahay", in *Forêt wallonne*, No. 67, 2003, p. 2–11.

10 Rolande Depoortere, "La Belgique et les réparations allemandes", p. 127–128.

11 R. Gobyn, "La crise du logement et le problème du logement provisoire en Belgique après la Première Guerre mondiale", in *Resurgam: La reconstruction après 1918 en Belgique*, Brussels, 1985, p. 169–188.

12 Sven Carnel gives a series of figures put forward at the time in *La reconstruction des régions dévastées après la Première Guerre mondiale: le cas de Neuve-Église*, Brussels, Archives générales du Royaume, 2002, p. 48–50.

13 *Het Ypersche/La Région d'Ypres*, "Waar is de rechtvaardigheid", 14 August 1920, p. 1.

14 André De Naeyer, "La reconstruction des monuments et des sites en Belgique après la Première Guerre mondiale", in *Monumentum*, 20–22, 1982, p. 172.

15 *La Cité*, "Les urbanistes des pays amis soutiennent nos efforts", No. 1, July 1919, p. 4.

16 André De Naeyer, "La reconstruction des monuments et des sites en Belgique après la Première Guerre mondiale", p. 168.

17 Camille Joset, *Une grande œuvre de guerre belge. Le Fonds du Roi Albert,* Brussels, 1925; *Fonds Roi Albert. Habitations pour les Belges sans-abri*, Paris, 1917.

18 G. Smets, "Les Régions dévastées et la réparation des dommages de guerre", in Ernest Mahaim, *La Belgique restaurée*, Brussels, 1926, p. 112.

19 Sven Carnel, *La reconstruction des régions dévastées*, p. 56.

20 Alexandre Notebaert, Christel Neumann and Willem Vanden Eynde, *Inventaire des archives de l'Office des Régions dévastées*, Brussels, Archives Générales du Royaume, 1986, p. 39; *Moniteur belge*, 24–26 October 1918, p. 866–876; G. Smets, "Les régions dévastées et la réparation", p. 78–79.

21 Sven Carnel, "Entre espoir et désillusion. Le retour des sinistrés dans les régions dévastées après la Première Guerre mondiale", in *Une guerre totale? La Belgique dans la Première Guerre mondiale: nouvelles tendances de la recherche historique*, minutes of the international colloquium held at ULB from 15 to 17 January 2003, Brussels, Archives générales du Royaume, 2005, p. 495.

22 André De Naeyer, "La reconstruction des monuments et des sites", p. 170.

23 Extract from the Law on the national adoption of towns and the restoration of devastated regions, quoted here by the Mayor of Ypres, René Colaert. Ypres, Ieper Stadsarchief, Verslagen gemeenteraad, Boek 1, Session of 12 July 1919, p. 23.

24 *Moniteur belge*, 22–23 April 1919, p. 1657–1660.

25 Alexandre Notebaert, Christel Neumann and Willem Vanden Eynde, *Inventaire des archives*, p. 14–17.

26 Sophie De Schaepdrijver, *La Belgique et la Première Guerre mondiale*, p. 294.

27 Emmanuelle Danchin, *Le temps des ruines, 1914–1921*, Rennes, 2015.

28 Kervyn De Lettenhove, "Les ruines en Belgique", extract from the *Gazette des Beaux-Arts*, Paris, [1916], p. 244–246.

29 Hugh Clout, "The Great Reconstruction of Towns and Cities in France 1918–35", in *Planning perspectives*, Jan. 2005, vol. 20, p. 2.

30 The Union of Belgian towns and cities met every week in occupied Belgium. "Discours de M. le Gouverneur Béco, Président", in *Mouvement communal*, No. 9–10, July 1919, p. 99–101. For the circulation of modernist ideas during the War, see: Pieter Uyttenhove, "Les efforts internationaux pour une Belgique modern", in *Resurgam*, p. 33–70.

31 Council of Ministers, Minutes of Meetings, Meeting of 16 January 1919, p. 4–5.

32 Koen Baert, "De terugkeer. Aspecten van de herbevolking van Ieper na 1918", in *Ieper, de herrezenstad, de wederop-bouw in Ieper na 14-18*, Kortrijk, 1999, p. 9–20; Sven Carnel, "Entre espoir et désillusion. Le retour des sinistrés dans les régions dévastées après la Première Guerre mondiale", in *Une guerre totale?...*, p. 503–505.

33 There were a few exceptions, such as the building of a Cubist church by Architect Huib Hoste at Zonnebeke, which was greeted with anything but unanimity by the locals. Aleks A. M. Deseyne, *Huib Hoste en de wederop-bouw te Zonnebeke*, Zonnebeke, 1981. See also: Marcel Smets, *L'avènement de la cité-jardin en Belgique: histoire de l'habitat social en Belgique de 1830 à 1930*, Brussels, 1977.

34 Johan Meire, *De stilte van de Salient, herinnering van de eerste wereldoorlog rond Ieper*, Tielt, 2003, p. 118–126.

35 Dominiek Dendooven, *Menin Gate & Last Post: Ypres as Holy Ground*, Koksijde, 2001; Delphine Lauwers, *Le Saillant d'Ypres entre reconstruction et construction d'un lieu de mémoire. Un long processus de négociations mémorielles de 1914 à nos jours*, PhD thesis in preparation, European University Institute, Florence.

36 *Het Ypersche*, "Yper's triomfdag", 4.08.1934, p. 1.

37 Robert Baccarne and Jan Steen, *Poelkapelle 1914–1918*, Wervik, 1965, p. 155–162; Franky Bostyn and Dominiek Dendooven, "Landschap en Wereldoorlog I", in *Landschap en Herinnering in de Zuidelijke Westhoek*, Ypres, 2004, p. 2–5; Sven Carnel, *La reconstruction des régions dévastées après la Première Guerre Mondiale. Le cas de Neuve-Eglise*, Brussels, 2002, p. 58, 151; Dries Claeys, "World War I and the Reconstruction of Rural Landscapes in Belgium and France. A Historiographical Essay", in *Agricultural History Review*, 2017 (65), p. 108–129; Hugh Clout, *After the Ruins: Restoring the Countryside of Northern France after the Great War*, Exeter, 1996; André Deseyne and Aleks Deseyne, *Zonnebeke 1914–1918: Dood en heropstanding van een dorp*, Zonnebeke, 1976; Raphaël Verwilghen, L. Boereboom, et al., *Nieuw-Vlaanderen*, Antwerp, 1923.

38 Sven Carnel, *La reconstruction des Régions Dévastées*, p. 102–104, 159–161; Jeroen Cornilly and Chris Vandewalle, "Onzichtbare pleitbezorgers. Tussen bewoners en hogere overheden", in Jeroen Cornilly, et al., *Bouwen aan wederopbouw 1914/2050. Architectuur in de Westhoek*, Ypres, 2009, p. 51–73; Sofie De Caigny, et al., *Het Gekwetste Gewest. Onderzoeksgids van de wederopbouwarchitectuur in de Westhoek*, Antwerp, 2009; John Desreumaux, *Land van schroot en knoken. Slachtoffers van ontploffingen in de frontstreek 1918-heden*, Louvain, 2011, p. 11–15; Mathieu Gilot, *Onze Werking in Verwoest Vlaanderen. Beknopt overzicht der werkzaamheden van onzen 'Dienst voor herstel van West-Vlaanderen'*, Roeselare, 1921, p. 39–41; Steven Heyde, "Het herstel van het bocagelandschap in de zuidelijke Westhoek na de Eerste Wereldoorlog", in *M&L. Monumenten, Landschappen en Archeologie*, 33, 2014, p. 28–41; Lambertus Hortensius, *Burgers, boeren. Hun goed, hun vee. De frontstreek na 1914–1918*, Louvain, 1989, unpushlished master's thesis, p. 121–125; Marcel Pauwels and Norman Vanoverbeke, "De wederopbouw", in *Halfweg Menin Road en Ypernstrasse. Gheluvelt 1914–1918*, Voormezele, 2002, p. 240–253; Patricia Vyvey, *De landbouw in het arrondissement Veurne (1880–1930)*, unpublished master's thesis, Ghent University, 1982.

39 Koen Baert. "Wonen in de verwoesting. Omstandigheden en getuigen", in *Bouwen aan wederopbouw 1914/2050*, Ypres, 2009, p. 17–41; Jean-Marie Bailleul, *Problematiek omtrent de wederopbouw van België na de Eerste Wereld-oorlog. Casus Ieper en omgeving (1918–1924)*, unpublished master's thesis, Ghent University, 1976; André Deseyne and Aleks Deseyne, *Zonnebeke 1914–1918*; Dominiek Dendooven, "Het terrein effenen. Aanleg, infrastructuur en landbeheer", in *Bouwen aan wederopbouw 1914/2050. Architectuur in de Westhoek*, Ypres, 2009, p. 81–106; Steven Heyde, "Het herstel van het bocagelandschap in de zuidelijke Westhoek na de Eerste Wereldoorlog", p. 37–38; Steven Heyde, et al., *Kasteeldomeinen 1795–2015. Historische tuinen en parken in de zuidelijke Westhoek*, Tielt, 2015; Lieven Stubbe, "Planten en de Eerste Wereldoorlog", in *De Bron*, 2008 (3), p. 19–22; Pierre-Alain Tallier, "La reconstruction du patrimoine forestier Belge après 1918", in *Forêt et Guerre*, Paris, 1994, p. 215–311; J. Verpaalen, *Molens van de Frontstreek*, Koksijde, 1995.

40 Franky Bostyn, "De ijzeren oogst", in *Halfweg Menin Road en Ypernstrasse. Gheluvelt 1914–1918*, Voormezele, 2002, p. 286; Franky Bostyn and Dominiek Dendooven, "Landschap en Wereldoorlog I", p. 2–5; Sven Carnel, "La reconstruction agricole dans les régions dévastées", in *Memoires de la société d'histoire de Comines-Warneton et*

de la region, 38, 2008, p. 257–276; Sofie De Caigny, "Tussen filantropie en macht. In de bres voor de belangen van hun achterban", in *Bouwen aan wederopbouw 1914/2050, Architectuur in de Westhoek Ieper*, 2009, p. 149–170; Mathieu Gilot, *Onze Werking in Verwoest Vlaanderen*; Raphaël Verwilghen, L. Boereboom, et al., *Nieuw-Vlaanderen*, p. 32 ff.; Patricia Vyvey, *De landbouw in het arrondissement Veurne (1880–1930)*; Marc Van Meirvenne, Bert Van Goidsenhoven, et al., *Studie naar de aanwezigheid van zware metalen in de bodem rond Ieper als gevolg van de Eerste Wereldoorlog*, Mechelen, 2009.

41 Franky Bostyn and Jan Vancoillie, *Bayernwald: Het Croonaertbos in de Eerste Wereldoorlog*, Zonnebeke, 2000, p. 85–87; Franky Bostyn, "De ijzeren oogst", in *Halfweg Menin Road en Ypernstrasse. Gheluvelt 1914–1918*, Voormezele, 2002, p. 287; Pieter Craenen, *Historiek van de Belgische Ontmijningsdienst*, unpublished master's thesis, Royal Military Academy, 1989; Siegfried Debaeke, *Oud ijzer. De frontstreek bedolven onder levensgevaarlijke oorlogsmunitie*, Bruges, 2010; John Desreumaux, *Land van schroot en knoken. Slachtoffers van ontploffingen in de frontstreek 1918-heden*, Louvain, 2011; Jean-Pascal Zander, "The Destruction of Old Chemical Munitions in Belgium", in Thomas Stock and Karlheinz Lohs (eds.), *The Challenge of Old Chemical Munitions and Toxic Armament Wastes*, Oxford, 1997, p. 201–206.

42 Franky Bostyn, Frans Descamps, et al., *Passchendaele 1917: Het verhaal van de doden en Tyne Cot Cemetery*, Roeselare, 2007, p. 223–231; Jan Vancoillie, *De Duitse militaire begraafplaats Menen Wald. Geschiedenis van de Duitse militaire graven van de eerste Wereldoorlog in Zuid-West-Vlaanderen*, Wevelgem, 2013, p. 31–53.

43 Robert Baccarne, et al., *Poelcapelle 1917, een spoor van tankwrakken*, Poelkapelle, 2007; Franky Bostyn and Dominiek Dendooven, "De Westhoek en het stenen erfgoed van de Eerste Wereldoorlog", in *Steen in de Zuidelijke Westhoek*, Ypres, 2003, p. 3–4; Robert Baccarne, et al., *Poelcapelle 1917, een spoor van tankwrakken*, Poelkapelle, 2007.

44 Delphine Lauwers, *Le tourisme de guerre en Belgique 1918–1939*, unpublished master's thesis, ULB, 2005.

45 Franky Bostyn and Dominiek Dendooven, "Landschap en Wereldoorlog I", p. 2–5; Franky Bostyn, Steven Heyde, et al., "Naar een integrale benadering van het oorlogslandschap. Bijdrage tot de ontwikkeling van een waarderingsmethodiek voor landschap en cultuurhistorie op lokale schaal – Proefproject Zonnebeke-Passendale (W.Vl.)", in *Relicta*, 11, 2015, p. 351–383; Dries Claeys, *World War I and the Reconstruction of Rural Landscapes in Belgium and France*, p. 108–129.

A new Belgium

1   Sophie de Schaepdrijver, *La Belgique et la Première Guerre mondiale*, Brussels, 2004; Serge Jaumain, et al. (eds.), *Une Guerre totale? La Belgique dans la Première Guerre mondiale. Nouvelles tendances de la recherche historique*, Brussels, 2005.

2   Emmanuel Gerard, *La démocratie rêvée, bridée et bafouée: 1918–1939. Nouvelle histoire de Belgique*, Brussel, 2006, vol. 2.

3   Jean Puissant, René Leboutte and Denis Scuto, *Un siècle d'histoire industrielle: Belgique, Luxembourg, Pays-Bas; Industrialisation et sociétés 1873–1973*, Paris, 1998, p. 137–160.

4   Dirk Luyten, "Guerre, dépression économique et contestation de la démocratie (1914-1944)", in Els Witte, Alain Meynen and Dirk Luyten, *Histoire politique de la Belgique*, Brussels, 2017, p. 177–285; Eliane Gubin, "Les femmes et la citoyenneté en Belgique. Histoire d'un malentendu", in *Sextant*, 7, 1997, p. 163–187.

5   Antoon Vrints, "Offers in balans. Hoop en wanhoop van de Belgische soldaten (1914–1918)", in *Bijdragen tot de Eigentijdse Geschiedenis*, 17, 2006, p. 237–251.

6   A.P. Chamber, 1920–1921, question De Beuckelaere, No. 219, 12 April 1921.

7   Gita Deneckere, "Oudstrijders op de vuist in Brussel. Het amnestieconflict tijdens het Interbellum", in *Belgisch Tijdschrift voor Nieuwste Geschiedenis*, 25, 1995, 3-4, p. 273–277.

8   Stefan De Bock, *De oud-strijders van de Eerste Wereldoorlog en de Belgische maatschappij (1918–1923)*, unpublished master's thesis, Ghent University, 2009, p. 54–67.

9   Jos Declerck, *Histoire Anecdotique de la Fédération Nationale des Combattants*, Brussels, 1920, p. 30.

10 Martin Schoups, *Woekeraars, uithongeraars, accapareurs, sjacheraars, opkopers, uitzuigers en zeepbaronnen. Prijscontestatie in België na de Eerste Wereldoorlog, 1918–1924*, unpublished master's thesis, Ghent University, 2016, p. 195–202.

11 Antoine Prost, *Les anciens combattants et la société française: Mentalité et idéologie*, Paris, 1977; Alain Colignon, *Les Anciens combattants en Belgique francophone, 1918–1940*, Liège, 1984; Bruno Cabanes, *La victoire endeuillée: la sortie de guerre des soldats français 1918–1920*, Paris, 2004; Bruno Cabanes and Guillaume Piketty, *Retour à l'intime au sortir de la guerre*, Paris, 2009; Stefan De Bock, *Erkenning voor "onze helden van den IJzer"?*

De oud-strijders van de Eerste Wereldoorlog en de Belgische maatschappij (1918–1923), unpublished master's thesis, Ghent University, 2009; Dominique Fouchard, "Le retour des soldats de la Première Guerre mondiale: l'impossible démobilisation intime", in *Les Chemins de la Mémoire*, Defence Ministry, Paris, May 2009, 194, p. 7–10.

12 Deborah Cohen, *The War Comes Home. Disabled Veterans in Britain and Germany, 1914–1939*, Berkeley/Los Angeles, 2001; Sophie Delaporte, "Le corps et la parole des mutilés de la Grande Guerre", in *Guerres mondiales et conflits contemporains*, 205, March 2002, p. 5–14; Marina Larsson, *Shattered Anzacs, Living with the Scars of War*, Sidney, 2009.

13 Broeders van liefde, Ghent, Zelzate archives. Box "Hist. Overzicht, Instituut Sint-Jan-Baptist in Zelzate. Een beknopt historisch overzicht." Broeder Warner, "Psychiatrisch Instituut Sint-Jan-Baptist in Zelzate", in *Sint Laurensklok, driemaandelijks tijdschrift Broeders van liefde*, 45, 2 (1972–1973), p. 19–20.

14 A.P. Chamber, 1918–1919, Proposal by Minister of Finance L. Delacroix (also Prime Minister) on 09.04.1919 (p. 760), adopted by the Chamber on 02.07.1919 (p. 1168–1174), adopted by the Senate on 29.07.1919 (p. 490).

15 *L'invalide belge*, 10.05.1919; *Le Soir*, 21.07.1919, 23.10.1919, 02.11.1919; *Vingt-cinq années d'activité, 1919–1945*, Œuvre Nationale des Invalides de la guerre, Brussels, 1945; JMO 1921 (1), Circular regarding the medical care to provided for disabled war veterans, 08.06.1921, p. 851–853; Dr. Léon Wilmaers, "L'hôpital militaire de Bonsecours", in *Archives médicales belges*, December 1919; Sophie Delaporte, *Le corps et la parole des mutilés*, Paris, 2003, p. 5–14.

16 Published in the *Moniteur* on 06.12.1919.

17 Luc Somerhausen, *Essai sur les origines et l'évolution du droit à réparation des victimes militaires des guerres*, Centre for Military History, 11, Brussels, 1974, p. 60–61; Sonja Van 'T Hof, "A Kaleidoscope of Victimhood. Le Cas de la Belgique", in Jolande Withuis and Annet Mooij (eds.), *The Politics of War Trauma. The aftermath of World War II in eleven European countries*, Amsterdam, 2010, p. 63–66.

18 A. Dorteuil, *Mémento du démobilisé. Guide pratique, simple et complet d'après les documents officiels*, Brussels, 1919.

19 A.P. Chamber, 1920, 27.07.1920, p. 2116.

20 *Le rapport Francqui et les pensions d'invalidité*, Fédération Nationale des Invalides de Guerre, Brussels, 1932.

21 *L'invalide belge*, 25.02.1919; Alain Colignon, *Les Anciens combattants en Belgique francophone, 1918–1940*, Liège, 1984, p. 50–57; Stefan De Bock, *Erkenning voor "onze helden van den IJzer"? De oud-strijders van de Eerste Wereldoorlog en de Belgische maatschappij (1918–1923)*, unpublished master's thesis, Ghent University, 2009, p. 29.

22 *L'invalide belge*, May 1919. The ONIG was the forerunner of the INIG, which, as of 1ˢᵗ May 2017, is one of the members of the War Heritage Institute.

23 For example, the *Maison des Invalides* at the rue de Laeken, which was opened in July 1919 thanks to the intervention of Countess Jean de Merode.

24 Sophie de Schaepdrijver, "Death is Elsewhere: the Shifting Locus of Tragedy in Belgian Great War Literature", in *Yale French Studies*, 102, 2002, p. 94–114.

25 Regarding a soldier interned at Zelzate, memo to the Pension Department, 03.02.1925, MRA, military record.

26 Sabine Keintz, "Quelle place pour les héros mutilés? Les invalides de guerre entre intégration et exclusion", in *14–18 Aujourd'hui*, 4, 2001, p. 151–165.

27 The East Cantons consisted of the nine communities of the present German-speaking Community of Belgium plus the two communities of Malmedy and Waimes; the historic development of La Calamine was different.

28 Quoted from Klaus Pabst, "Eupen-Malmedy in der belgischen Regierungs- und Parteienpolitik 1914–1940", in *Zeitschrift des Aachener Geschichtsvereins*, 76, 1964, p. 267–268.

29 Louis de Brouckère, "Eupen et Malmédy", in *Le Peuple*, 7.1.1919, p. 1.

30 Jean Stengers, "Histoire de la législation électorale en Belgique", in *Revue belge de philologie et d'histoire*, 82, 2004, p. 254.

31 Anne-Emmanuelle Bourgaux, *La démocratisation du gouvernement représentatif en Belgique: une promesse oubliée?*, unpublished PhD thesis, ULB, 2013.

32 Richard Boijen, *De taalwetgeving in het Belgische leger (1830–1940)*, Brussels, 1992, p. 76.

33 Henri Carton de Wiart, *Souvenirs politiques (1918–1951)*, Brussels, 1981, p. 48–49.

34 José Gotovitch, "La peur du rouge dans les dossiers de la justice belge: la signification du procès de 1923", in Pascal Delwit and José Gotovitch (eds.), *La peur du rouge*, Brussels, 1996, p. 87–97.

35 Gita Deneckere, "Het 'rode gevaar' tijdens het interbellum. Of hoe de waan van een wereldwijd communistisch complot de werkelijkheid beïnvloedde", in *Brood en Rozen*, 2, 1997, No. 4, p. 49–65; Marc Swennen, *Les mouvements anticommunistes dans les années 1920*, Brussels, 2010.

36 National Archives of Belgium, Archive, Belgian Ministry of Foreign Affairs, *Question flamande* (1918–1934), B.257, Letter from *Lt.-gen.* Coppejans to Chief of Staff of the occupying army in the Rhineland, 3ʳᵈ of March 1919;

Idem, letter from Paul Hymans to Rolin-Jacquemyns, 15ᵗʰ of March 1920; *Idem, Auswärtiges Amt, Akten Belgien,* Microfilms FNRS, 44, Bd. 16, no. 63, A4259: telegram 11 February 1919.

37 Paul van Ostaijen, *Verzameld werk. Deel 4: proza. Besprekingen en beschouwingen,* Amsterdam, 1979, p. 118–126.

38 Emmanuel Gerard, *De schaduw van het interbellum. België van euforie tot crisis 1918–1939,* Tielt, 2017, p. 67.

39 Paul Aron, «Romain Rolland, Henri Barbusse et leurs amis belges: l'efficacité d'un réseau politico-littéraire», in Robert Frickx (ed.), *Les relations littéraires franco-belges de 1914 à 1940,* Brussels, 1990, p. 29–54; Geert Buelens, Matthijs de Ridder and Jan Stuyck (eds.), *De trust der vaderlandsliefde. Over literatuur en Vlaamse Beweging, 1890–1940,* Antwerp, 2005; Bibiane Fréché, "L'Art Libre (1919–1921) et les réseaux intellectuels internationalistes", in Hubert Roland and Stéphanie Vanasten (eds.), *Les nouvelles voies du comparatisme,* Ghent, 2010, p. 71–83.

40 Hubert Roland, "Paul Colin et la réception de l'expressionnisme en Belgique francophone dans l'entre-deux-guerres", in *Textyles,* No. 20, 2001, p, 45.

41 Francine Bolle, "L'extrême gauche syndicale dans les mouvements de grève (1919–1924). Les contestataires radicaux et la Belgique", in Anne Morelli and José Gotovitch (eds.), *Contester dans un pays prospère. L'extrême gauche en Belgique et au Canada,* Brussels, 2007, p. 37–63.

42 Hendrik Elias, *Vijfentwintig jaar Vlaamse beweging 1914–1939, dl. 2,* Antwerp, 1971–1972, p. 74, 80–81.

43 Jozef Simons, *Eer Vlaanderen vergaat,* Kapellen, 1999 (1927), p. 118–120.

The remembrance of war

1 Burr Price, *Louvain Liége [sic],* Brussels, 1919, p. 5.

2 *Itinéraire descriptif des champs de bataille de Belgique, avec carte détaillée. Itinéraire n° 1: Vilvorde - Pont-Brûlé – Eppeghem – Weerde – Elewyt – Hofstade - Houthem-Perck,* Brussels, [1914].

3 Foske Rozeboom, *Oorlog als attractie. De musealisering van de Eerste Wereldoorlog: Sanctuary Wood Museum Hill 62,* Amsterdam, 2009, p. 12.

4 *Bulletin officiel du Touring Club de Belgique,* 1 October 1920, p. 456.

5 Regarding school field trips, see: Tine Hens in collaboration with Saartje Vanden Borre and Kaat Wils, *Oorlog in tijden van vrede. De Eerste Wereldoorlog in de klas, 1919–1940,* Kalmthout, 2015.

6 Death becomes taboo for pilgrims as well. See: Dominique Vanneste and Caroline Winter, "First World War Battlefield Tourism: Journeys Out of the Dark and Into the Light", in Philip Stone, Rudi Hartmann, Tony Seaton, Richard Sharpley and Leanne White (eds.), *The Palgrave Handbook of Dark Tourism Studies,* London, 2018, p. 443–467.

7 *L'Echo d'Ostende,* 10 October 1920, p. 3.

8 *Bulletin officiel du Touring Club de Belgique,* 15 August 1920, p. 379.

9 George Mosse, *Fallen Soldiers. Reshaping the Memory of the World Wars,* New York, 1990, p. 126.

10 Ralph Hale Mottram, *Journey to the Western Front. Twenty Years After,* London, 1936, p. 44.

11 Annette Becker, *Oubliés de la Grande Guerre 1914–1918: Populations occupées, déportés civils, prisonniers de guerre,* Paris, 1998.

12 Mariette Jacobs, *Zij die vielen als helden... Cultuurhistorische analyse van de oorlogsgedenktekens van de twee wereldoorlogen in West-Vlaanderen,* vol. 1, Bruges, 1995.

13 Bruno Benvindo and Evert Peeters, *Les décombres de la guerre: mémoires belges en conflit, 1945–2010,* Waterloo, 2012.

14 Unless otherwise stated, we refer for all sources and references to Wannes Devos, *Het gealiëneerd museum. Musealisering van oorlog en geschiedenis in militaire musea. De casestudy van het Koninklijk Legermuseum,* ongoing PhD research, Ghent University. Quote from: Minutes from a letter Théophile Théodore baron Jamblinne de Meux, director of Royal Army Museum, to the director of the *Commission Centrale de la Récupération,* 19 September 1919, War Heritage Institute, Documentation Centre of the Royal Army Museum, Archives of the Institution.

15 Jay Winter, *Remembering War: The Great War and Historical Memory in the Twentieth Century,* New Haven, 2006; Liesbet Nys, *De intrede van het publiek: museumbezoek in België, 1830–1914,* Louvain, 2012, p. 253–272.

16 For the operation of other Belgian museums during the First World War, see: Anneleen Arnout, "Archimedes achterna. De Belgische musea tijdens de Eerste Wereldoorlog", in *Bijdragen tot de Eigentijdse Geschiedenis,* 22, 2010, p. 55–92. For the operation of the Military Museum in Brussels (and an alternative Military Museum in Le Havre), see: Wannes Devos, "Het Koninklijk Legermuseum: een pantheon voor de natie", in Chantal Kesteloot and Laurence Van Ypersele (eds.), *La Belgique et la Grande Guerre: du café liégeois au soldat inconnu,* Brussels, 2018.

17   Note from Théophile Théodore baron Jamblinne de Meux, director of the Royal Army Museum, February 1921, War Heritage Institute, Documentation Centre of the Royal Army Museum, Archives of the Institution.

18   Royal Decree of 17 June 1919. Published in *Belgisch Staatsblad* (Belgian Official Gazette), 11 July 1919, p. 3210.

19   Commonly, a distinction is made between four dimensions of remembrance: individual, social, political and cultural. See Aleida Assmann, *Der lange Schatten der Vergangenheit*, Munich, 2006, p. 21–61.

20   Wetsontwerp aangaande de politie over de militaire begraafplaatsen, Memorie van Toelichting, Chamber of Representatives, No. 430, 7 October 1919, accessible online via www.dekamer.be, p. 1–5.

21   Tanja Luckins, *The Gates of Memory, Australian People's Experiences and Memories of Loss and the Great War*, Fremantle, 2004, p. 15.

22   Émile S. Fouda and Ève Comandé, *Corps à corps, Essai de transmission mémorielle par le cimetière militaire*, 2015, p. 69.

23   Richard Allen Hulver, "Bereavement and Mourning (USA)", in Daniel Ute, et al. (eds.), *1914–1918-online*, Berlin, 2014-10-08; Béatrix Pau, *Le Ballet des morts, État, armée, familles: s'occuper des corps de la Grande Guerre*, Paris, 2016, p. 287.

24   Wetsontwerp aangaande de politie over de militaire begraafplaatsen, Memorie van Toelichting, Chamber of Representatives, No. 430, 7 October 1919, accessible online via www.dekamer.be, p. 3; *De Volksstem,* 4 April 1922, p. 2; *Fernand Delhaye*, War Dead Register, accessible online via www.wardeadregister.be.

25   Koninklijk Besluit betreffende de militaire grafsteden, No. 298, 18 August 1920, published in the *Belgian State Journal* of 10 Septembre 1920, No. 254; Wetsontwerp betrekkelijk het toezicht over de militaire grafsteden, Memorie van Toelichting, Chamber of Representatives, No. 267, 11 May 1920, accessible online via www.dekamer.be, p. 5.

26   Grafsteden der onder den oorlog overleden militairen, *Belgian State Journal*, 6–7 September 1920, p. 6657; *De Volksstem,* 21–22 November 1920, p. 1; Grafsteden der onder den oorlog overleden militairen, *Belgian State Journal*, 30–31 August 1920, p. 6426.

27   Julie Summers, *Remembered; History of the Commonwealth War Graves Commission*, London, 2007, p. 25.

28   Béatrix Pau, *Le Ballet des morts*, p. 94.

29   Oliver Janz, "Mourning and Cult of the Fallen (Italy)", in Daniel Ute, et al. (eds.), *1914–1918-online*, Berlin, 2016-03-23.

30   Jussi Jalonen, Klaus Richter and Piotr Szlanta, "Commemoration, Cult of the Fallen (East Central Europe)", in Daniel Ute, et al. (eds.), *1914–1918-online*, Berlin, 2014-10-08.

31   Jan Huijbrechts, "De heldenhuldezerkjes 1914–1918", in Frank Seberechts (ed.), *Onsterfelijk in uw steen, soldatengraven, Heldenhulde en de Groote Oorlog*, Antwerp, 2016, p. 39–42, 70–71 and 126.

32   Jan Vancoillie, *De Duitse militaire begraafplaats Menen Wald, Geschiedenis van de Duitse militaire graven van de Eerste Wereldoorlog in Zuid-West-Vlaanderen*, Wevelgem, 2013, p. 32–33; Florian Greiner, "Volksbund Deutsche Kriegsgräberfürsorge", in Daniel Ute, et al. (eds.), *1914–1918-online*, Berlin, 2017-07-19.

33   Jan Huijbrechts, "De heldenhuldezerkjes 1914–1918", p. 72–74.

34   Koninklijk Besluit waarbij de dienst betreffende de grafsteden der onder den oorlog 1914–1918 gestorven Belgische militairen overgedragen wordt aan het Ministerie van Binnenlandsche Zaken en Volksgezondheid, No. 365, 28 September 1927, published in the *Belgian State Journal* of 24–25 October, 1927, No. 297–298.

The Roaring Twenties

1   Paul van Ostaijen, *Verzameld werk. 2: Poëzie. Bezette Stad en Nagelaten Gedichten*, Amsterdam, 1979, p. 15.

2   Jean Brismé, *Cinema. Honderd jaar film in België*, Liège, 1995, p. 33–45.

3   Matthijs de Ridder, "Charlot is geboren aan het front. Charlie Chaplin en het ontstaan van de nieuwe tijd", in *Zacht Lawijd*, 13, No. 4, December 2014, p. 45–69.

4   Matthijs de Ridder, *De eeuw van Charlie Chaplin*, Amsterdam, 2017, p. 291.

5   Xavier Canonne, "Het parelmoeren scherm", in *Avant-garde 1927–1937. Surrealisme en experiment in de Belgische cinema*, Brussels, 2009, p. 17.

6   Xavier Canonne, "Het parelmoeren scherm", p. 19–23.

7   "Those were exhilarating days: in between a world war and what we thought, what we hoped to be, a world revolution a pure liberating revolution." Achilles Mussche quoted in: August J. Bal, *Het leven in de jaren 20*. Documentation brochure, 20–29 August 1963, Brussels, 1963.

8   In his extensive PhD thesis, Dennis van Mol describes the hesitating first steps towards innovation in Belgium. Regarding the meaning of the first Futuristic exhibition in Belgium and The Great Zwans Exhibition, see:

Dennis van Mol, "*(persoonlijk ben ik er niet voor)*", *Over de moeizame doorbraak van de modern –ismen en het ontstaan van een activistische tegentraditie in Vlaanderen, 1906–1933*, unpublished PhD thesis, Antwerp University, Antwerp, 2017, p. 259–520.

9   Leo Picard, "De jaren '20, jaren van opstanding", in August J. Bal, *Het leven in de jaren* 20, p. 1–4.

10   Karel van Isacker, *Mijn land in de kering 1830–1980, deel 2, De enge ruimte / 1914–1980*, Antwerp-Amsterdam, 1983, p. 39.

11   The influence of humanitarian Expressionism on Flemish avant-garde is explored in Kris Humbeek, "God geve dat wij Staatsgevaarlijk wezen! Mijn kleine oorlog en de retoriek van het linkse activisme", in Hubert F. Van den Berg and Gillis J. Dorleijn (eds.), *Avantgarde! Voorhoede? Vernieuwingsbewegingen in Noord en Zuid opnieuw beschouwd*, Nijmegen, 2002, p. 103–112.

12   The important position of one of the few female avant-garde artists in Belgium is increasingly acknowledged internationally, e.g., through the publications by Peter J.H. Pauwels. See: Peter J.H. Pauwels, Kristien Boon and Marcel Daloze, *A Woman Artist in the Avant-Garde*, Ghent, 2015.

13   Van Doesburg gives several lectures, extremely meaningful for the emergence of geometric abstraction in Antwerp and Brussels. The lecture *Klassiek, barok, modern* is delivered in Antwerp on the 13th of February 1920 at the *Lugardiszaal;* one month later to the day a lecture on *De Stijl* is given in the Brussels *Centre d'Art*. On the 2nd of December 1921 Van Doesburg gives a lecture entitled *Tot Stijl* at the Antwerp Royal Athenaeum.

14   The uninominal vote in 1919 and the breakthrough of unions with the law of the 24th of May 1921 both give a new demographic entity an increased social influence.

15   The group including Kloos, called *De Tachtigers*, emphasized personal experiences and sensorial impressions, a characteristic of Impressionism and all resulting movements, such as Fauvism. This adoration of "beauty" will be heavily debated after the First World War, particularly the fact that explicit aestheticism precluded social commitment.

16   For a documented review of the animosity between the various avant-gardes in the early 1920s, see: Jean F. Buyck, "Het Interbellum: 'kunst van heden' en het debat omtrent het Vlaams expressionisme", in *In dienst van de kunst. Antwerps mecenaat rond 'Kunst van Heden'*, Antwerp, 1991, p. 129–142.

17   *Het Roode Zeil* put its programme in perspective in a flyer: "(t)o obtain personal purification, to widen our literary horizons, to participate in the now created artistic movements that have totally outgrown the local scene, to take a position in, at and against the multiple questions raised by art today, to define the many modern phenomena that influence our artistic life, we try to rise above." Quoted in: Manu van der Aa, *Tatave! Paul-Gustave Van Hecke. Kunstpaus, modekoning en salonsocialist*, Tielt, 2017, p. 181.

18   Johan Meylander, "Fashion", in *Het Roode Zeil*, No. 1, Brussels, 1920, p. 13.

19   Herman Vos, "Een dekadent Vlaanderen?", in *Ruimte*, No. 10-11-12, December 1920, p. 118–121.

20   About Peeters and the Flemish movement, see: Sergio Servellón, "Van toen Vlaams-nationaal, progressief engagement en avant-garde samenklitten", in *Zuurvrij, berichten uit het Letterenhuis*, No. 26, June 2014, Letterenhuis Antwerp, p. 22–31.

21   The *Kring Moderne Kunst* is created by Jozef Peeters and some fellow academy members in analogy with the *Kunstkring Moderne Kunst* in Amsterdam. The three congresses on modern art organised by the society will promote Peeters as the pioneer of avant-garde in Flanders. The "1st Congress for Modern Art" is held in Antwerp on October 10 and 11; the "2nd Congress for Modern Art" takes place from January 21 till 23 1922 also in Antwerp; the "3rd Congress for Modern Art" takes place from July 30 till August 15 1922 in Bruges.

22   About the international significance of *Het Overzicht*, see: Bob Coppens, *Het Overzicht. Een Antwerps avant-garde tijdschrift (1921–1925)*, unpublished master's thesis, Catholic University Louvain, 1974.

23   After the First World War the ideas behind the conferences *Architectuur en Maatschappij* given by Hendrik Petrus Berlage at the ULB in 1913 witnessed a revival, particularly in Brussels. Architects such as Louis Herman De Koninck, Victor Bourgeois and artist Marcel-Louis Baugniet vented their progressive ideas through a series of initiatives and associations.

24   This is completely in keeping with the "primitivistic" foundation of the group around *Sélection*, as opposed to the call for all things contemporary by the *7 Arts* group. An Paenhuysen, *De nieuwe wereld. De wonderjaren van de Belgische avant-garde, 1918–1939*, Antwerp, 2010, p. 146.

25   The Surrealists will often make public "threats" in Brussels in order to disrupt the "usual state of affairs", also regarding the relationship between spectator and public. *Idem*, p. 174.

26   Van Hecke opens a new gallery in 1926, *L'Epoque*, that he entrusts to the management of former composer E.L.T. Mesens. Together they launch the magazine *Variété*, that alongside *Distances* will become the face of Surrealism in Belgium from 1928 onwards. Mesens is the one putting the *Correspondance* group (with Magritte, Louis Scutenaire, Paul Colinet and Marcel Mariën) in contact with Paris.

27 Billie Melsman, *Women and the Popular Imagination in the Twenties. Flappers and Nymphs*, Hampshire-London, 1988; Alys Eve Weinbaum, et al. (eds.), *The Modern Girl Around the World: Consumption, Modernity and Globalization*, Durham-London, 2008; Kelly Boyer Sagert, *Flappers: A Guide to an American Subculture*, Santa Barbara-Denver-Oxford, 2010.

28 Valerie Steele, *The Corset: A Cultural History*, New Haven, 2001.

29 Emmanuelle Dirix, "Veren en franjes. De spectaculair moderne flapper: ode aan een veranderend icoon", in Eve Demoen, et al., *Jazz Age. Mode in de bruisende jaren 20*, exh. cat. Fashion Museum Hasselt, Ghent, 2015, p. 115–129.

30 Nancy Troy, *Couture Culture: a study in modern art and fashion*, Cambridge (MA), 2003; Idem, "Paul Poiret's minaret style: originality, reproduction, and art in fashion", in *Fashion Theory* 6, 2, 2002, p. 117–144; Madelief Hohé, "Paul Poiret. Mode door 'Le Magnifique'", in *Art deco Paris*, exh. cat. Gemeentemuseum The Hague, Zwolle, 2017, p. 184–203.

31 Emmanuelle Polle, "Sportswear: een levensstijl à la Patou", in Eve Demoen, et al., *Jazz Age. Mode in de bruisende jaren 20*, exh. cat. Fashion Museum Hasselt, Ghent, 2015, p. 55–73.

32 Sophie Grossiord, et al., *Jeanne Lanvin*, exh. cat. Palais Galliera, Paris, 2015.

33 Véronique Pouillard, "Mode en luxe in België. Tussen periferie en onafhankelijkheid", in Hettie Juda (ed.), *Delvaux 1829–2009. 180 jaar Belgische luxe*, exh. cat. Fashion Museum Province Antwerp, 2009, p. 41–45.

34 Nele Bernheim, "Maison Norine, Brussels: Belgian Avant-Garde Couture, c. 1916–1952", in *Symposium 1: Modus Operandi. State of affairs in Current Research on Belgian Fashion. 18/10/2007. MoMu – Fashion Museum Province of Antwerp*, Antwerp, 2008, p. 17–35.

35 Raymond Murray Schafer, *The Tuning of the World (The Soundscape)*, New York, 1977.

36 Christopher Brent Murray, "Rethinking Musical Life in Post-Armistice Brussels", in *Revue belge de Musicologie – Belgisch Tijdschrift voor Muziekwetenschap*, 68, 2014, p. 186.

37 *Idem*, p. 176.

38 Daniel Berger, et al., *L'Heure bleue. La vie nocturne à Bruxelles de 1830 à 1940*, Brussels, 1987, p. 77.

39 A. Sykes, "Le jazz band", in *L'Arstiste musicien*, August 1924, p. 118–119.

40 Félicie Lécrivain, *Le phénomène des 'dancings' à Bruxelles durant l'entre-deux-guerres*, unpublished paper, ULB, 2013, p. 19.

41 Robert Goffin, *Aux frontières du jazz*, Paris, 1932, p. 31.

42 *Idem*, p. 22.

43 In 1924, this became the *Bistrouille Amateur Dance Orchestra*.

44 Initially entitled *Musique Magazine*, it took its definitive name, *Music*, in 1925.

45 Robert Goffin, *Aux frontières du jazz*.

46 Auguste Getteman, "Belgique. La musique à Bruxelles et en Belgique", in *La Revue musicale*, January 1926, p. 87.

47 Robert Wangermée, "La vie musicale d'une guerre à l'autre", in Dominique Favart (ed.), *Au bonheur des musiciens. 150 ans de vie musicale à Bruxelles*, Tielt, 1997, p. 53–74.

48 Malou Haine, "La vie musicale en Belgique de 1920 à 1940 dans La Revue musicale de Henry Prunières", in *Revue belge de Musicologie – Belgisch Tijdschrift voor Muziekwetenschap*, 67, 2013, p. 151.

49 Kristin Van den Buys, "L'importance d'un orchestre de radio", in Dominique Favart (ed.), *Au bonheur des musiciens. 150 ans de vie musicale à Bruxelles*, Tielt, 1997, p. 209–224.

Epilogue

1 About this period, see Emmanuel Gerard, *La Démocratie rêvée, bridée et bafouée, Nouvelle Histoire de Belgique 1918–1939*, Brussels, 2010.

2 Ronny Gobyn and Winston Spriet, *La séduction des masses. Les années 30 en Belgique,* Brussels, 1994.

BIBLIOGRAPHY

- Anon., *Beknopte Bekendmakingen nopens den Dienst der Verwoeste Gewesten*, Brussels, 1921.
- Anon., *Fonds Roi Albert. Habitations pour les Belges sans-abri*, Paris, 1917.
- Anon., "Les urbanistes des pays amis soutiennent nos efforts", in *La Cité*, 1 July 1919, p. 4.
- Anon., "Belgian Mandate for East Africa", in *The American Journal of International Law*, vol. 17/3, Suppl. Official Documents, 1923, p. 149.
- Amara, Michaël, "Des exilés à l'heure du retour. Les réfugiés en Belgique à la fin de la Première Guerre mondiale (1918–1919)", in Pierre-Alain Tallier and Patrick Nefors (eds.), *Quand les canons se taisent – En toen zwegen de kanonnen,* Brussels, 2010, p. 217–218.
- Amara, Michaël, *Des Belges à l'épreuve de l'Exil. Les réfugiés de la Première Guerre mondiale (France, Grande-Bretagne, Pays-Bas)*, Brussels, 2008.
- Arnout, Anneleen, "Archimedes achterna. De Belgische musea tijdens de Eerste Wereldoorlog", in *Bijdragen tot de Eigentijdse Geschiedenis*, 22, 2010, p. 55–92.
- Aron, Paul, "Romain Rolland, Henri Barbusse et leurs amis belges: l'efficacité d'un réseau politico-littéraire", in Robert Frickx (ed.), *Les relations littéraires franco-belges de 1914 à 1940*, Brussels, 1990, p. 29–54.
- Artaud, Denise, and André Kaspi, *Histoire des Etats-Unis,* Paris, 1969.
- Assmann, Aleida, *Der lange Schatten der Vergangenheit*, Munich, 2006.
- Baccarne, Robert, and Jan Steen, *Poelkapelle 1914–1918*, Wervik, 1965.
- Baccarne, Robert, and Jan Steen, *Boezinge na 1914–1918*, Wervik, 1974.
- Baccarne, Robert, et al., *Poelcapelle 1917, een spoor van tankwrakken*, Poelkapelle, 2007.
- Baert, Koen, "De terugkeer. Aspecten van de herbevolking van Ieper na 1918", in *Ieper, de herrezen stad, de wederopbouw in Ieper na 14–18*, Kortrijk, 1999, p. 9–20.
- Baert, Koen, "Wonen in de verwoesting. Omstandigheden en getuigen", in Jeroen Cornilly, et al., *Bouwen aan wederopbouw 1914/2050. Architectuur in de Westhoek*, Ypres, 2009, p. 17–41.
- Bailleul, Jean-Marie, *Problematiek omtrent de wederopbouw van België na de Eerste Wereldoorlog. Casus Ieper en omgeving (1918–1924)*, unpublished master's thesis, Ghent University, 1976.
- Baudhuin, Fernand, *Histoire économique de la Belgique, 1914–1939*, v. 1, Brussels, 1946.
- Bean, Charles, *The Australian Imperial Force in France during the Allied Offensive, 1918*, Sydney, 1942.
- Becker, Annette, *Oubliés de la Grande Guerre 1914–1918: populations occupées, déportés civils, prisonniers de guerre*, Paris, 1998.
- Becker, Jean-Jacques, "Les conséquences des traités de paix", in *Revue historique des armées* [online], 254, 2009.
- Benvindo, Bruno, and Evert Peeters, *Les décombres de la guerre: mémoires belges en conflit, 1945–2010*, Waterloo, 2012.
- Berger, Daniel, et al., *L'Heure bleue. La vie nocturne à Bruxelles de 1830 à 1940*, Brussels, 1987.
- Bernheim, Nele, "Maison Norine, Brussels: Belgian Avant-Garde Couture, c. 1916–1952", in *Symposium 1: modus operandi. State of affairs in current research on Belgian fashion. 18/10/2007. MoMu – Fashion Museum Province of Antwerp*, Antwerp, 2008, p. 17–35.
- Blomme, Jan, *The Economic Development of Belgian Agriculture, 1880–1980. A Quantitative and Qualitative Analysis*, Brussels, 1992.
- Boemeke, Manfred Bo, Gerald D. Feldman, and Elisabeth Glaser, *The Treaty of Versailles. A Reassessment after 75 Years*, Cambridge, 2006.
- Boijen, Richard, *De taalwetgeving in het Belgische leger (1830–1940)*, Brussels, 1992.

- Bolle, Francine, "L'extrême gauche syndicale dans les mouvements de grève (1919–1924). Les contestataires radicaux et la Belgique", in Anne Morelli and José Gotovitch (eds.), *Contester dans un pays prospère. L'extrême gauche en Belgique et au Canada*, Brussels, 2007, p. 37–63.
- Bostyn, Franky, and Jan Vancoillie, *Bayernwald: Het Croonaertbos in de Eerste Wereldoorlog*, Zonnebeke, 2000.
- Bostyn, Franky, "De ijzeren oogst", in Jan Vancoillie (ed.), *Halfweg Menin Road en Ypernstrasse. Gheluvelt 1914–1918*, Voormezele, 2002, p. 283–290.
- Bostyn, Franky, and Dominiek Dendooven, "De Westhoek en het stenen erfgoed van de Eerste Wereldoorlog", in *Steen in de Zuidelijke Westhoek*, Ypres, 2003, p. 2–6.
- Bostyn, Franky, and Dominiek Dendooven, "Landschap en Wereldoorlog I", in *Landschap en Herinnering in de Zuidelijke Westhoek*, Ypres, 2004, p. 2–5.
- Bostyn, Franky, Frans Descamps, et al., *Passchendaele 1917: Het verhaal van de doden en Tyne Cot Cemetery*, Roeselare, 2007.
- Bostyn, Franky, Steven Heyde, et al., "Naar een Integrale Benadering van het Oorlogslandschap: Bijdrage tot de Ontwikkeling van een Waarderingsmethodiek voor Landschap en Cultuurhistorie op Lokale Schaal – Proefproject Zonnebeke-Passendale (W.Vl.)", in *Relicta*, 11, 2015, p. 351–383.
- Bourgaux, Anne-Emmanuelle, *La démocratisation du gouvernement représentatif en Belgique: une promesse oubliée?*, unpublished PhD thesis, Université Libre de Bruxelles, 2013.
- Boyer Sagert, Kelly, *Flappers: A Guide to an American Subculture*, Santa Barbara-Denver-Oxford, 2010.
- Brent Murray, Christopher, "Rethinking Musical Life in Post-Armistice Brussels", in *Revue belge de Musicologie – Belgisch Tijdschrift voor Muziekwetenschap*, 58, 2014, p. 169–192.
- Brion, René, and Jean-Louis Moreau, *De Generale Maatschappij van België, 1822–1997*, Antwerp, 1998.
- Brismé, Jean, *Cinema. Honderd jaar film in België*, Liège, 1995.
- Buelens, Geert, Matthijs de Ridder, and Jan Stuyck (eds.), *De trust der vaderlandsliefde. Over literatuur en Vlaamse Beweging, 1890–1940*, Antwerp, 2005.
- *Bulletin officiel du Touring Club de Belgique*, 1918-1928.
- Bullock, Nicholas, and Luc Verpoest (eds.), *Living with history, 1914-1964: rebuilding Europe after the first and second World Wars and the role of heritage preservation*, Louvain, 2001.
- Bussière, Eric, *La France, la Belgique et l'organisation économique de l'Europe, 1918–1935,* Paris, 1992.
- Buyck, Jean F., "Het Interbellum: 'kunst van heden' en het debat omtrent het Vlaams expressionisme", in *In dienst van de kunst. Antwerps mecenaat rond 'Kunst van Heden'* (exh. cat.), Royal Museum of Fine Arts Antwerp, 1991, p. 129–142.
- Cabanes, Bruno, *La victoire endeuillée: la sortie de guerre des soldats français 1918–1920*, Paris, 2004.
- Cabanes, Bruno, and Guillaume Piketty, *Retour à l'intime au sortir de la guerre*, Paris, 2009.
- Canonne, Xavier, "Het parelmoeren scherm", in *Avant-garde 1927–1937. Surrealisme en experiment in de Belgische cinema*, Brussels, 2009, p. 12–49.
- Carnel, Sven, "Entre espoir et désillusion. Le retour des sinistrés dans les régions dévastées après la Première Guerre mondiale", in *Une guerre totale? La Belgique dans la Première Guerre mondiale: nouvelles tendances de la recherche historique,* Acts of the international colloquium, organised at the Université Libre de Bruxelles from 15 to 17 January 2003, Brussels, 2005, p. 495–505.
- Carnel, Sven, "La reconstruction agricole dans les régions dévastées", in *Memoires de la société d'histoire de Comines-Warneton et de la région*, 38, 2008, p. 257–276.
- Carnel, Sven, *La reconstruction des régions dévastées après la Première Guerre mondiale: le cas de Neuve-Église*, Brussels, 2002.
- Cartier, Raymond, *Le Monde entre deux guerres, 1919–1939*, Paris, 1969.
- Carton de Wiart, Henri, *Souvenirs politiques (1918–1951)*, Brussels, 1981.
- Claeys, Dries, "World War I and the reconstruction of rural landscapes in Belgium and France. A historiographical essay", in *Agricultural History Review*, 65, 2017, p. 108–129.

- Clout, Hugh, *After the Ruins: Restoring the Countryside of Northern France after the Great War*, Exeter, 1996.
- Clout, Hugh, "The Great Reconstruction of Towns and Cities in France 1918–35", in *Planning perspectives*, 20, 2005, p. 1–33.
- Cohen, Deborah, *The War Come Home. Disabled Veterans in Britain and Germany, 1914–1939*, Berkeley/Los Angeles, 2001.
- Colignon, Alain, *Les Anciens combattant en Belgique francophone, 1918–1940*, Liège, 1984.
- Coolsaet, Rik, *België en zijn buitenlandse politiek 1830-2015*, Leuven, 6th edition, 2014.
- Coppens, Bob, *Het Overzicht. Een Antwerps avant-garde tijdschrift (1921–1925),* unpublished master's thesis, Catholic University of Leuven, 1974.
- Cornilly, Jeroen, and Chris Vandewalle, "Onzichtbare pleitbezorgers. Tussen bewoners en hogere overheden", in Jeroen Cornilly, et al., *Bouwen aan wederopbouw 1914/2050. Architectuur in de Westhoek*, Ypres, 2009, p. 51–73.
- Cornilly, Jeroen, "Tussen traditie en moderniteit: de wederopbouw van parochiekerken in West-Vlaanderen na de Eerste Wereldoorlog", in *In de Steigers*, 3, 2008, pp. 71-95.
- Cornilly, Jeroen, "Aspecten van de wederopbouwarchitectuur in het arrondissement Ieper", in *Open Monumentendag. 20ᵉ eeuw in de Zuidelijke Westhoek*, Ypres, 2008, pp. 3-12.
- Cornilly, Jeroen, "Gevraagd: architecten. Kiezen tussen alternatieven", in Jeroen Cornilly, et al., *Bouwen aan wederopbouw 1914-2050: architectuur in de Westhoek*, Ypres, 2009, pp. 115-141.
- Smets, Marcel, et al., Resurgam. De Belgische wederopbouw na 1914, Brussels, 1985.
- Craenen, Pieter, *Historiek van de Belgische Ontmijningsdienst*, unpublished master's thesis, Royal Military Academy, Brussels, 1989.
- Crowell, Benedict, and Robert Forrest Wilson, *Demobilization. Our Industrial and Military Demobilization after the Armistice, 1918–1920*, New Haven, 1921.
- Danchin, Emmanuelle, *Le temps des ruines, 1914–1921*, Rennes, 2015.
- De Bock, Stefan, *De oud-strijders van de Eerste Wereldoorlog en de Belgische maatschappij (1918–1923)*, unpublished master's thesis, Ghent University, 2009.
- De Caigny, Sofie, et al., *Het Gekwetste Gewest. Onderzoeksgids van de wederopbouwarchitectuur in de Westhoek*, Antwerp, 2009.
- De Caigny, Sofie, "Tussen filantropie en macht. In de bres voor de belangen van hun achterban", in Jeroen Cornilly, et al., *Bouwen aan wederopbouw 1914/2050, Architectuur in de Westhoek Ieper*, 2009, p. 149–170.
- De Naeyer, André, "La reconstruction des monuments et des sites en Belgique après la Première Guerre mondiale", in *Monumentum*, 20–22, 1982, p. 167–188.
- De Ridder, Matthijs, "Charlot is geboren aan het front. Charlie Chaplin en het ontstaan van de nieuwe tijd", in *Zacht Lawijd*, 13/4, 2014, p. 45–69.
- De Ridder, Matthijs, *De eeuw van Charlie Chaplin*, Amsterdam, 2017.
- De Schaepdrijver, Sophie, "Death is Elsewhere: the Shifting Locus of Tragedy in Belgian Great War Literature", in *Yale French Studies*, 102, 2002, p. 94–114.
- De Schaepdrijver, Sophie, *La Belgique et la Première Guerre mondiale*, Brussels, 2004.
- De Vos, Luc, and Franky Bostyn, et al., *14–18. Oorlog in België*, Leuven, 2014.
- De Waele, Jan, *Voor Vorst en Vaderland: de situatie van zwarte soldaten en dragers in dienst van het Belgisch Leger (Force Publique) tijdens de Eerste Wereldoorlog in Centraal-Afrika*, unpublished master's thesis, Vrije Universiteit Brussel, 2001.
- Debaeke, Siegfried, *Oud ijzer. De frontstreek bedolven onder levensgevaarlijke oorlogsmunitie*, Bruges, 2010.
- Declerck, Jos, *Histoire Anecdotique de la Fédération Nationale des Combattants,* Brussels, 1920.
- Delahaye, Claire, and Serge Ricard, *L'héritage de Théodore Roosevelt: impérialisme et progressisme (1912–2012)*, Paris, 2012.
- Delaporte, Sophie, "Le corps et la parole des mutilés de la Grande Guerre", in *Guerres mondiales et conflits contemporains*, 205, 2002, p. 5–14.

- Delaporte, Sophie, *Le corps et la parole des mutilés*, Paris, 2003.
- Dendooven, Dominiek, *Menin Gate & Last Post: Ypres as Holy Ground*, Koksijde, 2001.
- Dendooven, Dominiek, Koen Baert, et al., *Ieper: De Herrezen Stad*, Koksijde, 1999.
- Dendooven, Dominiek, and Piet Chielens (eds.), *Wereldoorlog I: vijf continenten in Vlaanderen*, Tielt, 2008.
- Dendooven, Dominiek, "Het terrein effenen. Aanleg, infrastructuur en landbeheer", in Jeroen Cornilly, et al., *Bouwen aan wederopbouw 1914/2050. Architectuur in de Westhoek*, Ieper, 2009, p. 81–106.
- Deneckere, Gita, "Het 'rode gevaar' tijdens het interbellum. Of hoe de waan van een wereldwijd communistisch complot de werkelijkheid beïnvloedde", in *Brood en Rozen*, 2/4, 1997, p. 49–65.
- Deneckere, Gita, "Oudstrijders op de vuist in Brussel. Het amnestieconflict tijdens het Interbellum", in *Belgisch Tijdschrift voor Nieuwste Geschiedenis*, 25/3-4, 1995, p. 273–277.
- Deperchin, Annie, "La conférence de paix" – "Les traités de paix" – "L'application des traités", in Stéphane Audoin-Rouzeau and Jean-Jacques Becker (eds.), *Encyclopédie de la Grande Guerre 1914–1918: Histoire et culture*, Paris, 2004, p. 993–1030.
- Depoortere, Rolande, *La question des réparations allemandes dans la politique étrangère de la Belgique après la première guerre mondiale 1919–1925*, Brussels, 1997.
- Depoortere, Rolande, "La Belgique et les réparations allemandes: la grande illusion", in Sophie Claisse et al. (eds.), *Comment (se) sortir de la Grande Guerre. Regards sur quelques pays "vainqueurs": la Belgique, la France et la Grande-Bretagne*, Paris, 2005, p. 127–154.
- Deseyne, Aleks, *Huib Hoste en de wederopbouw te Zonnebeke*, Zonnebeke, 1981.
- Deseyne, André, and Aleks Deseyne, *Zonnebeke 1914–1918: Dood en Heropstanding van een Dorp*, Zonnebeke, 1976.
- Desreumaux, John, *Land van schroot en knoken. Slachtoffers van ontploffingen in de frontstreek 1918-heden*, Leuven, 2011.
- Devos, Wannes, "Het Koninklijk Legermuseum: een pantheon voor de natie", in Chantal Kesteloot and Laurence Van Ypersele (eds.), *La Belgique et la Grande Guerre: du café liégeois au soldat inconnu*, Brussels, 2018.
- Devos, Wannes, *Het gealiëneerd museum. Musealisering van oorlog en geschiedenis in militaire musea. De casestudy van het Koninklijk Legermuseum*, ongoing PhD, Ghent University.
- Dirix, Emmanuelle, "Veren en franjes. De spectaculair moderne flapper: ode aan een veranderend icoon", in Eve Demoen et al. (eds.), *Jazz Age. Mode in de bruisende jaren 20*, (exh. cat.) Fashion Museum Hasselt, Ghent, 2015, p. 115–129.
- Dorteuil, A., *Mémento du démobilisé. Guide pratique, simple et complet d'après les documents officiels*, Brussels, 1919.
- Elias, Hendrik, *Vijfentwintig jaar Vlaamse beweging 1914–1939*, v. 2, Antwerp, 1971–1972.
- Ferguson, Niall, *Empire: How Britain Made the Modern World*, London, 2004.
- Fink, Carole, "The Peace Settlement, 1919–1939", in John Horne (ed.), *A Companion to World War I* (Blackwell Companions to World History), Chichester, 2010, p. 544–557.
- Fouchard, Dominique, "Le retour des soldats de la Première Guerre mondiale: l'impossible démobilisation intime", in *Les Chemins de la Mémoire*, 194, 2009, p. 7–10.
- Fouda, Émile S., and Ève Comandé, *Corps à corps, Essai de transmission mémorielle par le cimetière militaire*, 2015.
- Fréché, Bibiane, "L'Art Libre (1919–1921) et les réseaux intellectuels internationalistes", in Hubert Roland and Stéphanie Vanasten (eds.), *Les nouvelles voies du comparatisme*, Ghent, 2010, p. 71–83.
- Gerard, Emmanuel, *De schaduw van het interbellum. België van euforie tot crisis 1918–1939*, Tielt, 2017.
- Gerard, Emmanuel, *La démocratie rêvée, bridée et bafouée: 1918–1939. Nouvelle histoire de Belgique*, v. 2, Brussels, 2006.
- Getteman, Auguste, "Belgique. La musique à Bruxelles et en Belgique", in *La Revue musicale*, January 1926, p. 87.

- Gille, Louis, Alphonse Ooms and Paul Delandsheere, *Cinquante mois d'occupation allemande*, v. 4, Brussels, 1919.
- Gilot, Mathieu, *Onze Werking in Verwoest Vlaanderen. Beknopt overzicht der werkzaamheden van onzen "Dienst voor herstel van West-Vlaanderen"*, Roeselare, 1921.
- Gobyn, R., "La crise du logement et le problème du logement provisoire en Belgique après la Première Guerre mondiale", in *Resurgam: La reconstruction après 1918 en Belgique*, Brussels, 1985, p. 169–188.
- Goffin, Robert, *Aux frontières du jazz*, Paris, 1932.
- Gotovitch, José, "La peur du rouge dans les dossiers de la justice belge: la signification du procès de 1923", in Pascal Delwit and José Gotovitch (eds.), *La peur du rouge*, Brussels, 1996, p. 87–97.
- Greiner, Florian, "Volksbund Deutsche Kriegsgräberfürsorge", in Daniel Ute, Peter Gatrell, et al. (eds.), *1914–1918-online, International Encyclopedia of the First World War*, Berlin, 2017-07-19.
- Grossiord, Sophie, et al., *Jeanne Lanvin* (exh. cat.), Palais Galliera, Paris, 2015.
- Gubin, Eliane, "Les femmes et la citoyenneté en Belgique. Histoire d'un malentendu", in *Sextant*, 7, 1997, p. 163–187.
- Haag, Henri, "Le choix du roi Albert à Loppem", in Carlos Wyffels (ed.), *Actes du colloque roi Albert*, Brussels, 1976, p. 169–191.
- Haine, Malou, "La vie musicale en Belgique de 1920 à 1940 dans *La Revue musicale* de Henry Prunières", in *Revue belge de Musicologie – Belgisch Tijdschrift voor Muziekwetenschap*, 67, 2013, p. 135–158.
- Haslinger, Peter, "Saint-Germain, Treaty of", in Daniel Ute, Peter Gatrell, et al. (eds.), *1914–1918-online, International Encyclopedia of the First World War*, Berlin, 2016-12-06.
- Hens, Tine, Saartje Vanden Borre, and Kaat Wils, *Oorlog in tijden van vrede. De Eerste Wereldoorlog in de klas, 1919–1940*, Kalmthout, 2015.
- Heyde, Steven, "*Het herstel van het bocagelandschap in de zuidelijke Westhoek na de Eerste Wereldoorlog*", in *M&L. Monumenten, Landschappen en Archeologie*, 33, 2014, p. 28–41.
- Heyde, Steven, et al., *Kasteeldomeinen 1795–2015. Historische tuinen en parken in de zuidelijke Westhoek*, Tielt, 2015.
- Hobsbawn, Eric J., *Nations and Nationalism since 1780. Programme, Myth, Reality*, Cambridge, 1990.
- Hohé, Madelief, "Paul Poiret. Mode door 'Le Magnifique'", in *Art deco Paris* (exh. cat.), Gemeentemuseum The Hague, Zwolle, 2017, p. 184–203.
- Hortensius, Lambertus, *Burgers, boeren. Hun goed, hun vee. De frontstreek na 1914–1918*, unpublished master's thesis, Catholic University of Leuven, 1989.
- Huijbrechts, Jan, "De heldenhuldezerkjes 1914–1918", in Frank Seberechts (ed.), *Onsterfelijk in uw steen, soldatengraven, Heldenhulde en de Groote Oorlog*, Antwerp, 2016.
- Hulver, Richard Allen, "Bereavement and Mourning (USA)", in Daniel Ute, Peter Gatrell, et al. (eds.), *1914–1918-online, International Encyclopedia of the First World War*, Berlin, 2014-10-08.
- Humbeek, Kris, "God geve dat wij Staatsgevaarlijk wezen! Mijn kleine oorlog en de retoriek van het linkse activisme", in Hubert F. Van den Berg and Gillis J. Dorleijn (eds.), *Avantgarde! Voorhoede? Vernieuwingsbewegingen in Noord en Zuid opnieuw beschouwd*, Nijmegen, 2002, p. 103–112.
- Jacobs, Mariette, *Zij die vielen als helden... Cultuurhistorische analyse van de oorlogsgedenktekens van de twee wereldoorlogen in West-Vlaanderen*, v. 1, Bruges, 1995.
- Jalonen, Jussi, Klaus Richter, and Piotr Szlanta, "Commemoration, Cult of the Fallen (East Central Europe)", in Daniel Ute, Peter Gatrell, et al. (eds.), *1914–1918-online, International Encyclopedia of the First World War*, Berlin, 2014-10-08.
- Janssen, Erik, *Inventaris van het archief van de Dienst voor de Duitse Krijgsgevangenen van de Belgische Middendienst voor de Krijgsgevangenen, 1914–1924 (1922–1926)*, Royal Army Museum, unpublished inventory, Brussels, 2011.
- Janssen, Erik, *Inventaris van het archief van het Korps van de Krijgsgevangenen [1914] 1918–1921*, Royal Army Museum, unpublished inventory, Brussels, 2011.

- Janssens, Valéry, *De Belgische frank. Anderhalve eeuw geldgeschiedenis*, Antwerp, 1976.
- Janz, Oliver, "Mourning and Cult of the Fallen (Italy)", in Daniel Ute, Peter Gatrell, et al. (eds.), *1914–1918-online, International Encyclopedia of the First World War*, Berlin, 2016-03-23.
- Jaumain, Serge, et al. (eds.), *Une Guerre totale? La Belgique dans la Première Guerre mondiale. Nouvelles tendances de la recherche historique*, Brussels, 2005.
- Joset, Camille, *Une grande œuvre de guerre belge. Le Fonds du Roi Albert*, Brussels, 1925.
- Keintz, Sabine, "Quelle place pour les héros mutilés? Les invalides de guerre entre intégration et exclusion", in *14–18 Aujourd'hui*, 4, 2001, p. 151–165.
- Kesteloot, Chantal, "Een nieuwe Blijde Intrede in het bevrijde Brussel", in *Albert & Elisabeth. De film van een koninklijk leven*, Brussels, 2014, p. 86–97.
- Kissinger, Henry, *Diplomatie*, Paris, 1996.
- Konrad, Helmut, "Bâtir la paix", in Jay Winter (ed.), *La Première Guerre mondiale; t. II: Etats*, Paris, 2014, p. 647–678.
- Larsson, Marina, *Shattered Anzacs, Living with the Scars of War*, Sydney, 2009.
- Lauwers, Delphine, *Le tourisme de guerre en Belgique 1918–1939*, unpublished master's thesis, Université Libre de Bruxelles, 2005.
- Lauwers, Delphine, *Le Saillant d'Ypres entre reconstruction et construction d'un lieu de mémoire. Un long processus de négociations mémorielles de 1914 à nos jours*, unpublished PHD thesis, European University Institute, Florence, 2014.
- Lécrivain, Félicie, *Le phénomène des 'dancings' à Bruxelles durant l'entre-deux-guerres*, unpublished paper, Université Libre de Bruxelles, 2013.
- Lloyd, David W., *Battlefield Tourism. Pilgrimage and the Commemoration of the Great War in Britain, Australia and Canada, 1919-1939*, Oxford, 1998.
- Louis, William Roger, *Ruanda-Urundi 1884–1919*, Oxford, 1963.
- Luckins, Tanja, *The Gates of Memory, Australian People's Experiences and Memories of Loss and the Great War*, Fremantle, 2004.
- Luyten, Dirk, "Guerre, dépression économique et contestation de la démocratie (1914–1944)", in Els Witte, Alain Meynen, and Dirk Luyten, *Histoire politique de la Belgique*, Brussels, 2017, p. 177–285.
- MacMillan, Margaret, *Paris 1919. Six Months that Changed the World*, New York, 2002.
- Mahaim, Ernest, *La Belgique restaurée: étude sociologique*, Brussels, 1926.
- Marinov Minkov, Stefan, "Neuilly-sur-Seine, Treaty of", in Daniel Ute, Peter Gatrell, et al. (eds.), *1914–1918-online, International Encyclopedia of the First World War*, Berlin, 2017-02-20.
- Marks, Sally, *Innocent Abroad. Belgium at the Paris Peace Conference of 1919*, Chapel Hill, 1981.
- Meire, Johan, *De stilte van de Salient, herinnering van de eerste wereldoorlog rond Ieper*, Tielt, 2003.
- Melsman, Billie, *Women and the Popular Imagination in the Twenties. Flappers and Nymphs*, Hampshire-London, 1988.
- Meylander, Johan, "Fashion", in *Het Roode Zeil*, 1/1, Brussels, 1920, p. 13.
- Michael, Hardt, and Antonio Negri, *Empire*, Cambridge/London, 2000.
- Monballyu, Jos, *Slechte Belgen! De repressie van het incivisme na de Eerste Wereldoorlog door het Hof van Assisen van Brabant (1919–1927)*, Brussels, 2011.
- Monnet, Jean, *Mémoires*, Paris, 1976.
- Mosse, George, *Fallen Soldiers. Reshaping the Memory of the World Wars*, New York, 1990.
- Mottram, Ralph Hale, *Journey to the Western Front. Twenty Years After*, London, 1936.
- Ndaywel è Nziem, Isidore, and Pamphile Mabiala Mantuba-Ngoma, *Le Congo belge dans la Première Guerre mondiale (1914–1918)*, RDC, 2015.
- Nicholson, G.W.L., *Canadian Expeditionary Force, 1914–1919*, Ottawa, 1964.
- Notebaert, Alexandre, Christel Neumann, and Willem Vanden Eynde, *Inventaire des archives de l'Office des Régions dévastées*, National State Archives, Brussels, 1986.
- Nys, Liesbet, *De intrede van het publiek: museumbezoek in België, 1830–1914*, Leuven, 2012.

- Orts, Pierre, "The Claim for Colonies: A Belgian View", in *Journal of the Royal African Society*, 36/142, 1937, p. 25.
- Pabst, Klaus, "Eupen-Malmedy in der belgischen Regierungs- und Parteienpolitik 1914–1940", in *Zeitschrift des Aachener Geschichtsvereins*, 76, 1964, p. 267–268.
- Paenhuysen, An, *De nieuwe wereld. De wonderjaren van de Belgische avant-garde, 1918–1939*, Antwerp, 2010.
- Pau, Béatrix, *Le Ballet des morts, État, armée, familles: s'occuper des corps de la Grande Guerre*, Paris, 2016.
- Pauwels, Marcel, and Norman Vanoverbeke, "De wederopbouw", in *Halfweg Menin Road en Ypernstrasse. Gheluvelt 1914–1918*, Voormezele, 2002, p. 240–253.
- Pauwels, Peter J.H., Kristien Boon, and Marcel Daloze, *A Woman Artist in the Avant-Garde*, Ghent, 2015.
- Pawley, Margaret, *The Watch on the Rhine. The Military Occupation of the Rhineland, 1918–1930*, London, 2007.
- Pedersen, B. Susan, "The Meaning of The Mandates System: An Argument", in *Geschichte und Gesellschaft*, 32, 2004, p. 560–582.
- Pirard, Joseph, *L'extension du rôle de l'Etat en Belgique aux XIXᵉ et XXᵉ siècles*, Brussels, 1999.
- Polle, Emmanuelle, "Sportswear: een levensstijl à la Patou", in Eve Demoen, et al., *Jazz Age. Mode in de bruisende jaren 20* (exh. cat.), Fashion Museum Hasselt, Ghent, 2015, p. 55–73.
- Pouillard, Véronique, "Mode en luxe in België. Tussen periferie en onafhankelijkheid", in Hettie Juda (ed.), *Delvaux 1829–2009. 180 jaar Belgische luxe* (exh. cat.), Fashion Museum Province of Antwerp, 2009, p. 41–45.
- Price, Burr, *Louvain Liége [sic]*, Brussels, 1919.
- Prost, Antoine, *Les anciens combattants et la société française: Mentalité et idéologie*, Paris, 1977.
- Provoost, Guido, *Vlaanderen en het militair politiek beleid in België tussen de twee wereldoorlogen*, v. 1–2, Leuven, 1976–1977.
- Puissant, Jean, René Leboutte, and Denis Scuto, *Un siècle d'histoire industrielle: Belgique, Luxembourg, Pays-Bas; Industrialisation et sociétés 1873–1973*, Paris, 1998.
- Roland, Hubert, "Paul Colin et la réception de l'expressionnisme en Belgique francophone dans l'entre-deux-guerres", in *Textyles*, 20, 2001, p. 45.
- Rousseaux, Xavier, and Laurence van Ypersele (eds.), *La patrie crie vengeance! La répression des "inciviques" belges au sortir de la guerre 1914–1918*, Brussels, 2008.
- Rozeboom, Foske, *Oorlog als attractie. De musealisering van de Eerste Wereldoorlog: Sanctuary Wood Museum Hill 62*, Amsterdam, 2009.
- Rumiya, Jean, *Le Ruanda sous le régime du mandat belge (1918–1931)*, Paris, 1992.
- Said, Edward, *Culture and Imperialism*, New York, 1998.
- Schafer, Raymond Murray, *The Tuning of the World (The Soundscape)*, New York, 1977.
- Schoups, Martin, *Woekeraars, uithongeraars, accapareurs, sjacheraars, opkopers, uitzuigers en zeep-baronnen. Prijscontestatie in België na de Eerste Wereldoorlog, 1918–1924*, unpublished master's thesis, Ghent University, 2016.
- Servellón, Sergio, "Van toen Vlaams-nationaal, progressief engagement en avant-garde samenklitten", in *Zuurvrij, berichten uit het Letterenhuis*, 26, 2014, p. 22–31.
- Sharp, Alan, "The Paris Peace Conference and its Consequences", in Daniel Ute, Peter Gatrell, et al. (eds.), *1914–1918-online, International Encyclopedia of the First World War*, Berlin, 2014-10-08.
- Sieben, Luc, "De novemberdagen van 1918 in Brussel: revolutie en ordehandhaving", in Patrick Lefevre and Piet De Gryse (eds.), *Van Brialmont tot de Westeuropese Unie. Bijdragen in de militaire geschiedenis aangeboden aan Albert Duchesne, Jean Lorette en Jean-Léon Charles*, Brussels, 1988, p. 155–176.
- Simons, Jozef, *Eer Vlaanderen vergaat*, Kapellen, 1999 (1927).
- Smets, G., "Les Régions dévastées et la réparation des dommages de guerre", in Ernest Mahaim (ed.), *La Belgique restaurée, Etude sociologique*, Brussels, 1926, p. 71–139.

- Smets, Marcel, *L'avènement de la cité-jardin en Belgique: histoire de l'habitat social en Belgique de 1830 à 1930*, Brussels, 1977.
- Smets, Paul-F., *Paul Hymans, un authentique homme d'État*, Brussels, 2015, p. 237–238.
- Smith, Leonard V., "Post-war Treaties (Ottoman Empire/ Middle East)", in Daniel Ute, Peter Gatrell, et al. (eds.), 1914–1918-online, *International Encyclopedia of the First World War*, Berlin, 2014-10-08.
- Somerhausen, Luc, *Essai sur les origines et l'évolution du droit à réparation des victimes militaires des guerres*, Centre for Military History, 11, Brussels, 1974.
- Steele, Valerie, *The Corset: a Cultural History*, New Haven, 2001.
- Stengers, Jean, "Histoire de la législation électorale en Belgique", in *Revue belge de philologie et d'histoire*, 82, 2004, p. 247–270.
- Stevenson, David, *With our Backs to the Wall: Victory and Defeat in 1918*, London, 2011.
- Stewart, H., *The New Zealand Division 1916–1919: A Popular History Based on Official Records*, Auckland, 1921.
- Stubbe, Lieven, "Planten en de Eerste Wereldoorlog", in *De Bron*, 2008 (3), p. 19–22.
- Summers, Julie, *Remembered; History of the Commonwealth War Graves Commission*, London, 2007.
- Swennen, Marc, *Les mouvements anticommunistes dans les années 1920*, Brussels, 2010.
- Sykes, A., "Le jazz band", in *L'Arstiste musicien*, August 1924, p. 118–119.
- Tallier, Pierre-Alain, "L'annexion des cantons d'Eupen-Malmedy et la reconstitution du patrimoine forestier belge après la Première Guerre mondiale. Le rôle prépondérant de l'administration forestière et de son directeur général Nestor Iris Crahay", in *Forêt wallonne*, 67, 2003, p. 2–11.
- Tallier, Pierre-Alain, "La reconstruction du patrimoine forestier Belge après 1918", in Andrée Corvol and Jean-Paul Amat (eds.), *Forêt et Guerre*, Paris, 1994, p. 215–225.
- Troy, Nancy, *Couture Culture: A study in modern art and fashion,* Cambridge (MA), 2003.
- Troy, Nancy, "Paul Poiret's minaret style: Originality, reproduction, and art in fashion", in *Fashion Theory*, 6/2, 2002, p. 117–144.
- Uyttenhove, Pieter, and Jo Celis, *De wederopbouw van Leuven na 1914*, Louvain, 1991.
- Vaesen, Joost, "Hergebruik of oorlogstoerisme? De omgang met Belgische militaire sites als sporen van de strijd, 1918-1940", in Pierre-Alain Tallier and Patrick Nefors (eds.), *En toen zwegen de kanonnen. Akten van het internationaal colloquium georganiseerd door het Rijksarchief van België en het Koninklijk Museum van het Leger en de Krijgsgeschiedenis (Brussel, 3-6 november 2008)*, Brussels, 2010, pp. 483-518.
- Valluy, Général J. E., and Pierre Dufourcq, *La Première Guerre mondiale, t. 2, 1916–1918*, Paris, 1968.
- Van 'T Hof, Sonja, "A Kaleidoscope of Victimhood. Le Cas de la Belgique", in Jolande Withuis and Annet Mooij (eds.), *The Politics of War Trauma. The aftermath of World War II in eleven European countries*, Amsterdam, 2010, p. 63–66.
- Van den Buys, Kristin, "L'importance d'un orchestre de radio", in Dominique Favart (ed.), *Au bonheur des musiciens. 150 ans de vie musicale à Bruxelles*, Tielt, 1997, p. 209–224.
- Van der Aa, Manu, *Tatave! Paul-Gustave Van Hecke. Kunstpaus, modekoning en* salonsocialist, Tielt, 2017.
- Van der Fraenen, Jan, *Voor den kop geschoten: spionage en executies in het bezette België, 1914–1918*, Roeselare, 2009.
- Van der Fraenen, Jan, and Pieter-Jan Lachaert, *Spioneren voor het vaderland. De memoires van Evarist De Geyter*, Kortrijk, 2011.
- Van Isacker, Karel, *Mijn land in de kering 1830–1980, dl 2, De enge ruimte / 1914–1980*, Antwerp-Amsterdam, 1983.
- Van Kalken, Frans (ed.), *Paul Hymans: mémoires*, v. 1 and 2, Brussels, 1958.
- Van Meerten, Michelangelo, "Tussen herstel en vernieuwing: de spoorwegen na de Grote Oorlog", in Paul Van Heesvelde, et al., *Bestemming front. Spoorwegen in België tijdens de Grote Oorlog*, Tielt, 2014, p. 119-140.

- Van Mol, Dennis, "*(persoonlijk ben ik er niet voor)*", *Over de moeizame doorbraak van de moderne -ismen en het ontstaan van een activistische tegentraditie in Vlaanderen, 1906–1933*, unpublished PhD thesis, University of Antwerp, 2017.
- Van Ostaijen, Paul, *Verzameld werk. Deel 2: Poëzie. Bezette Stad en Nagelaten Gedichten*, Amsterdam, 1979.
- Van Ostaijen, Paul, *Verzameld werk. Deel 4: Proza. Besprekingen en beschouwingen*, Amsterdam, 1979.
- van Ypersele,Laurence, "Tourisme de mémoire, usages et mésusages: le cas de la Première Guerre mondiale", in *Témoigner. Entre histoire et mémoire. Revue pluridisciplinaire de la Fondation Auschwitz*, 116, 2013, pp. 13-21.
- Vancoillie, Jan, *De Duitse militaire begraafplaats Menen Wald, Geschiedenis van de Duitse militaire graven van de Eerste Wereldoorlog in Zuid-West-Vlaanderen*, Wevelgem, 2013.
- Vanden Bosch, Hans, *Inventaris van het archief van de Belgische Middendienst voor de krijgs-gevangenen, 1914–1925*, Brussels, 2009.
- Vanlangenhove, Fernand, *L'élaboration de la politique étrangère de la Belgique entre les deux guerres mondiales*, Brussels, 1980.
- Vanneste, Dominique, and Caroline Winter, "First World War Battlefield Tourism: Journeys Out of the Dark and Into the Light", in Philip Stone, Rudi Hartmann, Tony Seaton, Richard Sharpley and Leanne White (eds.), *The Palgrave Handbook of Dark Tourism Studies*, London, 2018, p. 443–467.
- Vanthemsche, Guy (ed.), *Le Congo belge pendant la Première Guerre mondiale. Les rapports du Ministre des Colonies Jules Renkin au roi Albert Iᵉʳ 1914–1918*, Brussels, 2009.
- Velaers, Jan, *Albert I. Koning in tijdens van oorlog en crisis 1909–1934*, Tielt, 2009.
- Verpaalen, John, *Molens van de Frontstreek*, Koksijde, 1995.
- Verwilghen, Raphaël, L. Boereboom, et al., *Nieuw-Vlaanderen,* Antwerp, 1923.
- Vierset, Auguste, *Mes souvenirs sur l'occupation allemande en Belgique*, Paris, 1932.
- Vos, Herman, "Een dekadent Vlaanderen?", in *Ruimte*, 1/10-11-12, 1920, p. 118–121.
- Vrints, Antoon, "Offers in balans. Hoop en wanhoop van de Belgische soldaten (1914–1918)", in *Bijdragen tot de Eigentijdse Geschiedenis*, 17, 2006, p. 237–251.
- Vrints, Antoon, and Xavier Rousseaux, "La répression étatique d'un phénomène de crise sociale. Le banditisme pendant et après la Première Guerre mondiale en Belgique", in Pierre-Alain Tallier and Patrick Nefors (eds.), *Quand les canons se taisent – En toen zwegen de kanonnen,* Brussels, 2010, p. 271–303.
- Vyvey, Patricia, *De landbouw in het arrondissement Veurne (1880–1930)*, unpublished master's thesis, Ghent University, 1982.
- Walberg, Eric, *Postmodern Imperialism: Geopolitics and the Great Games*, Atlanta, 2011.
- Wangermée, Robert, "La vie musicale d'une guerre à l'autre", in Dominique Favart (ed.), *Au bonheur des musiciens. 150 ans de vie musicale à Bruxelles*, Tielt, 1997, p. 53–74.
- Weemaes, Marcel, *Van de IJzer tot Brussel. Het bevrijdingsoffensief van het Belgisch leger. 28 September 1918*, Brussels, 1970.
- Weinbaum, Alys Eve, et al. (eds.), *The Modern Girl Around the World: Consumption, Modernity and Globalization*, Durham-London, 2008.
- Winter, Jay, *Remembering War: The Great War and Historical Memory in the Twentieth Century*, New Haven, 2006.
- Zabecki, David, *The German 1918 Offensives*, Abingdon, 2006.
- Zander, Jean-Pascal, "The Destruction of Old Chemical Munitions in Belgium", in Thomas Stock and Karlheinz Lohs (eds.), *The Challenge of Old Chemical Munitions and Toxic Armament Wastes*, Oxford, 1997, p. 197–230.
- Zeidler, Miklós, "Trianon, Treaty of", in Daniel Ute, Peter Gatrell, et al. (eds.), *1914–1918-online, International Encyclopedia of the First World War*, Berlin, 2014-10-08.

AUTHORS

Michaël Amara has a PhD in Contemporary History from Université libre de Bruxelles (ULB). A specialist in the Great War, he wrote his PhD thesis on Belgian refugees during the First World War. He is currently head of department at the National State Archives.

Franky Bostyn started out as curator at the Memorial Museum Passchendaele 1917. He has organised many heritage events and exhibitions about the First World War in Flanders, and has published many books on the subject. Since 2017, he has been acting co-general director of the War Heritage Institute, Brussels.

Christoph Brüll is senior research scientist at the Centre for Contemporary and Digital History at the University of Luxembourg. He studied History and International Relations at the University of Liège and obtained a PhD at Friedrich Schiller University Jena. He has published numerous articles on the history of the relationship between Belgium and Germany.

Erik Buyst is a professor with the Economy Research Unit at KU Leuven. His academic research focuses on macro-economic history and the history of private corporations. His work has been published in, among others, the *Journal of Economic History, Financial Review History* and *Journal of Interdisciplinary History*. He has contributed to several books, such as on the history of the National Bank of Belgium. He co-authored *Het gestolde land: Een economische geschiedenis van België* (2016).

Rik Coolsaet is emeritus professor of International Relations at Ghent University and senior associate fellow at EGMONT – Royal Institute for International Relations (Brussels).

Jeroen Cornilly is a staff member with Letterenhuis (Antwerp). He obtained master's degrees in both Science of the Arts and Conservation Studies, as well as a PhD in Engineering Sciences–Architecture (KU Leuven). He has worked for the heritage service of the province of West Flanders and was collections manager at the Westflandrica Provincial Heritage Library. He writes on 19th- and 20th-century architecture in Belgium, focusing on the administrative and institutional aspects of architecture, architecture as a profession and artistic architecture. He coordinated the book *Bouwen aan wederop-bouw* (2008) on reconstruction in the Westhoek after the First World War.

Karolien De Clippel is director of the Hasselt Fashion Museum. Between February 2015 and September 2017 she was the museum's curator. An academic for 15 years before that, she was a professor in the History and Art History departments at Utrecht University. Her research focuses on early modern painting in the Low Countries, with special attention on individual artists such as Pieter Paul Rubens and Adriaen Brouwer, as well as on genre, classical mythology, the artistic exchange between the Southern and Northern Netherlands, "undress", fashion and clothing.

Matthijs de Ridder is a writer and a critic. He has written about Louis Paul Boon, Gaston Burssens, Kurt Köhler and Paul van Ostaijen. In his work he looks for creative points of view that tell the story of our times. *Rebelse ritmes* (2012) is a swinging cultural history in tune with jazz. In *De eeuw van Charlie Chaplin* (2017) he presents the 20th century as seen by Charlie Chaplin. He is currently working on a biography of Paul van Ostaijen.

Wannes Devos was awarded master's degrees in both History and Administration Management. He currently works as a historian at the War Heritage Institute, Brussels, and is doing a PhD at Ghent University on the representation of war and history in national military museums, in particular at the Royal Museum of the Armed Forces and of Military History (1911–2017).

Luc De Vos is emeritus professor of Foreign Affairs at KU Leuven, and has also taught at the Royal Military Academy, Brussels, for many years as chair of the department of Conflict Studies. From 2000 to 2010 he was president of the International Commission of Military History (ICMH).

Géry Dumoulin is a musicologist and curator of the wind and percussion instruments at the Musical Instruments Museum (MIM) in Brussels. He has a special interest in 19th-century copper instruments.

Manuel Duran is a political scientist and historian. He earned a master's degree in Medieval History at Ghent University and a master's degree in International Relations & Diplomacy at Antwerp University. His PhD thesis (Antwerp University, 2014) was published by Brill/Martinus Nijhoff as *Mediterranean Paradiplomacies: The Dynamics of Diplomatic Reterritorialization*. He is currently working as a collections manager of the mobile collections at the Royal Museum of the Armed Forces and of Military History, Brussels. He has published articles on diplomacy and military history.

Emmanuel Gerard is a historian, emeritus professor at KU Leuven and honorary chairman at KADOC (Documentation and Research Center on Religion, Culture and Society). His publications have covered the inter-war era, Christian democracy, the monarchy, parliament, the assassination of Julien Lahaut and the crisis in the Congo.

Kevin Gony has a degree in History from the University of Liège (2008) and has been working at the Royal Museum of the Armed Forces and of Military History, Brussels, since 2009. He collaborated on the Kemmel Command Bunker project on the Cold War in Belgium. Since 2010, he has also been working on the European Forum of Contemporary Conflict at the War Heritage Institute – a project for a permanent exhibition on the end of World War II, focusing in particular on the Eastern Front and the Pacific War, which opens in 2019.

Serge Jaumain is professor in Contemporary History at Université libre de Bruxelles (ULB), where he also co-directs AmericaS, the interdisciplinary centre for American studies. His current research focuses on the history of travel guides and on the relationship between Belgium and Canada.

Michel Jaupart, political scientist and history enthusiast, pursued a career in several state departments and cabinets. As chairman of the non-profit organization SRAMA-KVVL, he supported the creation of the gallery displaying the treasures of imperial Russia at the Royal Military Museum. As RMM administrator, he was associated with the institution's conversion into a state service with separate management. Until recently he was acting senior officer at the Veterans Institute and as such involved in the commemoration mission for the victims of Nazism. Today (2018) he is acting chief executive officer at the War Heritage Institute.

Chantal Kesteloot has a PhD in Contemporary History, is head of the public history department at CEGESOMA (Centre for Historical Research and Documentation on War and Contemporary Society)/State Archives, and a specialist in remembrance linked to the two world wars and in the history of Brussels. She recently edited, with Laurence van Ypersele, *Du café liégeois au soldat inconnu: La Belgique et la Grande Guerre* (2018).

Catherine Lanneau holds a PhD in History and a DEA in International Relations and European Integration. She is a professor at the University of Liège and secretary of the F.R.S-FNRS contact group "Belgium and contemporary worlds". Her research focuses on the history of Belgium and of Wallonia, and on the relationship between Belgium and France in the 19th and 20th centuries. She has published *L'inconnue française: La France et les Belges francophones 1944-1945* (2008) and co-edited several works, including (with Francis Depagie) *De Gaulle et la Belgique* (2015) and (with Michel Dumoulin) *La biographie individuelle et collective dans le champ des relations internationales* (2016).

Delphine Lauwers is currently a post-doctoral researcher at the National State Archives on the Brain project Jusinbellgium. Her PhD from the European University Institute in Florence (2014) focused on remembrance in relation to the First World War in the Ypres Salient from 1914 to 2014 (to be published by ULB in 2019). In the framework of the Jusinbellgium project she is now particularly interested in the judgment of war crimes committed during the two world wars in Belgium.

Pierre Lierneux obtained a PhD in History at Université catholique de Louvain (UCL) and specialised in military history at the Royal Military Academy, Brussels. He curated the uniform collections at the Royal Museum of the Armed Forces and of Military History and is now in charge of the exhibition department at the War Heritage Institute. He is a member of the Royal Academy of Art and Archaeology of Belgium.

Enika Ngongo has a degree in Contemporary History from Université catholique de Louvain (UCL, 2012). After a stint as a research assistant with the *Centre d'histoire du droit et de la justice* (CHDJ-UCL), she wrote a PhD thesis on the Belgian Congo during the First World War at the *Centre de recherches en histoire du droit et des institutions* (CRHiDI) at Université Saint-Louis in Brussels. She is also interested in juvenile delinquents in the Belgian Congo and the teaching of colonial history in Belgium.

Natasja Peeters has a PhD in Art History and a BA in History from Vrije Universiteit Brussel (VUB). In 2004, she curated the exhibition *De uitvinding van het landschap. Het Vlaamse landschap van Patinir tot Rubens, 1520–1700*, at the Royal Museum of Fine Arts Antwerp, in collaboration with the Kunsthistorisches Museum in Vienna. From 2004 to 2006 she was a researcher in the Rubensproject (Royal Museums of Fine Arts of Belgium) culminating in the Rubens exhibition (2008). Her book on journeymen was published in 2007, and her monograph on the painter Frans Francken in 2014. She was a guest professor at VUB from 2009 to 2011. In 2006, she became curator of the Arts department at the Royal Museum of the Armed Forces and of Military History, and in 2017 she became acting director of Collections.

Marc Reynebeau is editor at *De Standaard* newspaper and has written books on politics and culture, history theory, and the history of Belgium and Flemish nationalism. His latest book (published in autumn 2018) is on the significance of the First World War for the 20th century.

Martin Schoups is a researcher at FWO (Research Foundation – Flanders) and works within the history taskforce at Ghent University (Research Group Social History after 1750). He has published on Belgian food policy after the First World War, and the political actions by Belgian veterans during the inter-war period. For his PhD thesis he analyses how and why city dwellers took to the streets in Antwerp between 1880 and 1940.

Sergio Servellón is director of the FeliXart Museum in Drogenbos. Under his direction, the museum migrated from a monographic to a thematic institution focusing on the Belgian inter-war avant-garde. He has organised retrospective exhibitions on Karel Maes, Paul Joostens, Paul Van Hoeydonck, Michel Seuphor and Luc Peire. He is editor for the website Abstract Modernism of the Flemish Art Collection, and has published a catalogue of Felix de Boeck's drawings and a monograph of author/artist Michel Seuphor. He spent two years as training coordinator for the Conservation–Restoration department at KASKA-Artesis. He has also been chair of ICOM Belgium Flanders and the PAS Foundation.

Tom Simoens teaches history at the Royal Military Academy in Brussels. He specialises in the First World War with a particular focus on the Belgian army and Belgian military justice.

Jean-Michel Sterkendries was a student at the Royal Military Academy, Brussels (1974–1978) and is officer with the armoured troops. He obtained a PhD in History at Université libre de Bruxelles (ULB). He now is a professor at the Royal Military Academy, where he teaches historical criticism, history of international relations, history of Belgium and history of conflicts. He became head of the Conflicts Study department at the Royal Military Academy in 2012.

Jan Van der Fraenen is a scientific researcher at the War Heritage Institute, Brussels. He has written several pieces on the First World War and the Cold War, and curated several exhibitions, including on the Kemmel Command Bunker and the Trench of Death in Dixmude. He is currently doing a PhD at Ghent University on the Trench of Death.

Christine Van Everbroeck has a PhD in History from the Université libre de Bruxelles (ULB), and is head of the educational service at the Royal Museum of the Armed Forces and of Military History, Brussels. With Pieter Verstraete she co-authored the book *Le silence mutilé: Les soldats invalides belges de la Grande Guerre/Verminkte stilte: De Belgische invalide soldaten van de Groote Oorlog* (2014).

Laurence van Ypersele is professor at Université catholique de Louvain (UCL), where she teaches contemporary history and historical criticism. Her speciality is the First World War and its remembrance.

Piet Veldeman studied History and Archival Heritage. In 2008 he became assistant researcher at the Royal Museum of the Armed Forces and of Military History, now part of the War Heritage Institute, Brussels. He specialises in 19th-century political and military history and is currently working on a PhD on the Belgian Civic Guard (1830–1920). He has been acting director for the sites at the War Heritage Institute since 2017.

Antoon Vrints is chief docent at Ghent University (Research Group Social History after 1750). He has written on First World War social history and on long-term conflict settlement. He has published *Het theater van de straat: Publiek geweld in Antwerpen tijdens de eerste helft van de twintigste eeuw* (2011) and, with Maarten Van Ginderachter and Koen Aerts, *Het land dat ooit was: Een tegenfeitelijke geschiedenis van België* (2014).